"Directness, coherence, and [illegible] *The Significance of Ethical Criticism in a Global Age* as Choo opens [illegible] fields of inquiry about the central purposes and practices of Literature education and its complex relationship to ethics. Drawing upon a wide variety of resources from histories of literary criticism, reception theories, pedagogical practices and into the particularities of classroom exchanges, Choo demonstrates that only through transforming the very purposes and structures of Literature education will ethical dispositions – 'listening to the heart' of others and Confucius's teachings of *shu* (not to impose one's will on others) – be cultivated. This timely book is a bold reconsideration of how readers create, in company with literature, ethical encounters and dilemmas and how teachers may encourage or discourage ethical imagination. What links the work of teaching literature to experiencing and feeling *with and for* others? Choo has an answer to this question as she considers her signature theorizing about how we might hone the *hospitable imagination* in order to grapple with ways to understand the purposes of ethical response and action. Just what does it take to nurture the narrative imagination that allows one to step into the river of another's experiences, to transmigrate into their wishes and desires, and to understand their positionalities – that is, to be an ethical reader of others' stories, desires, and experiences? The gift of Choo's explorations might just be that she exposes the nervous system of literature where the hand and mind of writer perturb a fictional shell game which requires a *hospitable imagination* in order for readers to feel distanced from their own lives and find familiarity and possibility in the lives of others."

– **Ruth Vinz**, *Professor at Teachers College, Columbia University, USA*

"In this book, Choo has defined a serious problem with precision and she has devised a comprehensive and creative solution. She has deftly exposed two dangerous myths: first, the myth that academic scholarship and literature can be value-free; and, second, the myth that learning is a solitary experience. Her solutions show up in the diverse classroom practices which help students learn how to communicate with each other about subtle ideas in literature. She analyzes those practices skilfully and humanely. In doing so she is not only helping a generation create the kind of habits that are urgently needed in a global age, but are needed in an electronic age which constantly emphasizes quickness. Choo's approach enriches the reading and teaching of literature that spark conversation and collaboration essential to any thorough understanding of how stories unfold as they do – stories in fiction and stories in daily, real life."

Stephan Ellenwood, *Professor at Boston University, USA*

"This remarkable book provides a supremely timely reminder of the importance of teaching literature to young people, whilst recognising that we need to argue more emphatically for literature's place in the curriculum. Suzanne S. Choo inspires teachers and scholars to regain their belief in the fundamental seriousness of literature as an ethical change agent in young people's lives, helping them to see, as no other curriculum area can, that they are part of a global humanity that requires a vision of international, cultural understanding. Literature, she passionately argues, and based on her substantive research in real classrooms, illuminates the world and human behaviour so that young people can enjoy texts and feel the questioning power that literary texts demand, texts invite young people to scrutinise human behaviour and moral integrity. The book includes a remarkable review of literary traditions that have influenced the teaching of literature and finds them all important but with too strong an emphasis on reducing texts to either aesthetic icons or troubling sites of discourse. She draws intensely on her own experiences of the extraordinary richness of the multilingual and cultural diversities of Singapore. There 'English Literature' occupies a significant position for her and for its young people leading to her developing a vision of the ultimate value of all literatures and their extraordinary importance to the ethical development of young people in a post-COVID world."

– **Andy Goodwyn**, *Professor at University of Bedfordshire, UK*

TEACHING ETHICS THROUGH LITERATURE

Teaching Ethics through Literature provides in-depth understanding of a new and exciting shift in the fields of English education, Literature, Language Arts, and Literacy through exploring their connections with ethics. The book pioneers an approach to integrating ethics in the teaching of literature. This has become increasingly relevant and necessary in our globally connected age. A key feature of the book is its integration of theory and practice. It begins with a historical survey of the emergence of the ethical turn in Literature education and grounds this on the ideas of influential Ethical Philosophers and Literature scholars. Most importantly, it provides insights into how teachers can engage students with ethical concerns and apply practices of Ethical Criticism using rich on-the-ground case studies of high school Literature teachers in Australia, Singapore and the United States.

Suzanne S. Choo is Associate Professor in the English Language and Literature Group at National Institute of Education, Nanyang Technological University, Singapore. Her book *Reading the world, the globe, and the cosmos: Approaches to teaching literature for the twenty-first century* (Peter Lang, 2013) was awarded the 2014 Critics Choice Book Award by the American Educational Studies Association. She co-edited the book *Literature Education in the Asia-Pacific: Policies, Practices and Perspectives in Global Times* (Routledge, 2018).

Citizenship, Character and Values Education

Edited by Wing On Lee

Executive Director of Institute for Adult Learning Singapore

This series provides a platform for discussion and debate on the latest issues, challenges and developments in Citizenship, Character and Values Education across the globe. The series facilitates continued conversation on policy and politics, curriculum and pedagogy, review and reform, and provides a comparative overview of the different conceptions and approaches to Citizenship, Character and Values Education around the world. The volumes in this series will appeal to teacher educators, researchers, teachers, school leaders and policymakers. They will also facilitate decision-making in the practical steps necessary to develop Citizenship, Character and Values Education curricula in different national contexts.

The State of Global Education
Edited by Brad Maguth and Jeremy Hillburn

Teaching Character and Virtue in School
James Arthur, Kristján Kristjánsson, Tom Harrison, Wouter Sanderse & Daniel Wright

Moral Education in Japan: Values in a global context
Marie Højlund Roesgaard

Contesting Education and Identity in Hong Kong
Liz Jackson

Teaching Ethics through Literature: The Significance of Ethical Criticism in a Global Age
Suzanne S. Choo

TEACHING ETHICS THROUGH LITERATURE

The Significance of Ethical Criticism in a Global Age

Suzanne S. Choo

LONDON AND NEW YORK

First published 2021
by Routledge
2 Park Square, Milton Park, Abingdon, Oxon OX14 4RN

and by Routledge
605 Third Avenue, New York, NY 10158

Routledge is an imprint of the Taylor & Francis Group, an informa business

British Library Cataloguing-in-Publication Data
A catalogue record for this book is available from the British Library

Library of Congress Cataloging-in-Publication Data
Names: Choo, Suzanne S., author.
Title: Teaching ethics through literature: the significance of ethical criticism in a global age / Suzanne S. Choo.
Description: Abingdon, Oxon; New York, NY: Routledge, 2021. | Series: Citizenship, character and values education | Includes bibliographical references and index. | Summary: "Teaching Ethics through Literature provides in-depth understanding of a new and exciting shift in the fields of English education, Literature, Language Arts, and Literacy through exploring their connections with ethics. The book pioneers an approach to integrating ethics in the teaching of literature. This has become increasingly relevant and necessary in our globally connected age. A key feature of the book is its integration of theory and practice. It begins with a historical survey of the emergence of the ethical turn in Literature education and grounds this on the ideas of influential Ethical Philosophers and Literature scholars. Most importantly, it provides insights into how teachers can engage students with ethical concerns and apply practices of Ethical Criticism using rich on-the-ground case studies of high school Literature teachers in Australia, Singapore and the United States."—Provided by publisher.
Identifiers: LCCN 2021001001 | ISBN 9780367262228 (hardback) | ISBN 9780367262266 (paperback) | ISBN 9780429292101 (ebook)
Subjects: LCSH: Moral education. | Ethics—Study and teaching. | Literature—Study and teaching. | Ethics in literature.
Classification: LCC LC268. C46 2021 | DDC 370.11/4—dc23
LC record available at https://lccn.loc.gov/2021001001

ISBN: 978-0-367-26222-8 (hbk)
ISBN: 978-0-367-26226-6 (pbk)
ISBN: 978-0-429-29210-1 (ebk)

Typeset in Bembo
by Apex CoVantage, LLC

CONTENTS

ILLUSTRATIONS

Tables

Figures

ACKNOWLEDGEMENTS

I published my first monograph *Reading the world, the globe and the cosmos: Approaches to teaching literature for the twenty-first century* in 2013. This work sought to provide a comprehensive historical analysis of the development of Literature education from the eighteenth century to the present. Seven years have passed between then and now and during this time, I have built on my initial research focusing particularly on the integration of cosmopolitan ethics in the teaching of literature and have published over 30 book chapters, edited books, and journal articles from 2014 to the present. This book is my second monograph featuring new work on ethics and Ethical Criticism in Literature education while also adapting from my recently published work. I thank the editorial team of the following journals for allowing me to reproduce parts from my paper:

Chapter 3 – The sections regarding debates about the Literature curriculum and historical emergence of World Literature in schools are reproduced with permission from:

- Choo, S. S. (2021). Expanding the imagination: Mediating the aesthetic-political divide through the third space of ethics in Literature education. *British Journal of Educational Studies, 69*(1), 65–82.
- Choo, S. S. (2014a). Cultivating a hospitable imagination: Re-envisioning the world literature curriculum through a cosmopolitan lens. *Curriculum Inquiry, 44*(1), 68–89.

Chapter 4 – The first part of the chapter describing the historical development of Ethical Criticism is reproduced with permission from:

- Choo, S. S. (2017a). Globalizing literature pedagogy: Applying cosmopolitan Ethical Criticism to the teaching of literature. *Harvard Educational Review, 87*(3), 335–356.

Chapter 5 – Case studies of Literature teachers are reproduced with permission from the following:

- Choo, S. S. (2014a). Cultivating a hospitable imagination: Re-envisioning the world literature curriculum through a cosmopolitan lens. *Curriculum Inquiry, 44*(1), 68–89.
- Choo, S. S. (2016). Fostering the hospitable imagination through cosmopolitan pedagogies: Re-envisioning Literature education in Singapore. *Research in the Teaching of English, 50*(4), 400–421.
- Choo, S. S. (2017a). Globalizing literature pedagogy: Applying cosmopolitan Ethical Criticism to the teaching of literature. *Harvard Educational Review, 87*(3), 335–356.
- Choo, S. S. (2020a). The cosmopolitan turn in Literature education and its resulting tensions in Singapore schools. *Critical Studies in Education, 61*(4), 512–527.

Chapter 6 – The first part of the chapter theorizing Confucian cosmopolitanism is reproduced with permission from:

- Choo, S. S. (2020b). Examining models of twenty-first century education through the lens of Confucian Cosmopolitanism. *Asia Pacific Journal of Education, 40*(1), 20–34.

This book would not have been possible without the support of my colleagues in the field. I thank Prof Lee Wing On for inviting me to contribute to the series he is editing with Routledge on Citizenship, Character and Values Education and for the enriching discussions on values education and philosophy. I am grateful to Prof Thomas Bean, Prof Stephan Ellenwood, and Prof Andy Goodwyn for their encouraging words and endorsement of this work.

A few of the international case studies stemmed from the work of the Global Learning Alliance in the early years of its founding and I am thankful for the mentorship and creative vision of Prof Ruth Vinz as well as my colleagues and friends, Deb Sawch, and Alison Villanueva, who I had the opportunity to travel and collaborate with. Most of the case studies would not have been possible without the Start-up grant (SUG 21/16 CSL) and Education Research Funding Programme grants (OER 60/12 CSL & OER 22/17 CSL) from my university – the National Institute of Education, Nanyang Technological University, Singapore.

I am appreciative of the professionalism and hard work of the editorial team at Routledge, particularly Katie Peace and Jacy Hui, who have patiently addressed my questions as well as my research assistants Ismath Beevi and Dominic Nah for their assistance in collecting data for some of the case studies discussed in this book.

I am grateful to Wilson Tan, my husband, for his unwavering love and support. I dedicate this work to our daughter, Gracelyn – may you always read widely, care deeply, and live your life purposefully that the world may be fairer, more just and hospitable. Finally, I thank God for His grace and favour in seeing this work come to fruition.

SERIES EDITOR'S FOREWORD

This is a valuable and insightful book, written by Suzanne S. Choo, who has offered a critical review of the value proposition of Literature education and proposed a Cosmopolitan Literature Pedagogic Framework for teaching English Literature. Her presentation of arguments and analyses is sound and clear, and deserve serious reading, from both the perspective of her mastery of the concepts and philosophy of Literature education, and from her analysis of teaching approaches that supports her proposed Cosmopolitan Literature Pedagogic Framework.

The books starts with a thorough literature review on the topic of ethics in Literature Education, covering all major theories and the leading thinkers of the various streams of thoughts in related arguments. Choo starts off by pointing out the present multicultural landscape in most cosmopolitan cities, mainly due to mass migrations across the globe with increased globalization and cross country economic activities. As a result, many cosmopolitan cities have increasingly diverse workforce and clientele, and the teaching of English Literature, with English as a lingua franca, needs to have this awareness to make Literature education relevant to the cosmopolitan environment of today, and thus meaningful to the students whom we are preparing to face this cosmopolitan world as well.

Choo points out that the current dominant approach in Literature education has been strongly influenced by the apolitical method of Aesthetic Criticism, leading to today's Literature education emphasizing literary techniques such as symbolism, personification hyperbole, enjambment, etc. Choo points out that a consequence of this approach is that the Literature classroom is perceived as disconnected from the real world as literary engagement is then fixated on the aesthetic appreciation of texts rather than on its relevance to the contextual environment and implications for today's societal situation. More importantly, this approach neglects the ethical implications of teaching literature.

Based on her comprehensive research, Choo argues that the philosophical end of Literature education is ethics, through considering the views of major philosophers such as Immanuel Kant, Martin Heidegger, and Emanuel Levinas. In addition to the rationality endpoint that will ultimately lead to certain fundamental grounds in values and morality, Choo points out that there are transcendental elements in literature beyond aesthetic appreciation. Strictly speaking, aesthetic appreciation has a transcendental dimension as well. And this transcendental element is closely imbued with values and ethics. Thus, her conclusion is that there is no value-free Literature education. Her strong stand on this viewpoint makes me recall a compelling statement made by Leo Ward (1971)

> Education is turning towards values. It is for values – it has to be. As soon as we delete values, we delete education. No values, no education; and where there is real education, there are genuine human values.
>
> *(p. 428)*

Choo concedes that in teaching literature, we need a cosmopolitan orientation that shares an existential concern about what it means to live with others in the world, and is correspondingly characterized by an intentional willingness to invest in the other. In this light, Choo suggests a cosmopolitan Ethical Criticism approach to Literature education, which involves aesthetic–political–ethical analysis of texts, readers, and others in an interactional process. To enable students to bring about these connections, one practical approach to teaching literature, as Choo suggests, is to adopt intertextual and dialogic strategies that seek to develop informed and engaged interpretive communities through literature discussions.

The cosmopolitan Ethical Criticism approach to Literature education is important as this will enable students to realize the significance of cosmopolitan love as the grounds of human respect in a diverse cosmopolitan age. This cosmopolitan love will form the foundation for the respect of human rights and dignity, and will enhance students' connections with others in the society and the world.

I sincerely congratulate Choo for achieving this work, which stands out from her solid research and obviously from her years of experience and deep reflection about the teaching of literature. I sincerely recommend this work to all readers who are engaged with Literature education – this is a must read book for you.

Wing On Lee
Series Editor & Professor and Executive Director
Institute for Adult Learning
Singapore University of Social Sciences
Singapore 599494

Reference

Ward, L. (1971). Education and values. In J. P. Strain (Ed.), *Modern philosophies of education* (pp. 428–438). Cambridge, MA: Harvard University Press.

FOREWORD

As a college English major steeped in Literature classes, I can still recall New Criticism as a driving force in how we were introduced to close reading and particular interpretations of the literary canon. Indeed, along with my classmates we tried often in vain to figure out what our professors viewed as the "correct" and defensible interpretation. Then, as Reader Response came into vogue, a small space was created for reader and text connections but that movement came with its own baggage of idiosyncratic, self-centred interpretations.

Now, with a variety of global risk factors that include climate change and, most recently the COVID-19 pandemic, it becomes readily apparent that we are living in a highly connected world. And, we are living in a world that, of necessity, limits travel and the open border lifestyle that defines a world citizen who may embrace a cosmopolitan disposition that values social difference. As I write this foreword, it is hard to reconcile instances of isolation, social distancing, aloneness, and tragedy. So, where does Literature "fit" within this new world?

Author and scholar Professor Suzanne S. Choo has, based on over ten years of case study research, come up with a powerful antidote to separatist and isolationist times. Indeed, she argues that the arts must have a place in this deliberation to move beyond the narrow confines of New Criticism. She demonstrates in this book how we can engage students from a variety of levels in critical literacy practices rooted in cosmopolitan ethics. She argues that the "primary focus in this book is how ethics can be taught and ethical dispositions cultivated through literature" (p. 2).

As a starting point, Choo traces the major schools of thought that have influenced pedagogy in Literature classes, including New Criticism and Reader Response. One would think we have moved beyond these constraints but this form of literary exegesis to unearth correct interpretations still persists in Literature classes and assessments.

Rather than stay mired in pedagogy that treats texts as sacred, canonical entities, Choo's research takes up global citizenship with Literature that moves beyond discussions of character, plot, and setting to consider moral and ethical issues (e.g. justice, friendship), and ethical philosophy. This school of thought sees texts as cultural constructions with Literature taking up a position that values world literature.

At the applied end of this spectrum, Choo devoted ten years observing more than 80 classes and interviewing 140 teachers from various countries to understand their praxis. This research underpins the case studies she discusses to illustrate how to move Literature discussion into a more critical zone that centres on the global other and ethical dimensions.

For example, in an effort to move beyond early New Criticism as a framework for Literature discussion, World Literature programmes, along with a consideration of Human Rights education, have helped transform the Literature curriculum to take up critical pedagogy. As she notes: "Ethical Criticism disrupts art from its own closure and envisions reminding the spectator that art is part of the larger world and cannot escape its accountability to the other" (p. 24). Towards that end, she advocates close reading that pays attention to the gaps and silences that may mis represent others.

There is a need to reconstruct the Literature curriculum from a cosmopolitan lens to trouble stereotypes and Western colonial norms with a move towards cultural pluralism. Indeed, school curriculum should align with multiple diverse scholars. Adolescents deserve to see their lives, cultures, languages, and ethnicities represented in contemporary young adult literature that moves beyond *Lord of the Flies*. Rather, possible themes might include gender roles, war and origin studies, concepts including power, the nature of good and evil, immigration stories, and a host of other topics. This move towards a transnational literacy is timely and badly needed to broaden the Western canon. To do so, Choo defines the terrain of Ethical Criticism as a:

> Critical hermeneutical approach to reading texts that analyzes the representation and construction of ethical values, how processes of othering and marginalization occur in specific social and geopolitical contexts and how texts can offer entry points to engaging with ethical issues in the community and the world.
>
> *(p. 61)*

In summary, this book will appeal to a wide range of educators interested in transforming a staid Literature curriculum rooted in older approaches to reading that fail to interrogate the fictional world of texts. This book spans both philosophical and practical domains with illustrative case studies that illustrate how to engage students in critical and ethical discussion in Literature. *Teaching Ethics through Literature: The Significance of Ethical Criticism in a Global Age* makes a significant contribution to the field by applying an in-depth understanding of ethics to reframing the philosophical objectives of teaching literature along with its curriculum design, critical reading of texts, pedagogy, and values for a more inclusive future.

Thomas W. Bean, Ph.D.
Professor of Reading/Literacy
Rosanne Keeley Norris Endowed Professor
Old Dominion University
Darden College of Education and Professional Studies
Department of Teaching and Learning
Norfolk, VA 23529

1

INTRODUCTION

The significance of ethics in the teaching of literature

At the start of the third decade of the twenty-first century, the world was gripped by news of a bushfire that rapidly evolved to an uncontrolled wildfire. At first, this appeared to be a national affair affecting Australia, where fires destroyed 3,000 homes and killed over a billion animals. Later, this devastation that started in such inconsequential ways became a preview to another kind of global inferno that would spread a few months later. The rapid combustion of the world began in small ways in the form of a novel respiratory disease that was first reported in Wuhan, a province in Hubei, China, in January 2020. Three months later, the Coronavirus had infected over half a million people in almost every continent in the world with the World Health Organization declaring it a pandemic (Sam et al., 2020).

In the race to treat the infections, governments and major transnational organizations have focused on providing funding to support scientific research and development. In the United States, Congress passed an $8.3 billion emergency response bill to support the development of medical countermeasures, vaccines, and purchase of diagnostic tests among others. The European Union opened an emergency call for research to treat Covid-19 with funding up to €47.5 million. Major companies and academic institutions have also rallied to support such scientific endeavours. The Gates Foundation, for example, partnered with credit card company MasterCard in a $125 million push to speed up the development of drugs for treating infections (European Union, 2020; Geulette, 2020).

In major global crisis, the prevailing view is that science needs to be invested in and counted on for providing informed evidence in tackling the unknown. While science is the harbinger of hope, the arts is dispensable and can be temporarily suspended. Thus, theatre companies, dance troupes, music ensembles, film and other arts groups have cancelled performances in the face of nation-wide lockdowns. Arts organizations have called on governments to provide emergency funding in response to closures, cancelled tours, international festivals, and the probability of bankruptcy. Yet, the perception remains that the arts is associated with an "entertainment" industry which, in disaster situations, is deemed "non-essential" and should take a backseat. In Maslow's Hierarchy of Needs (1943), the arts address higher levels of need for love and belonging and are less crucial to meeting basic physiological and safety needs.

This age-old view of the arts as connected to pleasure and of literature as associated with an elitist appreciation of *belles letters* or beautiful writing should today be problematized. If not, the arts risk becoming obsolete and marginalized in an age when global risks are increasingly becoming part and parcel of everyday realities. As Ulrich Beck (2014) argues, "Being at risk is the way of being and ruling in the world of modernity; being at global risk is the human condition at the beginning of the twenty-first century" (p. 80). As the world has become hyper-connected, globalization can no longer be conceived as an external phenomenon, the glocalization of the everyday pushes individuals to encounter, live with, and accommodate foreign others. Beck (2007) describes this as "enforced cosmopolitanization" in which "global risks activate and connect actors across borders, who otherwise don't want to have anything to do with one another" (p. 287).

While the arts perform multiple roles in society – to engage the senses, to expand the imagination, to entertain, to escape, to critique, and so on – in the context of an interconnected age, I argue that the arts must respond more prominently and intentionally to global risks. In this light, the most significant value of the arts is in developing the kinds of critical, social, and ethical dispositions that mitigate intolerance, discrimination, and forms of institutional, symbolic, social, and historical violence arising from global crisis. This book focuses specifically on the teaching of English Literature although its principles may be applied to other areas in arts education such as Drama, Dance, Film, Fine Arts, and Music. For the sake of clarity, I capitalize the term "Literature" to refer to the subject English Literature while the non-capitalized form "literature" refers to literary texts. The primary focus in this book is how ethics can be taught and ethical dispositions cultivated through Literature.

For much of the twentieth century, engagements with ethical concerns and moral values have largely been excluded from the Literature curriculum. This may be attributed to two dominant approaches to teaching literature particularly in schools – New Criticism and Reader Response Criticism. New Criticism became popular around the 1930s and 1940s as influenced by I. A. Richards, T. S. Eliot, John Crowe Ransom, among others. The New Critics advanced a disconnected practice of close reading and positioned the text as an autonomous, self-contained entity. A Literature student is to avoid the intentional fallacy, which involves considerations of the author's context and his or her intentions in literary analysis; similarly, the student is to avoid the affective fallacy by leaving impressionistic feelings at bay and remaining a disinterested reader of texts (Wimsatt & Beardsley, 1947/2001).

In the 1970s, Reader Response Criticism countered New Criticism's passive approach to interpretation. Louise Rosenblatt (1988), a leading scholar of the movement, highlights the point that texts are not isolated entities and that readers bring to the text past linguistic and life experiences. Readers and texts coexist in a transactional relationship. In contrast to "efferent reading" in which the reader approaches the text in a utilitarian manner such as the way one treats a recipe or car manual, literary reading can promote "aesthetic reading" in which the reader's emotions, experiences, and imagination are evoked leading to immersive rather than detached responses to texts (Rosenblatt, 1978).

Broadly, both approaches popularized text and reader-centric ways of teaching literature that emphasized aesthetic appreciation of the stylistic properties of texts and aesthetic engagement, tapping on readers' responses to texts. Both approaches continue to influence Literature curriculum and assessment. Take, for example, a typical question in the New York State's Regents High School Examination (2020) in English Language Arts:

> write a well-developed, text-based response of two to three paragraphs. In your response, identify a central idea in the text and analyze how the author's use of one writing strategy (literary element or literary technique or rhetorical device) develops this central idea.
>
> *(p. 21)*

To answer such a question, the student must apply New Criticism's close analysis of the stylistic properties of texts. Similarly, in the Cambridge International General Certificate of Secondary Education (IGCSE) Literature in English examination, some questions are entirely centred on the formal properties of text such as the following based on Jane Austen's *Northanger Abbey*:

> Mr and Mrs Allen are supposed to be looking after Catherine in Bath. To what extent does Austen's writing persuade you that they do this successfully?
>
> *(Cambridge Assessment International Education, 2020, p. 11)*

Other questions involve a blend of New Criticism and Reader Response Criticism such as the following based on an anthology of short stories:

> What does the writer make you feel about either Mr Twycott in *The Son's Veto* (by Thomas Hardy) or the husband in *Sandpiper* (by Ahdaf Soueif)?
>
> *(Cambridge Assessment International Education, 2020, p. 25).*

Here, students must explore their own responses to texts and support this through close textual exegesis. Such questions reflect two of the key aims of the syllabus that are for students to "communicate an informed personal response appropriately and effectively" and "appreciate different ways in which writers achieve their effects" (Cambridge Assessment International Education, 2019, p. 5).

Absent from text and reader-centric-type questions are what I term "other-centric" questions (Choo, 2013) that push students to bridge the gap between fictional texts and real-world in order to empathize and engage with diverse others and their ethical concerns. Today, there is even greater pressure to challenge Literature's absorption in the fictional lifeworld of texts and validation of readers' responses. Recovering the close interconnection between Literature and ethics has become especially crucial today because of what I proceed to describe as the three pressure points that have countered traditional approaches to teaching literature.

The three pressure points catalyzing reform in Literature

The pressure to reclaim relevance

The first concerns the increasing pressure to reclaim Literature's relevance in the context of an intensely globalized twenty-first century. In recent years particularly, debates concerning the value of Literature have garnered increasing attention. Once described as the "supremely civilizing pursuit" and the most central subject in American and British schools (Applebee, 1974; Eagleton, 1996, p. 27), Literature appears to have now lost its place of prominence. Already in 1987, a report commissioned by the United States Congress found that History, Literature, and Languages were inadequately taught in public schools (Cheney, 1987). Years later, another influential report, *Reading at Risk*, by the National Endowment for the Arts (2004) provided a comprehensive survey of literary reading and reported "solid evidence of the declining importance of Literature to the [country's] populace" (p. ix). This decline had occurred among all education levels from grade school to college over the past 20 years. Three years later, another study found that nearly half of all Americans aged 18–24 read no books for pleasure and the percentage who read a book not required for work or school had declined at a rate of 12% from 1992 to 2002 (National Endowment for the Arts, 2007). Although the latest report (National Endowment for the Arts, 2009) revealed a reversal of this declining trend, figures still showed that students were turning away from majoring in Literature and the Humanities in favour of Sciences at colleges (Chace, 2009; Lewin, 2013; Simpson & Kelly, 2013).

Even in the United Kingdom, the number of students enrolled in GCSE English Literature Advanced Level examination, a high-stakes nationwide examination taken at the end of secondary education, dropped from 77% in 2004 to 72% in 2009, which is equivalent to one in four students opting out of taking the subject (Curtis, 2009). Further, a review of examination papers by the Office of Qualifications and Examinations Regulation, an independent watchdog, reported the lack of rigour in assessment since questions appeared too formulaic and predictable. Scholars also charged that the curriculum had not progressed since the 1950s and still continued to assess students on the traditional analysis of themes, plot, character, and style at the secondary level which was out of sync with the integration of literary theory at college level (Ballinger, 2003; Eaglestone & McEvoy, 1999). The most scathing attack was made by the National Association of Teachers of English (NATE) that recommended GCSE English Literature be discontinued at the Advanced Level since the subject relied on a narrow list of texts, failed to give students the requisite skills for college, and had little relevance to contemporary society (Bluett, Cockcroft, Harris, Hodgson, & Snapper, 2006; Garner, 2005).

In Australia, it is compulsory for high school students to take either English or English Literature. In 2018, only 1,400 Year 12 students opted to study Literature compared to 11,000 who opted to study English. The English Teachers Association of Western Australia reported that the percentage of Year 12 students plummeted from 26% in 1998 to 11% in 2017 and the number of schools offering Literature dropped from 135 in 2001 to 97 in 2017 (Hiatt, 2018).

Similarly, in Singapore where English Language is a compulsory first language subject and the main medium of instruction in primary and secondary schools, the number of students enrolled in the national Literature in English examination dropped from 48% in 2002 to 9% in 2012 (Heng, 2013).[1] A national survey on Singapore teenagers' reading habits found that more than once a week, only 25% read fiction books compared to 51% who read online articles posted on social media or websites (National Library Board, 2017, p. 15).

This bleak picture of Literature has spurred numerous books and opinion articles that range from grim prophesies about the death of Literature (Kernan, 1990; Scholes, 1998) and cynical questions concerning "Will the Humanities save us?" (Fish, 2008) to passionate defences about why democracy needs the Humanities (Nussbaum, 2010). As Alvin Kernan (1990) already anticipated, the decline would open the way for a renewed vision of Literature that would "claim for the traditional literary works a place of some importance and usefulness in individual life and society as whole" (p. 213). For Martha Nussbaum (1997), this usefulness must address the question of "what sorts of literary works, and what sort of teaching of those works, our academic institutions should promote in order to foster an informed and compassionate vision of the different" (p. 89).

Along these lines, organizations such as the American Academy of Arts & Sciences were commissioned by the United States government to counterbalance state investments in the STEM (Science, Technology, Engineering, and Mathematics) disciplines. Part of its goal was to propose ways in which the Humanities can empower students to contribute to twenty-first century democracy by expanding their understanding of diverse cultures. Essentially, these calls for Literature's relevance to social realities have meant that Literature can no longer remain purely insulated with its focus on aesthetic texts and language. Scholars have argued that the scope of Literature should expand to include newer textual modes such as video games, graphic novels, hypermedia, etc. (Swenson, Young, McGrail, Rozema, & Whitin, 2006). Other scholars have argued the need to emphasize textual and discourse analysis so that students would be equipped to read, interpret, and criticize texts in all forms of modes and media (Holden, 1999; Scholes, 1998). Broadly, the decline of Literature has revived new global positioning strategies in response to a fast-changing, increasingly complex and connected age.

The pressure to globalize

As an extension of the need to uncover new relevance for Literature, the second reason why ethics has become an important focus in teaching literature lies in the pressure to promote Global Citizenship Education. Growing consciousness of cross-cultural volatility has arisen as a result of the intensification of twenty-first century globalization. As the world headed into the third millennium, key globalization studies scholars concurred that there was now a greater perception of the world as a whole (Robertson, 1992), a growing movement "by which the peoples of the world are incorporated into a single world society" (Albrow & King, 1990, p. 9), and an "intensification of social relations throughout the world linking distant localities" (Giddens, 1991, p. 64). The "flattening" of the world (Friedman, 2007) also exacerbated rising instances of extremism, fundamentalism, and xenophobia worldwide.

Concerns about the effects of globalization led to increasing calls by governments, policymakers, and educators of the need to invest in Global Citizenship Education. This umbrella term encompasses Global Education, Human Rights Education, Peace Education, Environmental Education, among others (Fricke, Gathercole, & Skinner, 2015; Hicks, 2003). Global Citizenship Education essentially advocates that issues should be explored from a globally oriented perspective and that this should not just occur via subjects such as Social Studies or Civics Education but should be integrated into all subjects in the curriculum (Choo, 2017b). Frameworks by the Organisation for Economic Co-operation and Development (OECD) and Partnership for Twenty-first Century Learning (P21), founded by the United States Department of Education in collaboration with multinational corporations such as Apple Computer, Microsoft Corporation, Time Warner Foundation, etc., have been influential in spreading awareness about the need to infuse core twenty-first century skills and competencies in all aspects of teaching and learning. These twenty-first century competencies include intercultural competencies such as learning to "interact in heterogeneous groups" (OECD, 2005, p. 5) and "global awareness" (Partnership for 21st Century Skills (P21), 2013, p. 5).

Global Citizenship Education's influence in Literature is most evidently observed in the International Baccalaureate's (IB's) Literature syllabus, which is driven by the general aim "to develop internationally minded people who, recognizing their common humanity and shared guardianship of the planet, help to create a better and more peaceful world" (International Baccalaureate Organization, 2019, p. iii). Other than equipping students to appreciate aesthetic qualities of texts and form independent literary judgements, the IB's Literature syllabus encourages global awareness so that through the study of texts, students "experience representations of other realities and other people, allowing them to get acquainted with perspectives of the world that might be different from their own" (International Baccalaureate Organization, 2019, p. 10). Students have to study works in their original language as well as those in translation selected from an extensive prescribed reading list. As part of an internal assessment, students need to give an oral presentation of two works that involves identifying a global issue and examining how this is presented in the content and form of these texts.

Another major assessment accreditation body is the Cambridge Assessment International Education (CIE), which oversees the IGCSE offered in over 10,000 schools in 160 countries. CIE launched the World Literature syllabus in 2014 with one of the key aims to equip students to "explore wider and universal issues and gain skills of empathy, promoting students' better understanding of themselves and of the world around them" (Cambridge Assessment International Education, 2015, p. 3). In Singapore, the Ministry of Education (MOE) works with CIE to administer the high-stakes national examination, General Certificate of Education (GCE) Ordinary level, taken at the end of high school. Among recent changes has been a greater emphasis on developing global awareness as observed in the revised Literature in English 2019 syllabus by the MOE. The previous syllabus was overly centred on critical appreciation as highlighted in its opening paragraph – "Literature is the critical study of literary texts. Central to the subject is the critical analysis of how language is purposefully and creatively used in texts in order to create meaning and explore issues or themes" (Curriculum Planning and Development Division, 2013, p. 2). The previous syllabus advocated the teaching of the Literature around five areas of study – plot, character, setting and atmosphere, theme, and style. Conversely, the revised 2019 Literature syllabus is more holistic as it is centred on four student outcomes related to the development of empathetic and global thinkers, critical readers, creative meaning-makers, and convincing communicators (Curriculum Planning and Development Division, 2018, p. 6). The revised syllabus further adds,

> The study of literature is particularly suited to developing students' global awareness and critical and inventive thinking. Students study and discuss texts from different parts of the world that deal with a varied range of timeless human concerns, naturally broadening their global awareness.
>
> *(p. 7)*

The emphasis on extending literary engagement beyond the text is also observed in the newly proposed literary response framework where students are encouraged to expand their analysis of the text to connecting the text to self, other texts, other readers, and the world.

The pressure to engage with ethics

The impetus to infuse Global Citizenship Education in all subjects brings to light the third reason for the significance of ethics in Literature education. Unlike other Humanities subjects such as History, Civics, Social Studies where students already analyze global issues closely, Literature's approach to global engagement is different. Whereas in these other Humanities subjects, the focus is on key historic events, treaties, and significant figures, Literature often provides insights into the lived experiences of ordinary individuals experiencing trauma and other global injustices. The emphasis is on the ethical rather than the historical, on philosophical reflection rather than knowledge acquisition. In his essay "The Territory of Literature," George Hillocks (2016) begins with the argument about the close interconnection between Literature and ethical philosophy:

> What is the territory of Literature? What does it include? What are its boundaries? What is important to its understanding? First, high school curricula do not make it clear that, at the core, Literature is concerned not only with character, plot, and setting but with moral and philosophical issues. That is never a consideration given any serious thought. It is blithely ignored. However, if a curriculum is to be aimed at evidence-based argumentation in the disciplines, then in Literature, it will be of primary importance to pay particular attention to how the moral and philosophical issues of literature will be addressed.
>
> *(p. 110)*

Hillocks' call for closer alignment between Literature and ethical philosophy mirrors the growing interest in ethics in literary studies at universities around the world. Since the late twentieth century, scholars have noted the emergence of an ethical turn in literary studies. The reasons for this will be explored in chapter 4. Suffice to say that a number of prominent scholars in the field of Literature and Cultural Studies have been influential in prompting more serious attention to the connection between ethics and the teaching of literature.

The turn to ethics in Literature education

The turn to ethics is now more urgent than ever given the intensification of global interconnectedness that has led to greater efficiency and speed in the flows of knowledge and capital arising from the proliferation of digital culture. Trends in work places show increasingly diverse workforce and clientele. For example, between 2000 and 2050, new immigrants and their children will account for 83% of the growth of the working-age population in the United States (Burns, Barton, & Kerby, 2012); in 2011, between 30% and 40% of jobs in the business sector in Europe were sustained by consumers in foreign markets (OECD, 2016). By the time students graduate from schools and colleges, they are likely to find themselves in intercultural work environments and would have to work with others from different cultures and backgrounds. When surveyed, employers routinely list teamwork, collaboration, and oral communication skills as among the most valuable yet hard-to-find qualities of workers (Casner-Lotto & Barrington, 2006; Jerald, 2009). In an influential paper, Henry Jenkins (2006) highlights the rise of a participatory culture among youth, which necessitates educators lending more attention to how they can strengthen youth affiliations to physical and virtual communities, encourage creative forms of expression, promote collaborative problem solving, and empower them with new literacies (digital, multimodal, multilingual, etc.). Among the core skills needed in an age of participatory culture are the skills of navigation, networking, and negotiation of diverse perspectives.

At the same time, the darker side of globalization cannot be ignored. Beck (2007) argues that advanced industrialization has led to "risk societies" to the extent that global risks such as terrorism, extremism, xenophobia have permeated everyday realities. While some may celebrate the multicultural richness of a global village, others point to the disjunction between tourists and vagabonds or migrant labourers, between "flexible citizens" who inhabit multiple locations for work and pleasure and displaced refugees and asylum seekers who belong nowhere (Bauman, 1998; Ong, 1999). In 2018, the North Korean leader Kim Jung Un made a commitment to denuclearization and while many hailed his first meeting in Singapore with the President of the United States as a success, others questioned the silence surrounding ongoing human rights abuses in the country. Barely a week later, the United States announced its withdrawal from the United Nations Human Rights Council, and the White House has been criticized for separating children and even babies from parents at the United States' border control as part of a zero tolerance immigration policy. These are just some of the ethical dilemmas that people all over the word encounter on a daily basis.

The challenge for educators is how we can prepare students to navigate various moral ambiguities in the world, to be culturally sensitive to different values and beliefs, and to employ ethical reasoning to analyzing and critiquing global conflicts. Of all subjects in the curriculum, Literature provides the most opportune avenue for students to develop ethical sensitivity and reasoning.

First, Literature provides the gateway to understanding lived experiences of individuals at various times and places around the world and offers insights into cultures that students may not necessarily have access to. Most students, in their lifetime, would never travel to countries such as Syria, Afghanistan, and North Korea, or live among aboriginal communities in Australia. Perhaps the only access to understanding these cultures is through their narratives and oral histories. By encouraging an openness to the world, Literature attunes students to issues of justice and care for others, particularly those hurt by the excesses of global capitalism.

Second, literary texts, by providing insights into the lived experiences of others, inherently invite ethical contemplation. From issues of power in *Animal Farm* to the effects of vanity in *King Lear*, Literature is a prime site for applied ethics as students dialogue and debate about complex moral dilemmas. In the Literature class, as students study over a prolonged period how characters grow and change in various contexts, they are more able to contemplate the process of character formation, including their own.

Third, the infusion of ethical questions in Literature would empower students with ethical reasoning capacities as they examine the values underlying particular characters' motivations and behaviour, analyze the historical context informing such values, and compare values in one text with those from other cultures (Bauman, 1993; Eaglestone, 1997; Nie, 2015). Unlike formalist approaches to Literature that position texts as sacred and students as scholars, Lydia Brauer and Caroline Clark (2008) propose an alternative perspective – texts as culture, students as ethnographers. Culture encompasses the "array of signifying practices and is understood in relationship to social and economic economies of production and reception" (p. 304). By approaching texts as culture, teachers can facilitate the study of relationships between texts and their social, economic, and political contexts as well as their networks with cultural traditions and audiences. In this way, students do not merely read texts aesthetically, they read around texts by historicizing texts and comparing representation, production, and consumption of texts. Various scholars in Singapore have also called for a shift away from close reading of canonical works to including translated works from other ethnic groups such as Malay poetry (Yeo, 1999), to shift the curriculum from an English to World Literature focus (Holden, 1999), and to forge closer connections between literary texts studied and contemporary global realities (Choo, 2013; Liew, 2012; Loh, 2013; Poon, 2010).

In this book, I focus on how ethics can be a vital part of Literature education's DNA. Rather than a good-to-have topic of discussion only when one has covered the basics of literary analysis or when there is extra time at the end of class, ethics should be foregrounded and prioritized. This means that ethics should be the driving objective underlying the decisions made in organizing the curriculum, in teaching students to interpret texts, in enacting pedagogical practices and in cultivating values. Historically, Literature education has centred on training in literary criticism. From the late eighteenth century to the present, various movements have emphasized dominant forms of criticism, namely, New Criticism, Reader Response Criticism, and Poststructuralist Criticism. The deliberate effort to foreground ethics would mean training students in the relatively new approach of Ethical Criticism, which was popularized in the late twentieth century particularly by Wayne Booth and Martha Nussbaum and informed by key philosophers such as Emmanuel Levinas. It involves a critical hermeneutical approach to reading texts that analyzes how communities and their ethical values are represented, how ethical dilemmas are constructed and addressed, how the process of othering may be situated in local and global contexts, and how readers can engage with ethical issues in their communities and the world.

Ultimately, the infusion of ethics and Ethical Criticism in the Literature class is centred on an inquiry into how one should respond to and be responsible for others in the world. Human life is inherently social and human beings constantly make moral choices that influence others. The literary text itself has been crafted on the basis of key ethical decisions by the author who has selected an issue of concern to explore, to represent his or her viewpoint aesthetically through events, characters, and other stylistic elements, to depict ethical dilemmas in the fictional world, to persuade readers to share his or her point of view and so on. In his seminal work, *What Is Literature*, Jean-Paul Sartre (2001) argues that writers do not simply write for aesthetic reasons; their act of writing is inherently tied to an appeal for human freedom:

> Thus, whether he is an essayist, a pamphleteer, a satirist, or a novelist, whether he speaks only of individual passions or whether he attacks the social order, the writer, a free man addressing free men, has only one subject, freedom.
> (*p. 64*)

This innate concern with pushing the boundaries of freedom is the reason why literary texts are inextricability ethical, concerned essentially with the materiality of sociopolitical systems, and invested in provoking dissensus towards unjust epistemic underpinnings of hegemonic social orders.

Aims of the book and author's situatedness

Despite an evident turn to ethics in the field of Literature, several gaps remain unaddressed. First, such theorizations are predominantly observed among scholars working in university settings rather than at high schools, where contemporary literary theory, including Ethical Criticism, is rarely employed in Literature classrooms. Second, major scholarly texts on Literature and ethics tend to focus on literary texts that invite or provoke ethical responses such as Booth's (1988) *The Company We Keep: An Ethics of Fiction* and Nussbaum's (1990) *Love's Knowledge: Essays on Philosophy and Literature*. In most of these scholarly works, the examples used to support ethical engagement focus on literary texts and their effects on readers as though the transaction between them occurs in the private space of home. Absent from these examples is the fact that in the public sphere of the classroom, literary engagement occurs within a community of other readers. Here, students do not merely read literature but are socialized into what and how to read as decisions about the aims of teaching, the kinds of texts to study, the questions to ask about these texts, the ways to organize curricula units, the instructional and assessment strategies to employ are made by teachers in the classroom in connection to a broader community of students, parents, school leaders, curriculum specialists, scholars, etc. The lack of attention by scholars in literary studies to ethics and Ethical Criticism in practice may be a reason why it tends to be discussed more in theory and has been less pervasive in teaching.

The central aim of this book is to provide a comprehensive historical and theoretical understanding of the connection between Literature and ethics and its implications for teaching. Discussions are supplemented by on the-ground practices of how Literature teachers have engaged students in ethics and Ethical Criticism. The chapters in the book contain examples that stem from over ten years of my research into the teaching of literature. During this time, I had the opportunity to observe more than 80 classes and interview 140 teachers from various countries including Australia, Singapore, and the United States. Case studies of some of these teachers from the different schools and countries will be discussed. I also participated in curriculum review meetings as a consultant for the International Baccalaureate during their review of Language A subjects that includes Literature, Language and Literature, Literature and Performance as well as for the Ministry of Education in their review of the Literature in English syllabus for schools in Singapore. These experiences have contributed to my deeper understanding of the principles informing curriculum and assessment design.

My own background contains a complex fusion of East and West that is very much reflective of the history of Singapore. Formerly colonized by the British, Singapore gained independence in 1965. Given its small size, its lack of a viable domestic market and natural resources, the country was on the verge of becoming consumed with domestic divisiveness. The government's key strategy was to focus externally and rebrand Singapore as a global city. Then Minister of Foreign Affairs, S. Rajaratnam (1972) reiterated that Singapore's minuscule size and economic vulnerabilities were the very catalysts to securing its position as an ecumenopolis or world-embracing city. The English Language was to play a key role in the country's globalizing ambitions as the government prioritized it as a compulsory first language subject in all public schools while mother tongue languages could be studied either as a first or second language subject. The perception was that English was a language of business deemed essential for the city's success as a global financial hub. English would further serve as a lingua franca or bridge language unifying the different ethnicities that today comprise 74% Chinese, 13% Malays, 9% Indians, and 3% other minority groups such as Eurasians (Department of Statistics, 2019). Unlike other Asian nations, Singapore is the only country where the English language is accorded a privileged status as an official and first language for all citizens. English is the main medium of instruction in schools and the main mode of communication in all public spheres of society. Today, English is the language spoken most often at home in Singapore with about 37% of residents aged five or older using it most often at home as opposed to 35% using Mandarin (Department of Statistics, 2016). In key international reading assessments, Singapore students have taken these in English and outperformed students from other English-speaking countries such as Australia, Canada, New Zealand, the United Kingdom, and the United States. In OECD's 2018 Programme for International Student Assessment (PISA), 15-year-old Singapore students were ranked second for reading (Schleicher, 2019), and in the 2016 Progress in International Reading Literacy Study (PIRLS) assessment, fourth-grade Singapore students had the second highest reading achievement on average (International Association for the Evaluation of Educational Achievement, 2016).

The prioritization given to English has boosted Singapore's position as a global city fuelled by English as a global language and has contributed to the government's strategy of making it "the most open and cosmopolitan city in Asia" conducive to businesses especially from the West (Economic Review Committee, 2003, p. 5). While English has facilitated communicative efficiency among its multicultural residents and foreigners alike, it has also established ingrained cultural contradictions. Local Singaporeans, the majority of whom trace their ancestry to immigrants arriving from China, India, the Malay Archipelago in the early nineteenth century, have less historic and cultural affinity to English, which was regarded then as a language inherited from their British colonial rulers.

The cultural contradiction of a "non-native" first language English speaker became clear during my secondary school days in 1980s Singapore. I was educated in a conservative all-girls Chinese school. The school was founded by Chinese businessmen, merchants, and intellectuals who had been inspired by the revolutionary leader Sun Yat Sen when he visited Singapore in 1910 and observed the lack of participation by Singapore women in the revolutionary movement in China. Thus, he brought to light the importance of education in encouraging women to become actively involved in political matters. Morning assemblies, concerts, and school posters were in Chinese but all subjects taught in class, aside from Chinese Language, were in English. All students at the time had to study Literature, but this was centred on literatures in English from the West. Only a minority of students studied both English and Chinese Literature. Recollections of my Literature classes in secondary school included a British teacher who gave each of us a recording of his reading of *Silas Marner* and instructed us to listen to it in preparation for the final examination as well as a local teacher who taught us *Macbeth* and told us which lines we had to underline and memorize. Years after graduating from secondary school, I often wondered why we were never encouraged to question the texts and authors we studied. These texts were almost positioned as sacred, the author a revered genius whose lines we were encouraged to learn by heart. The fact that authors and their representation of cultures are inevitably flawed, fraught with bias, personal grievances, historical inaccuracies were seldom, if never, brought to light.

This book condenses many years of my own reflection on the nature and purposes of Literature education and it is my hope that the book will provoke a return to ethical language and ethical ways of seeing others at the heart of how we read, discuss, and think about literature in the classroom. If Literature is to break free from its traditional bonds of structuralism, formalism, and aestheticism, where texts are revered artefacts and discourse remains insulated within fictional worlds, then change must occur holistically. Put another way, ethics should be embedded in all spheres of Literature education beginning foremost with its philosophy of education to ways of designing curricula units, interpreting texts, enacting pedagogy, and cultivating values.

This book is targeted at scholars, graduate students, policymakers, and teachers involved in Literature education. It integrates my historical and philosophical research as well as my pedagogical work with teachers. It is my belief that theory without practice renders ideas as abstract and of less influence in effecting change while practical examples that are not grounded on theoretical justifications or an understanding of the historical evolution of the field, diminishes the rigour of the discipline. This book hopes to marry philosophy and practice, thereby itself demonstrating how ethical education is both philosophical and practical.

Aside from this introductory chapter which provides the rationale for the importance of teaching ethics through Literature, this book contains five other chapters with each chapter focusing on one aspect of Literature education – objectives, curriculum, texts, pedagogy, and values. Each aspect is further grounded on a core ethical principle as follows.

Objectives: ethics as the philosophical end of Literature education

At various points in the history of Literature, different objectives were prioritized – the cultivation of taste in good writing, the use of literature for language learning, the empowerment of reader's experiences and enjoyment of reading, and so on. While Literature teaching should encompass a holistic range of goals, in this book, I will argue that all other goals are means to a larger, more philosophical end and this end is centred on ethical engagement with others and in deepening understanding of how one can live in relation to diverse and multiple others in the world.

In chapter 2, I focus on the different philosophical views about the ends of literature and relatedly, Literature education. I begin with a discussion of the distinction between means and ends before proceeding to explore three dominant ends of Literature education. I begin with the transcendental end of Literature education, a view that became popular during the Enlightenment through the ideas of the German philosopher, Immanuel Kant. I then discuss the material end that lends attention to the ways art works disclose physical and social worlds through the work of another German philosopher, Martin Heidegger. The limitations of these ends point to the significance of the ethical end as the ultimate, culminating objective of Literature education. Grounded on the philosophy of Emmanuel Levinas, I argue that it is the cultivation of ethical response and responsibility to diverse others in the world that is the primary end of Literature education trumping but not necessarily excluding transcendental and materialist ends.

Curriculum: developing cosmopolitan-mindedness through ethical inquiry

The prioritization of ethics as a central objective in Literature education implies reorienting the design of the curriculum. For centuries, until today, Literature education has centred on training students in aesthetic appreciation of texts and equipping students to analyze literary language remains a fundamental skill they need to acquire in order for them to be discerning readers of texts. At the same time, the purpose of ethical engagement is at odds with the fundamental tenets of aestheticism, a movement that became prominent in the latter half of the nineteenth century and that was encapsulated by the slogan "art for art's sake." In other words, aestheticism subscribes to the view that art and beauty are ends in themselves and as Richard Posner (1998) claims, "the moral content of a work of art, including a work of literature, has little to do either with the value of the work, including such value as might be derived from the effect of the work on its readers or on society (or civilization, or humanity) as a whole, or with the pleasure to be derived from the work" (p. 1). To an extreme, aestheticism leads to an idolatry of the text inhibiting the development of relationships with others. Similarly, the popularity of Poststructuralist Criticism has also led to the privileging of scepticism and critical methods aimed at locating contradictions and gaps in texts. Political criticism, however, should be seen as an important stepping stone to deepening one's investedness in another. Thus, my proposed approach to ethical engagement positions aesthetic and political engagements not as ends but as launch pads and as means to deepening ethical relations with others in the world.

In chapter 3, I begin by exploring the aesthetic–political divide in Literature education and how this was reinforced by the movements of New Criticism and Poststructuralist Criticism from the early through late twentieth century. These critical approaches continue to wield significance in informing the design of the Literature curriculum till this day. Instead, I propose cosmopolitan ethics as a third space that is inclusive of but also extending aesthetic and political engagements with texts. In relation to organizing a curriculum of study, I discuss what a Cosmopolitan Literature curriculum can look like. Such a curriculum is informed by two significant precursor models – the early World Literature programme and Human Rights Education. These curricula models share close alignment with the goals of a Cosmopolitan Literature curriculum whose goals also extend beyond them. Some of its key curriculum guidelines would include introducing a range of critical pedagogies that support aesthetic, political, and ethical engagements with literature, organizing the curriculum around cross-cultural themes or issues rather than studies of a single text or culture, and not only organizing the curriculum around human rights and justice but also encouraging interrogations and forging of cross-cultural connections.

Texts: applying Ethical Criticism to interpreting literature

Literature education has historically focused on training students to critically read texts whether focusing on textual aesthetics, politics in texts, or ethical values and concerns. If ethics is the culminating end of Literature education and ethical inquiry the anchor that organizes the curriculum, then the teaching of critical reading should also be grounded in Ethical Criticism. Marshall Gregory (2010) describes literary art as encompassing a special agency or power in that they invite ethical inquiry into the lives and behaviour of others. If ethics is grounded on the question of how to live relationally, then such an inquiry is necessarily an open, ever-expanding, and ever-evolving effort to understand others in the world. Such inquiry is other-oriented rather than self-seeking. Self-seeking inquiry aims to arrive at a fixed understanding of the other in order to objectify, control, and manage the other. One example is of Arthur Jensen's controversial claim that racial differences in intelligence test scores have a genetic origin (Cianciolo & Sternberg, 2004). Conversely, other-oriented inquiry refrains from imposing one's own cultural lens to interpreting other communities. This may involve the capacity to suspend judgement of others, to examine issues from a different point of view, and even the willingness to confront the complicity of oneself and one's society in enacting violence on the other. The willingness to step into the shoes of the other involves an active inquiry aimed at disrupting prejudices about groups that have been stereotyped by mass media and nationalist/supremacist groups.

In chapter 4, I start by describing the turn to ethics and Ethical Criticism in Literature education from the late twentieth century before discussing principles that ground cosmopolitan Ethical Criticism. While it is important to equip students with the skills of close reading and to ensure they are familiar with the disciplinary language of Literature such as knowledge of its technical terminology, I argue that aesthetic language is a means to ethics as an end. That is, the appreciation of aesthetic language alone is insufficient. Aesthetic language provides an opening, an invitation for us to engage with the other. In practical terms, this would mean supplementing readings of aesthetic language with an ethical lens. I demonstrate how the application of cosmopolitan Ethical Criticism can occur through five ethical lenses to interpreting texts – descriptive ethics, normative ethics, analytical ethics, practical ethics, and virtue ethics. I also show how we can include additional ethical layers to traditional literary analysis. For example, I show how we can examine plot through the angle of ethical dilemmas, setting through its relation to border ethics, characters through the development of virtue, style through conceptual associations and their ethical intentions, and finally theme through explorations of ethical concepts.

Pedagogy: building a critical-ethical community of readers

Developing an interpretive community of readers is an important reason why Literature teachers should incorporate ethics in classroom discourse because this provides an avenue where students can learn to dialogue, collaborate, and negotiate with others who have different views. However, this is not an end in itself as overindulgence in building such a community can breed exclusivity and passivity. When empowered, the community of readers should transform into a community of actors who are globally conscious, attuned to human concerns and the needs of others, driven by a sense of responsibility and accountability not only to their own family and community but to the fraternity of human beings including the different and foreign.

Chapter 5 focuses on the kinds of pedagogies that teachers can use to develop active, ethical communities in the Literature class. I propose a Cosmopolitan Literature Pedagogic framework that highlights how teachers negotiate the range of knowledge, skills, approaches, and contextual influences. I propose that teachers be empowered with a repertoire of pedagogical approaches particularly the four Cs – Constructivist, Critical, Culturally Relevant, and Cosmopolitan pedagogies. In this chapter, I pay particular attention to cosmopolitan pedagogies. Utilizing case studies of Literature teachers from Australia, Singapore, and the United States,

I show how cosmopolitan pedagogies can facilitate four ethical forms of connections to texts, society, world, and philosophy. These connections involve strategies that deliberately resist and counter existing stereotypes of marginalized communities. They also involve intertextual and dialogic strategies that seek to develop informed and engaged interpretive communities through Literature discussions as well as provide opportunities for students to develop a greater commitment to defending others against social and global injustices.

Values: developing ethical character through dispositional routines

Discussions about values and Literature may alarm teachers with the fear that Literature may be used for purposes of indoctrination. Indeed, this has been commonplace throughout history and totalitarian governments have used Literature to promote propaganda and nationalistic rhetoric. Yet, we cannot at the same time ignore the fact that values permeate teaching whether implicitly or explicitly. Values direct students to that which is important to their lives and to fundamental ethical principles. Some examples common to Literature teachers are teaching students to enjoy reading or encouraging them to be independent critical readers. Underpinning these are social values about the worth of critical thinking and the value of reading. Given the reality of global interconnectedness, perhaps Literature's most significant value is tied to the promotion of cosmopolitan sensitivities demonstrated by a concern for the flourishing of others in the world. A cosmopolitan orientation to the world involves ethical resistance to forms of totalitarianism that impose moral values supporting a dominant power leading to the oppression of others.

Chapter 6 begins with the integral connection among values, character dispositions, and pedagogical routines in the classroom. Grounded on Confucian concepts of cosmopolitan love and ritual, I discuss how critical values of questioning, discernment, and deliberation as well as ethical values of empathy, hospitality, and responsibility to others can be cultivated through attending to everyday classroom routines. Today, discussions about routines have tended to centre on thinking routines rather than what I term dispositional routines. Using examples from the practices of Literature teachers I have observed, I show how attending to pedagogical routines can disrupt parochialism and foster a deeper commitment to others in the world.

In my concluding chapter, I reflect on the current effects of social distancing and disconnection as a result of the global pandemic and correspondingly, the devastating impact it has had on literary and performance arts industries all over the world. Literature teachers, too, find that unlike their colleagues in Science and Mathematics departments, they have to continually justify and defend the significance of their discipline. As we look to the future, the fact remains that technological, economic, and cultural globalization will continue to intensify and this provides a compelling reason for Literature education's niche in the school curriculum – to empower students with critical discernment, ethical attunement, and cosmopolitan consciousness to engage with diverse others for a more hospitable and inclusive world.

Note

1 The 9% figure refers to the number of students who enrolled in Literature in English as a full subject in 2012. There was another 9% who enrolled in the subject as an elective subject. Students taking Literature as a full subject have to complete two papers covering poetry, prose, and drama at the GCE Ordinary level examination. Students taking Literature as an elective subject have to complete only one paper covering poetry and prose.

2

OBJECTIVES

Ethics as the philosophical end of Literature education

After descending a ladder that reaches 40 feet into the depths of the cave, one is struck immediately by a sparkling array of crystal-like stalactites hanging from the roof. Following its path, one eventually encounters a series of paintings consisting of a pair of red bears, a cheetah eyeing its prey, and a majestic horse galloping towards a vanishing horizon. The path leads towards the back where the images take on a surrealistic form. Here, there is a painting of a human partly transformed into an animal with the head and horns of a large bison. Another painting consists of a female figure attracting a centaur-like figure in a long chamber that would have been used for rituals (Clottes, 2008).[1]

The above is a description of the interior of the Chauvet Cave, located in Southern France, first discovered by Jean-Marie Chauvet in 1994 to contain the world's earliest cave paintings dating approximately 31,000 years old. However, the Chauvet cave is significant for another reason since its discovery validated the theory that early cave art was closely intertwined with religious beliefs, particularly Shamanism that aims to foster direct interactions with the spiritual realm.[2] The discovery of the Chauvet paintings solidified this theory since it became clear that the paintings did not consist solely of animals in the natural world. It was proposed that the shaman, accompanied by a small band of followers, engaged in ritualistic practices, which allowed him to enter into the supernatural realm. The shaman's followers then painted these visionary images after the trance following his directions (Whitley, 2009). The hallucinatory feature of the Chauvet art can also be observed in the way that the art is integrated with the topography of the cave. For example, a panel of horses and a panel of lions located at the rear of the cave are spread along the natural features of the cave walls and are incorporated into its clefts or niches so that from certain angles, it seems as if the animals are literally emerging from the walls. David Whitley (2009), an American archaeologist and researcher involved in early expeditions to the cave, concludes that "Paleolithic art was then, in a sense, found art" (p. 48). Possibly, these imagined images emerged realistically from the walls to the minds of those engaged in rituals within the darkness and claustrophobic feel of the cave. Perhaps even more interesting is the fact that early Paleolithic man chose art as the conduit for the coexistence of the material and the spiritual. It was this extraterrestrial quality inherent in art that they found conducive as a mediator between the natural and supernatural world.

The Chauvet paintings suggest that early man saw art not merely as a means for pleasure or entertainment; rather, its main aim was to allow man to connect and possibly influence the spiritual realm. Centuries later, with the advent of modernity, this transcendental aim of art has declined in significance and been replaced by other aesthetic, cultural, and political aims. The focus of this chapter is on the philosophical ends of Literature education. The notion of a philosophical or teleological end has been expounded in Aristotle's (350 B.C.E./1985) *Nichomachean Ethics* which begins, "Every craft and every investigation, and likewise every action and decision, seems to aim at some good; hence the good has been well described as that which everything aims" (§1, p. 1). In other words, there is an ultimate, teleological end or philosophical purpose informing our quest for knowledge and skills and any other pursuit we set out to do. In education, however, the tendency is to focus on *episteme* (knowledge) and *techne* (craft or pedagogy) to the exclusion of the values underlying these. Take, for example, the repeated emphasis on developing critical and creative thinking skills in most twenty-first century education frameworks proposed by organizations such as the OECD or P21 (see Choo, 2017b). What are the culminating goals underlying the teaching of these skills? When one considers, for example, that terrorists and extremists often employ critical and creative thinking to strategize their attacks in unpredictable ways, we are bound to conclude that the knowledge and skills we seek to empower our students with must be connected to deeper, more ethical ends.

In this chapter, I begin with this transcendental end of Literature education which gained somewhat of a revival during the period of the Enlightenment. I then explore two ends that gained dominance subsequently – the material and ethical ends. Ultimately, I argue that the culminating end of Literature education is to empower students with the knowledge, skills, and dispositions to engage ethically with others in a global world. This is what I term the cosmopolitan ethical end of Literature education. Given that this chapter deals with philosophical ends, I will be comparing key philosophers who discussed a philosophy of art from transcendental, materialist, and ethical ends. I will then argue why the ethical aim provides the most compelling argument for the significance of Literature education and should direct its ultimate end.

The three ultimate ends of Literature education

As the renowned linguist Ferdinand de Saussure (1916) argues, "in a language, there are only differences, and no positive terms" (p. 118). Signs are determined by their differential relations with others in a linguistic system just as we understand light when juxtaposed with dark. Thus, words and concepts become meaningful only in their interconnections with others. In the same way, the notion of a "teleological end" can only be conceived in relation to the notion of "means."

The Greek *telos* denotes a final purpose, and thus a teleological end refers to a final purpose or good as juxtaposed with the means through which this may be achieved. For example, if one subscribes to the belief that the acquisition of wealth is a means to the flourishing of others in the world, then money earned would be invested in pursuits that support justice and security for others. However, it is often the case that the means become the end or their attractiveness override attention to ends. In recent Pandemic times, media reports emphasize new government rules about lockdowns and the race to find a vaccine. These, however, draw attention to the means of ensuring safety and security. Of course, the potential to reduce deaths through safe distancing and development of vaccines is important but hardly does one read about the ends these are directed towards. Is the goal to merely preserve human life? If this is so, other reports have highlighted the increase in domestic violence and mental health issues threatening lives in the supposed safety of lockdowns. Over-attention to means, which are often short-term solutions, discount discussions about ultimate ends that may provide more holistic understandings of material, social, and emotional solutions needed to solve problems.

In education, a common means that tends to become the all-consuming focus of administrators, teachers, students, and parents is the attainment of high test scores. In my interviews with teachers, I often hear them remarking that there is a shortage of curriculum time, which means less time can be given to peer discussions, inquiry-based projects, role-play, and other student-centred activities. On probing further, the common answer is that teachers feel pressed for time to complete the curriculum and tend to focus on content that is assessed in high-stakes assessments. Yet, the assessment is merely a means to an end. What exactly is that end? No doubt, these teachers subscribe to ideals such as the desire to inculcate a love for reading or to cultivate empathy for others in the world. Yet, when push comes to shove, the reality is that preparing students for the test overshadows more ethical ends. The means of performing well then becomes the end in itself.

If the means of learning (such as the test) does not lead to an ethical end but becomes the end itself, education becomes instrumental and schools function as sorting mechanisms, where those who perform well get access to better opportunities. In such a system, students are perceived as human capital, instruments to fuel the machinery of the state or corporation. To mitigate against utilitarian aims of education, there is a need to always keep the end in mind such as by showing explicitly how school policies and practices, including everyday routines, are connected to ultimate aims.

To reflect on the ultimate end of Literature education, I turn to philosophers who have debated and sought to theorize the teleological end of the arts. Though there have been many influential philosophers of art from classical antiquity to the present, I draw attention to three primarily because they explicate three well-known ends of the arts that we continue to adhere to – Immanuel Kant's transcendental end, Martin Heidegger's materialist end, and Emmanuel Levinas' ethical end.

The transcendental end

The German philosopher, Immanuel Kant (1724–1804), was a central figure in the age of Enlightenment and established many key concepts in modern philosophy related to metaphysics, ethics, political philosophy, aesthetics, and other fields. In ethics, he is often cited in textbooks as the figure of deontology or duty ethics. Deontology is one of the three common domains of normative ethics, the other two being Consequentialism and Virtue Ethics. One well-known branch of Consequentialism is utilitarianism, which subscribes to the view that an act is morally right if it leads to a desirable outcome. Conversely, Kant (1785/1995) considers consequences irrelevant to evaluating the moral worth of actions. He argues that actions should be evaluated according to principles that are universalizable: "Act only according to that maxim by which you can at the same time will that it should become a universal law" (§421, p. 38). In other words, an act is morally good if the rational agent, of his own free will and not by compulsion, based his or her action on universal moral principles. Thus, to Kant, lying would be morally wrong in all circumstances not because of its consequences (e.g. the potential harm it could cause to someone) but because lying can never be generalizable as a universal law. To Kant, the quintessential universal principle is encapsulated in this moral imperative: "Act so that you treat humanity, whether in your own person or in that of another, always as an end and never as a means only" (§429, p. 46).

The moral ethic of universality serves to advance Kant's vision of a "league of peace" outlined in his (1795/1963) essay, "Perpetual Peace." He describes this as a loose federation of nation-states committed to ensuring universal hospitality such as ensuring "the right of a stranger not to be treated as an enemy when he arrives in the land of another" (§358, p. 102).[3]

Kant's defence of deontology in relation to aesthetics entails an inherent teleological ethic directed towards the ethical end of human fulfilment. Such a teleological ethic is influenced by his views of human destiny as a process of spiritual growth (Ward, 1971). This transcendental end is also apparent in his discussions on aesthetics. In his seminal work, *Critique of Aesthetic Judgment (CJ)*, Kant (1790/1987) associates aesthetics as a science of the beautiful. The pleasure we attain from art is a "liking devoid of all interest" (§211, p. 53) and it is not driven by utilitarian purposes. This disinterested liking occurs because art works gesture towards the supersensible. Kant (1790/1987) provides an interesting explanation of how such gesturing occurs:

> Now I maintain that the beautiful is the symbol of the morally good; and only because we refer the beautiful to the morally good (we all do so naturally and require all others also to do so, as a duty) does our liking for it include a claim to everyone else's assent, while the mind is also conscious of being

> ennobled, by this, above a mere receptivity for pleasure derived from sense impressions, and it assesses the value of other people too on the basis of [their having] a similar maxim in their power of judgment.
>
> *(§353, p. 228)*

Three phrases in the first line necessitate a closer analysis – "the beautiful," "symbol of," and "morally good." First, Kant's use of the term "the beautiful" refers to a presentation of aesthetic concepts presented to the imagination that cannot be determined completely by language. Kant claims that beauty is the "exhibition [*Darstellung*, also translated "presentation"] or expression of aesthetic ideas" (Ginsborg, 2013, §2.6). By aesthetic idea, Kant refers to the presentation of the imagination to which no determinate concept can be adequate (1790/1987, §314, p. 182). Already, there is a hint that the beautiful transcends that material, discursive realm. The beautiful is closely tied to the realm of supersensible rather than ideas that can be perceived by the senses alone.

Second, it is worthwhile to ask why Kant refers the beautiful to the morally good through the mediating function of the symbol. Without the phrase "the symbol of," the statement would posit an equivalent relation, i.e. the beautiful in the form of sensible signs would characterize the concept of the morally good. Kant's reason for framing this relationship symbolically is essentially based on the interaction of analogous relations. On one hand, supersensible concepts (such as God or freedom) are exhibited in the form of aesthetic ideas which express the beautiful. On the other hand, these aesthetic ideas gesture the subject towards these supersensible concepts hence leading the subject engaged in contemplation of beauty from mere sensory contemplation to what can be akin to spiritual contemplation (Allison, 2001).

Third, the notion of "morally good," as he earlier explains in *Foundations of the Metaphysics of Morals*, requires a free and autonomous will to adhere, without any hidden agenda, to the principle of universality. "Morally good" does not refer simply to moral acts but more importantly, involves moral feeling. This is evident in Kant's connection of art to nature. Kant states that though art is different from nature, "the purposiveness of its form must seem as free from all constraint of chosen rules as if it were a product of mere nature" (CJ, §306, p. 173). Here, purposiveness is related to the gesturing capability that Kant argues is present in both art and nature. This purposiveness is akin to moral contemplation in which the subject, through art, is invited to contemplate what is beyond the sensible, material world. Though Kant does not specify the content of this moral contemplation, he provides several examples – a lily's white colour attunes the mind to ideas of innocence; art cultivates universal feelings of sympathy; the encounter with lightning, thunder, volcanoes with all their destructive power propels us to judge nature aesthetically and so attunes us to the notion of God's sublimity but also to our capacity to conceive of sublimity.

In essence, a teacher who subscribes to the transcendental end of Literature education believes that such an education can attune the mind of students to the sublime and spiritual. The literary text is then regarded as a sacred artefact and the artist deemed to have an enlightened revelation of a "higher" kind of knowledge (Brauer & Clark, 2008). Such a teacher may subscribe to the belief that literature lifts the soul, that it has that inherent power to take our minds away from sensual and earthly pleasures, directing us to contemplate such sublime concepts as love, freedom, nature, and God. Such a view may lead teachers to select only certain kinds of literature – those which would qualify as "sacred," canonical, and timeless. They may also encourage pedagogies that promote close reading and appreciation of texts as well as meditation and contemplative techniques.

The material end

While literature may gesture towards the sublime and transcendental, it also functions to reveal physical and social worlds. This material end of art is what distinguishes Martin Heidegger's philosophy of art from Kant's. Heidegger (1889–1976) was another influential German philosopher who, in his seminal work, *Being and Time*, sought to explore the question of the meaning of being. According to him, *Being or Dasein*, comes into existence when one is socialized into an understanding of what it is to be human (Dreyfuss, 1991). In the same way, things, including art works, exist and attain significance in terms of their use and involvement in society.

In "The origin of the work of Art" (*OWA*), Heidegger (1971a) begins by suggesting that the question of the origin of the work of art must be addressed by looking beyond the source of its nature – "the art work is something else over and above the thingly element" (p. 19). The art work points not only to the supersensible but the material work of art discloses the context of physical and social worlds. The working of art to bring forth is what Heidegger (1971b) terms, the poetic. While "poem" as a noun refers to the composition of words typically employing rhythmic and metrical patterns, "poetic" as a verb refers to the creative act of producing. Thus, the poetic, derived from the Greek, *poiesis*, is evidenced in the activity of an artist, craftsman, or any person who brings the new into existence. Heidegger also describes the poetic occurring in nature as when something arises out of itself like the blooming of a flower. Heidegger draws attention to the way art works demonstrate the creative force of the poetic in our world. His thesis on art is encapsulated in this statement: "Art is truth setting itself to work" (OWA, p. 38). Three terms call for careful examination: "Art," "is," and "truth setting itself to work."

At first glance, it is evident that Heidegger's use of the word "Art" contrasts with Kant's use of the term "the beautiful" when Kant claims, "the beautiful is the symbol of the morally good" (CJ, §353, p. 228). Unlike Kant, who relates the beautiful to the transcendental, Heidegger's focus is on the materiality of the art work itself. In this sense, Heidegger overturns Kant's gesturing towards the supersensible. Heidegger is not so much concerned with the art work as object as he is with the working of art, i.e. the poetic. The verb "is" in "Art is" focuses on the poetic process of art and reiterates the notion that the work of art is not a mere thing. Thus, when Heidegger (1971a) discusses art works, he is interested in things in their use:

> The art work is, to be sure, a thing that is made, but it says something other than the mere thing itself is. The work makes public something other than itself; it manifests something other; it is an allegory. In the work of art something other is brought together with the thing that is made. To bring together is, in Greek, *sumballein*. The work is a symbol.
>
> *(OWA, p. 19)*

The notion of the poetic operating at the metaphorical level is reiterated in Heidegger's claim that the "work is a symbol" (p. 19) although his use of "symbol" has a different meaning from Kant's use of the same term. This may be clarified in Heidegger's example of Van Gogh's painting of a pair of peasant shoes. He notes that the peasant woman who wears the shoes is not aware of it at all in her everyday use of the shoes. However, in the painting, this object is taken out of its context so that we begin to focus not on the equipment in its use but its equipmental nature. Thus, while Kant refers the term "symbol" to a gesturing towards the sublime via art, Heidegger employs the term "symbol" to refer to the act of defamiliarizing.

Art is "truth setting itself to work" (p. 38) because the poetic defamiliarizes aspects of physical and social worlds. Heidegger references the Greek term, *aletheia*, which means, to unconceal. For example, Van Gogh's painting invites us to see the social life of the peasant, her hard work and toiling in the fields, etc. Other works of art can point to historical times or different social worlds. Additionally, the poetic discloses earth by giving form to matter. He gives the example of how a temple's firm towering makes visible the invisible spaces of air. While matter has always existed, it is only the workings of the poetic that make matter intelligible. Would, for example, a particular kind of wood have come into existence for us, had we not required its use? In this way, art brings what *is* into the open.

Further, Heidegger argues that a thing is essentially formed matter – the matter affects the form and the form shapes matter in order that we may use it – "What is constant in a thing, its consistency, lies in the fact that matter stands together with a form. The thing is formed matter" (p. 26). Similarly, art is formed matter. For example, a poem exists through its interplay of form and content; a painting discloses not only the equipmentality of the image but also the action or technique of the work. Because of this form–matter relation, the art work must be grounded in its usefulness. As he says, "Usefulness is the basic feature from which this entity regards us, that is, flashes at us and thereby is present and thus is this entity. Both the formative act and the choice of the material – a choice given with the act – and therewith the dominance of the conjunction of matter and form, are all grounded in such usefulness" (p. 28).

Essentially, a teacher who subscribes to Heidegger's materialist view of Literature education would believe that such an education can defamiliarize students to physical and social worlds by sensitizing us, for example, to beauty in nature or to "truths" about other lives or cultures. As Heidegger explains, "If there occurs in the work a disclosure of a particular being, disclosing what and how it is, then there is here an occurring, a happening of truth at work" (p. 35). To borrow a metaphor from Brauer and Clark (2008), the literary text would be regarded as a window to the real world of nature and societies and students would perform the role of witnesses. Teachers may employ texts from a variety of times and places to expand students' worldview. They may supplement this with culturally responsive and multicultural pedagogical approaches to foster appreciation of other cultures.

Thus far, the question of ultimate ends of Literature education has been addressed according to two opposite axes (see Figure 2.1). On the vertical axis, the Kantian view posits the role of art in facilitating a shift from attending to pleasurable and sensual desires to more spiritual contemplation. On the horizontal axis, the Heideggerian view posits the role of art as disclosing physical and social worlds. Each of these ends privileges a particular belief about the purpose of art works and correspondingly, aesthetic education.

In the Kantian view, revelation of the divine is privileged. Kant states:

> [I]n order to set ourselves a final purpose in conformity with the moral law, we must assume a moral cause of the world (an author of the world); and to the extent that setting ourselves a final purpose is necessary, to that extent (i.e. to the same degree and on the same ground) it is also necessary that we assume [that there is] a moral cause of the world: in other words, that there is a God.
>
> *(CJ, §450, p. 340)*

Revelation of God is the "inner moral destination" (CJ, §447, p. 336) that propels one to strive for the highest good in all forms of human engagement.

In the Heideggerian view, it is knowledge of the world that is privileged instead. Knowledge forms the basis of man's creativity since man's ability to create

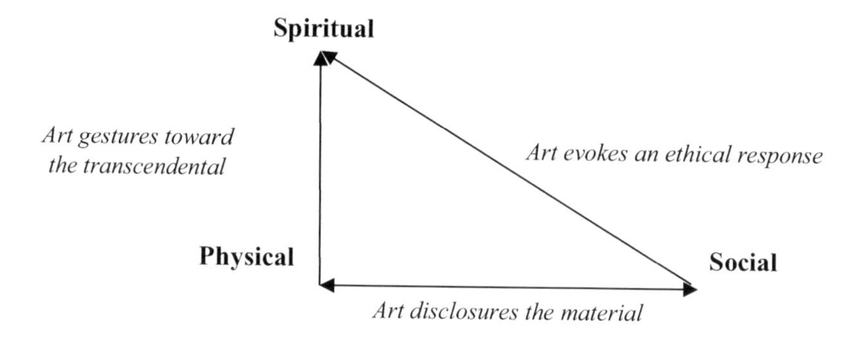

FIGURE 2.1 Three ultimate ends of art and aesthetic education

is determined by his poetic ability to take measure of the world. As Heidegger (1971b) asserts in his essay, ". . . Poetically Man Dwells . . .": "To write poetry is measure-taking, understood in the strict sense of the word, by which man first receives the measure for the breadth of his being" (p. 219). Thus, Heidegger argues that man's dwelling on the earth is not merely established by a need for survival; rather, it is man's capacity to create that distinguishes him from all other species. Yet, this creativity occurs only with a knowledge of the limitless potential of his being revealed through the poetic.

The ethical end

Emmanuel Levinas offers a third approach to the ultimate purpose of art and aesthetic education, one that focuses on an ethical end. Levinas (1906–1995) was born in Lithuania and grew up in a traditional Jewish family. Anti-Semitic persecution pushed his family to leave and settle in Ukraine where they again endured a wave of anti-Jewish progroms. Later, Levinas left for France and commenced his philosophical studies at the age of 17. He spent a year at the University of Freiburg in Germany working under the philosophers Husserl and Heidegger. Shortly after, war broke out and he joined the French army in 1939 becoming a prisoner of war a year later. While his wife and daughter survived the Holocaust, other members of his family were killed by the Nazis. Consciousness of suffering, of exile, and of the dehumanization of human beings have pervaded Levinas' major works that emerged after the Second World War, particularly *Totality and Infinity* (1969) and *Otherwise than Being or Beyond Essence* (1974). One of the most significant philosophers of the late twentieth century, Levinas has been described as a postmodern philosopher (Alford, 2002), Holocaust philosopher (Eaglestone, 2008), and philosopher of exile (Doukhan, 2012), among others.

Levinas regretted his enthusiasm for Heidegger given what he viewed as Heidegger's accommodation to Nazism. A core facet of his work was to critique the obsession of Western philosophy, especially Heidegger, with the meaning of being (ontology) as first philosophy. Throughout Western philosophy, first philosophy has been explored by various philosophers beginning with Aristotle through to Descartes, Husserl and Heidegger, among others. First philosophy, which concerns the question of what is being, how being came to be, and how being justifies itself, has been conceptualized in relation to universal principles, reason, time, and language, among others. Levinas observes that being's integral relation to the other has been largely absent from philosophical discourse and yet, responsibility to the Other pre-exists being's consciousness of itself. Levinas (1999) thus proposes ethics as first philosophy:

> When I speak of first philosophy, I am referring to a philosophy of dialogue that cannot not be an ethics. Even the philosophy that questions the meaning of being does so on the basis of the encounter with the other.
>
> *(p. 97)*

To Levinas, first philosophy is philosophy that prioritizes encounters with the other via dialogue which then determines language and philosophical reflection. This ethical encounter is not characterized by a set of rules but by a keen sense of and responsibility to the other (Doukhan, 2012).

Levinas views Kant's theorization of the poetic as gesturing towards a revelation of the divine as inadequate in capturing the totality and infinity of the transcendent. The divine God, the infinite or absolute Other, is non-thematizable and lies beyond ontological structures. It is an abstraction whose understanding cannot be obtained from the substance of beings since this would imply that God can be contained in form. Yet, the force of the divine penetrates being's core, disrupting any propensity for egoistic self-absorption while calling the self to respond to other beings in the world. As he (1987) explains:

> He [God] is neither an object nor an interlocutor. His absolute remoteness, his transcendence, turns into my responsibility – nonerotic par excellence – for the other.
>
> *(p. 165)*

Put another way, the poetic gestures not towards the transcendental God but the other who calls us to transcend our self-centredness in order to engage face to face with the other in the world (Perpezek, 1995). The voice of the Other manifests in ethical imperatives calling us to be morally accountable to and responsible for others in the world, particularly those who are suffering (Lingis, 1974).

Levinas also diverges from Heidegger's views of art as disclosing knowledge of the world. For Heidegger, a phenomenological account of being must begin from the notion of intentionality – being's interestedness in the world. It is the non-deliberate, non-self-referential, ongoing ways of everyday existing that being can be known (Dreyfuss, 1991). One way in which intentionality is made manifest is through language which opens a way for being to be unveiled. The poetic to Heidegger then refers to how art works to project being's involvement in the world. It is here that Levinas disagrees with Heidegger on two points.

First, an understanding of being cannot be located in expression that originates from culture. This may be clarified from Levinas' notion of "trace" which points to a beyond from which the face signifies but only incompletely in discourse. While Heidegger uses art as the means to which the poetic unconceals truth, Levinas (1989) argues that art is non-truth and rather than disclosing truth, it is "the very event of obscuring, a descent of the night, an invasion of shadow . . . art does not belong to the order of revelation, nor does it belong to the order of creation" (p. 132). Art is referred to as a "shadow," a resemblance of truth, bewitching us into replacing the copy or image for the real. The poetic thus works to unconceal non-truth.

Second, Levinas overturns another of Heidegger's arguments about the way the poetic works to defamiliarize by bringing into awareness the equipmentality of things. Conversely, Levinas observes that it is the "deformalization" by the poetic that occurs because of art's inadequate representation of the real (Levinas, 1974). This deformalization interrupts and ruptures all symbolic forms by its moral imperatives that is both beyond and more originary than culture (Cohen, 1974).

Herein lies the major difference between Levinas versus Kant and Heidegger's views of art which is the importance he gives to criticism as a way to interrupt art. Levinas does not romanticize the transcendental beauty of artworks or its poetic processes of disclosure. He offers a more sceptical view of art. To Levinas (1989), art substitutes reality for a representation that lures us into passivity, disengaging us from real encounters and commitment to action. Art charms, bewitches, and captivates the spectator who evacuates responsibility to the other (Crignon, Simek, & Zalloua, 2004). The spectator is lured into a position of passive disinterestedness such as by admiring the work, appreciating its composition, and even sympathizing with the characters of the work. What perpetuates this disinterestedness is the fact that art is timeless. While time may unfold within the world of the art but the work is still outside of real time (Eaglestone, 1997). As Levinas (1989) argues:

> The formula [art for art's sake] is false inasmuch as it situates art above reality and recognizes no master for it, and it is immoral inasmuch as it liberates the artist from his duties as a man and assures him of a pretentious and facile nobility. But a work would not belong to art if it did not have this formal structure of completion, if at least in this way it were not disengaged.
>
> *(p. 131)*

In this sense, art operates in the order of what Levinas (1974) terms, the said as opposed to the saying. The said is what has been culturally determined and through which language and cultural symbols are derived; the saying is what becomes subjected to the rules of cultural discourse but which resists this subjection at the same time.

> To say is to approach a neighbor, "dealing him signifyingness." This is not exhausted in "ascriptions of meaning," which are inscribed, as tales, in the said. Saying taken strictly is a "signifyingness dealt the other," prior to all objectification; it does not consist in giving signs.
>
> *(p. 48)*

For Levinas, the saying is located beyond phenomenology, in what is otherwise than being. It transcends totalizing systems and occurs before language: "Saying, taken strictly, is a signifyingness dealt with the other prior to all objectification" (p. 48). Levinas (1969) argues that "being is exteriority" (p. 290) and comes into existence through a conscious of the other calling us to respond. The ethical core of Levinas' philosophy is our originary encounter with the other occurring before language, art, and symbolic forms. Thus, ethics is first philosophy of art: "Before it is a celebration of being, expression is a relation with the one to whom I express the expression and whose presence is already required so that my cultural gesture of expression can be produced" (Levinas, 2006, p. 30).

How can the saying occur in concrete terms to interrupt the said? Levinas draws attention to the importance of criticism in interrupting art. He distinguishes two kinds of criticism – art criticism and philosophical criticism. The former examines art focusing on its aesthetic qualities while the latter pushes towards a committed criticism. He argues that "committed art cannot exist but committed criticism that can make art committed by leaving the world of art to appeal to the real world, can and must exist" (Eaglestone, 1997, p. 109). Thus, committed criticism is akin to "philosophical exegesis" (Levinas, 1989, p. 142), "ethical exegesis" (Cohen, 2016. p. 151) or, in other words, Ethical Criticism. Ethical Criticism exemplifies the saying that interrupts the said by evoking and placing the suffering face of the other continually before us. Through this evocation, Levinas (1974) states that we are "ordered toward the face of the other" (p. 11) which effects a "burning for the other" (p. 50) and a "suffering for his suffering" (p. 18). In the process, the self does not lose its own identity but is constantly challenged to move out of its own self-absorption and its desire to dominate the other, to make the other like his or her own self. The "ego loses its sovereign coincidence with self, its identification where consciousness comes back triumphantly to itself to reside in itself" (Levinas, 2006, p. 33).

In sum, Ethical Criticism disrupts art from its own closure, detachment, and evasions, reminding the spectator that art is part of the larger world and cannot escape its accountability to the other. All art must necessarily involve interpretation, intertextuality, and the interpersonal. A teacher who subscribes to the Levinasian ethical end of Literature education would complement appreciation of literature with Ethical Criticism. The latter involves close attentive reading of art that attends to silences, gaps, the ways it ethically misrepresents others as well as the way it calls us to real ethical encounters with others. Ethical Criticism must therefore complement any engagement with literature and the effect of Ethical Criticism is to draw us out of fictional worlds towards responsible engagement with the other. Here, response to literature via criticism, rather than contemplation, is integrally tied to responsibility to the other. As Levinas (1974) describes:

> The self is on the hither side of rest; it is the impossibility to come back from all things and concern oneself only with oneself. It is to hold on to oneself while gnawing away at oneself. Responsibility in obsession is a responsibility of the ego for what the ego has not wished, that is, for the others.
>
> *(p. 114)*

Even in attempts to respond, the other can never be totally grasped by any theoretical or thematic determination (Derrida, 2008). It is the very incomprehensibility of the other that allows for response to be manifested in responsibility. This reiterates Levinas' (1974) argument that "the neighbour that obsesses me is already a face, both comparable and incomparable, a unique face and in relationship with faces, which are visible in the concern for justice" (p. 158). It is also this incomprehensibility that ensures that a responsible response, including even an ethics of criticism, is never limited or closed but allows for continual creative interpretation and expression.

Towards ethics as the ultimate philosophical end of Literature education

The three ultimate ends of Literature education (see Figure 2.1) can be summed up as follows:

1 To gesture towards the transcendental;
2 To disclose the material (physical and social worlds); and
3 To evoke an ethical response via Ethical Criticism.

These three ends have attained significance at various points in history. There is no reason why these three objectives should not all be important goals of Literature education. In their study of texts, students should have opportunities to contemplate the beauty of nature and of the divine (whatever their beliefs about the transcendental may be). They should also explore the ways literary texts attune us to the world we live in such as by immersing ourselves in other cultures or drawing attention to everyday aspects of nature and objects. These objectives, while important, should be positioned as objective means rather than objective ends. In other words, they are key objectives that lead to an ultimate ethical end.

The transcendental and material objectives, if taken as ends, lead the reader to become absorbed in passive contemplation and disinterested appreciation of the literary text as sacred and cultural artefact. However, if positioned as an objective means, this allows the teacher to interrupt the process of contemplation to push students to consider how the literary text can relate to real communities in the world and how feelings of empathy evoked from the text can be connected to just actions in the world.

If all objectives are means to one end, it is ethics that is the culminating, ultimate philosophical end, of Literature education. The term "ethics" has been used interchangeably with "morality." However, there are some important distinctions. Morality, from the Latin, *moralis*, refers to customs or manners whereas ethics stems from the Greek, *ethos*, which denotes character (Thiroux, 2001). Thus, while morality is concerned with right and wrong according to specific social conventions, ethics is concerned with an individual's character and how one develops in relation to others. Teaching literature for moral education emphasizes the moral of the story or what one ought to do in given situations such as the principle that one should not lie as gleaned from Aesop's fable, "The boy who cried wolf." This form of teaching tends to be didactic in nature and, taken to the extreme, may be construed as indoctrination. For example, one is reminded about how German folktales were taught to young children in schools to inspire a nationalistic spirit and instil pride in the supremacy of the Aryan race (Kamenetsky, 1984).

Conversely, teaching literature as grounded on ethics as an end is inquiry-oriented and is concerned with how we relate to others in the world.

In short, I define ethics as the ultimate philosophical end of Literature education. This recentres the focus neither on some ephemeral transcendental quality in literature nor on the text's aesthetic beauty. Rather, Literature education grounded on ethics as an end is focused on an inquiry into how one should respond to and be responsible for others in the world. These would translate to the following key objectives of Literature education:

Objective 1: To expose students to diverse perspectives from around the world through literature and to enable students to inquire into ethical issues in connection to broader and more complex sociopolitical and historical factors.

Objective 2: To equip students to apply Ethical Criticism to uncovering ideological values in texts through analysis of aesthetic language as well as connect issues in texts to complex ethical realities in the world.

Objective 3: To encourage students' active ethical engagement in order that they may better empathize with the perspectives of others in the world.

Objective 4: To empower students with the agency to think critically and act responsibly to tackle injustices and effect transformative changes in society and the world.

Ethics as the ultimate end of Literature education entails an entire reorientation of its curriculum, texts, pedagogy, and values. Each of the four objectives above corresponds to these areas.

In the area of curriculum, objective 1 would mean rethinking the organization of the curriculum from a cosmopolitan lens. This would involve exploring how we can design a cosmopolitan Literature curriculum inclusive of diverse voices including works in translation and how we can encourage connections to cultural and intercultural dynamics beyond texts. This will be elaborated in chapter 3.

In the area of texts, objective 2 would mean recognizing the importance of training students with the skills to appreciate the nuances of language, form, meter, and other aesthetic techniques. At the same time, reading the text should be supplemented with reading against and beyond the text. Thus, Aesthetic Criticism should be complemented with Poststructuralist Criticism and Ethical Criticism. Specific ways of applying Ethical Criticism will be discussed in chapter 4.

In the area of pedagogy, objective 3 recognizes that literary engagement cannot be reduced to passive appreciation of texts but should activate students' involvement in the world. This could occur through intentionally surfacing and troubling stereotypes they have or that are commonly conveyed via mass media. It could also occur through dialogic exercises such as role-play and simulated forums, among others that provide opportunities for them to conduct more in-depth research into othered groups to see reality from their point of view. Examples of how teachers have employed such pedagogies will be described in chapter 5.

In the area of values, objective 4 extends the previous objective in recognizing that literary engagement should also activate students' involvement beyond the classroom to their community, their country, and the world. Ethical dispositions such as empathy, hospitality, and responsibility to others are important values that should be cultivated and explored as discussed in chapter 6.

In summary then, this suggested reorientation of Literature education as grounded on ethics as first philosophy would support the development of cosmopolitan-minded citizens. As Nussbaum (1997) observes, Literature and the Humanities play a vital role in developing in students' a sympathetic responsiveness to the needs of others. In particular, Literature fosters the "narrative imagination" which she defines as "the ability to think what it might be like to be in the shoes of a person different from oneself, to be an intelligent reader of that person's story, and to understand the emotions and wishes and desires that someone so placed might have" (p. 10). In contrast to Matthew Arnold's (1861/1993) proposition for a Literature education that gears towards spiritual perfection through the development of taste,[4] Literature education grounded on ethics orients students to seeing diverse others in the world as part of one's family and in so doing, intensifies their investedness in others beyond their community and nation.

The kind of ethical vision Nussbaum proposes aligns with an enlightenment notion of a cosmopolitan society involving Kant's (1795/1963) vision of "a universal cosmopolitan condition . . . wherein all the original capacities of the human race can develop" (§29, p. 23). Her conception of the narrative imagination is based on an ethics of empathy and identification with the other. It is premised on a celebration of life or affinity with others. On the other hand, Literature education anchored on ethics can also be centred on a consciousness of death. It is here that postcolonial scholar Edward Said's notion of democratic criticism finds resonance. At the beginning of his book, *Humanism and Democratic Criticism*, Said (2004) reminds us of the reality of September 11. This is followed by references to the Cold War, the conflict in the Middle East, ethnic cleansing in Rwanda, etc. Contrary to Nussbaum, Said's position is that criticism arises from the need to be conscious always of death, violence, and oppression. Said's critical tool is Philology, which involves a close reading and attentiveness to the ways in which language is used, the ways in which places, communities, and societies are named and the ideological implications behind these labels. Thus, while Nussbaum seeks cohesion and repair by pointing to a common humanity, Said seeks disruption and revision by pointing to cultural pluralism. Ultimately, it is a form of ethical engagement aimed at rupturing space within cultural discourse so as to recognize exiled, immigrant, unhoused populations who are silenced from this space.

Perhaps what it means when we propose ethics as the culminating philosophical end of Literature education is the need to negotiate a necessary tension between universality and plurality in our approach to ethics. In this global age where technology has vastly increased the avenues for multimodal communication resulting in the proliferation of information and the clashing of cultures, the need to empower students to navigate ethical complexities is even more crucial. In the end, such ethical engagements through Literature education should be understood as a continual project of response and responsibility.

Notes

1 This account is based on the experiences of John Robinson's expedition to the Chauvet cave in 1999 (see Bradshaw Foundation, n.d.).

2 Due to discrepancies in earlier theories, a new hypothesis began to emerge in the 1980s that connected early cave art with religious beliefs. David Whitley (2009) contends that the most popular theories of cave art from the late nineteenth century to the mid-twentieth century centred on hunting magic and structuralist aesthetics. While the first theory proposes that the cave paintings, consisting mostly of animals, were drawn to help early humans in conquest since their livelihood consisted of hunting and gathering, the second theory proposes that the paintings were aesthetic representations of the natural world. However, both these theories contain significant discrepancies. First, new archaeological findings reveal that the food these early humans ate had nothing to do with the animals they painted on the walls of the cave. Therefore, it is unlikely that the cave paintings were directly intended to have an effect on hunting activities. Second, these cave paintings are located in hard-to-reach parts of the cave which contradicts the rationale that they were created solely for aesthetic purposes since it is unlikely that many of the early humans had access to it.

3 Kant (1795/1963) theorizes cosmopolitan rights extending beyond the individual and nation-state in the third article of "Perceptual Peace" entitled, "The Law of World Citizenship Shall Be Limited to Conditions of Universal Hospitality" (§358, p. 102). Here, Kant expresses concern with rising nationalism in the late eighteenth century during the period which saw the emergence of the nation-state as an ideal political model for the rest of the world.

4 In discussing the function of criticism, Arnold (1861/1993) dichotomizes the practical and the spiritual. Criticism, he argues, must be independent of practical aims so as to "study and praise elements that for the fullness of spiritual perfection are wanted" (p. 47). Arnold's cultural criticism is centred on cultivating taste through pursuing perfection as associated with "an inward condition of the mind and spirit" (p. 63).

3

CURRICULUM

Developing cosmopolitan-mindedness through ethical inquiry

In 2014, reports surfaced that undergraduate students in Cambridge University were left baffled when they sat for their English Literature examination. This was a Practical Criticism paper and students were tasked to perform close reading on a given poem. The problem was that the poem, titled "Tipp-Ex-Sonate" by South African poet, Andre Letoit, has no words and is made up entirely of punctuation such as brackets, quotation marks, an exclamation mark and a question mark. For example, the second stanza begins "(   )!" and the second line"(   )?"

News sources describe students as feeling "shocked," "flustered," and "panicked" (Turnley, 2014, para 2). Perhaps this is because their training in practical criticism had taught them to critically appreciate the nuances of words, the connotations of figurative language, and the structural development of words in relation to form. Their incapacity to interpret such a poem also points to the limits of practical criticism, which has traditionally been a core aspect of English foundational courses in British universities since the 1930s. Practical Criticism emphasizes a form of disinterested and decontextualized reading of texts in which words on a page are deemed sufficient. While such a method of literary criticism applies well to canonical poems by the likes of Blake, Dickinson, and Wordsworth, etc., it is hermeneutically insufficient when applied to political poems such as Letoit's "Tipp-Ex-Sonate" where "tipp-ex" refers to a brand of correction fluid with the connotation of an erasure of voice. The BBC (2014) quoted Mark Ford, a professor of English at University College London, who said that understanding the poem involves recognizing the context of its writing and the background of the author. Kombius, an anti-apartheid activist, wrote the poem to protest against censorship laws imposed by White minorities in South Africa. The absence of words and punctuation then expresses oppressive silencing coupled with passive aggressive resistance. These absences also push readers into an active role encouraging them to fill the gaps by conducting research into the poet, his political protest and the historical context of apartheid. Not only would such an extended inquiry into the sociopolitical underpinnings of the text be impractical in a timed examination but it would also go against a core principle of Practical Criticism, namely, that aesthetic appreciation should be ahistorical and apolitical where the ideal critic is one who is disinterested and approaches the work scientifically as an object to be dissected.

For much of the twentieth century, this apolitical method of Aesthetic Criticism has triumphed over Poststructuralist Criticism and Ethical Criticism in Literature education. Equipping students to identify and discuss the effects of literary techniques such as symbolism, personification, hyperbole, enjambment, etc., was, and still is, a common approach to curriculum and teaching. One consequence is that the Literature classroom is perceived as disconnected from the real world as literary engagement continues to be fixated on aesthetic appreciation of texts rather than on their ethical implications. Indeed, the practice of literary criticism in schools is so closely connected to aesthetic appreciation of literary style and language that students rarely engage with discussions about human rights, social justice, the nature of suffering, and other ethical values that pervade the content of literature and often provide the primary motivation for literary writers in the first place.

In the first part of this chapter, I explore the aesthetic-political divide in Literature education paying particular attention to how this has been reinforced by New Criticism and Poststructuralist Criticism as these are key movements that have had significant influence on the teaching of literature in schools till this day. In the second part of the chapter, I then propose cosmopolitan ethics as the third space inclusive of but extending beyond aesthetics and politics. Following this, I proceed to discuss the features of a Cosmopolitan Literature curriculum and its connections to two important curricula – the World Literature programme and Human Rights Education.

The aesthetic–political divide in Literature education

Aestheticism as an ideological tool of colonization

The birth of English Literature as a public school subject began when a nationally organized system of education was established in Britain from the late eighteenth century. The primary aim was to cultivate taste in good writing as this was a mark of bourgeois English civility (Doyle, 1989). During this period, the rise of a middle class catalyzed the push to diffuse an education in polite social manners and habits of taste. Literature education gained new currency alongside the popularity of literary periodicals, coffee houses, guidebooks on manners, among others, in civilizing the masses (Eagleton, 1996). Essentially, Literature education provided the platform for the study of culture. As Arnold (1993) observes, culture is "a study of perfection" (p. 59) involving a sentiment for beauty that opposes "animality"

(p. 73). Immersion in high culture not only contributes to the development of an informed citizenry aware of the "best that is known and thought in the world" (p. 37) but the acquisition of taste also provides a necessary bulwark against utilitarian influences of an industrial age.

The lack of a systematic pedagogical approach to the critical appraisal of culture and cultural texts became the centre of scholarly attention in the 1930s. I. A. Richards (1929), then lecturer at Cambridge University, sought to provide a new technique "to prepare the way for educational methods more efficient than those we use now in developing discrimination and the power to understand what we hear and read" (p. 3). His book, *Practical Criticism*, was a seminal text that exemplified the importance of a systematic approach to close reading that would mitigate problems he had observed in his own students such as immaturity, stock responses, preconceptions, variability of responses, and a general lack of discrimination. The scholarly contributions of Richards, together with others such as T. S. Eliot, John Crowe Ransom, and Cleanth Brooks, fuelled the movement of New Criticism which came to dominate literary study in the universities and which then became a standard pedagogical approach in schools by the 1960s (Applebee, 1974).

New Criticism propagates an objective and disinterested close reading of texts that disregards any attention to the reader's impressions or extratextual concerns. To base one's interpretations on subjective opinions is to commit the affective fallacy; to consider the author's background or his or her authorial agenda is to commit the intentional fallacy (Wimsatt & Beardsley, 1947/2001). Equipped with the skills of critical analysis, the student is to focus on how form and style work in texts to convey meaning and literary analysis is to be scientific, objective, and disinterested.

Essentially, New Criticism reiterates the values of eighteenth-century aestheticism grounded on the "art for art's sake" doctrine that foregrounds the aesthetic value of the text to the exclusion of its sociopolitical ends. New Criticism was particularly conducive at a time when the British government sought for an alternative to Religious Studies, which had declined in popularity as a result of increasing cynicism towards the clergy in the late nineteenth century (Eagleton, 1996). English Literature provided a viable alternative for the moral education of the masses and subsequently became the most important subject in Britain and the "spiritual essence of the social formation" (Eagleton, 1996, p. 27). Its significance as a subject was due in part to the contributions of New Criticism which was a strategically appropriate pedagogy for two main reasons.

First, New Criticism's text-centred approach to literary analysis ensured that attention was centred on cultivating taste and appreciation of English culture. The 1921 Newbolt Report was Britain's first official report on English Literature and it proclaimed the subject as exemplary of "the native experience of [the Englishmen's] own race and culture" (Bacon, 1998, p. 302). English Literature thus exemplified an untainted "native experience" of English culture and New Criticism's insistence on close reading was conducive to deepening pride in English culture (Michael, 1987).

Second, New Criticism's apolitical stance was useful in masking the ideological uses of Literature education. Literature education had been accorded the quasi-religious function of civilizing the masses through perpetuating bourgeoisie values of Englishness. In schools, New Criticism perpetuated a culturally blinkered approach to teaching where attention to form and content drew attention away from ideology including such questions as how the curriculum was constructed, why particular texts were selected, and for what purposes. As Eagleton (1996) states, "Reading poetry in the New Critical way meant committing yourself to nothing: all that poetry taught you was 'disinterestedness', a serene, speculative, impeccably even-handed rejection of anything in particular. . . . It was, in other words, a recipe for political inertia, and thus for submission to the political status quo" (p. 43).

If Edward Said's (1979) *Orientalism* foregrounds the perpetuation of imperialism through discourses that reinforced the othering of the East, it is his student, Gauri Viswanathan's (2014) seminal book, *Masks of Conquest*, that demonstrates in concrete ways how this occurs via Literature education. Through detailed analysis of historical and government policy documents, Viswanathan (2014) shows how the British utilized Literature education in India to fashion an educated elite in awe of English culture and as a vehicle to convert students from Hinduism to Christianity. The push to replace pride in local with colonial culture is evident in Thomas Macaulay's (1835) calls for reform in his "Minute on Indian Education." Macaulay, a member of the British Parliament who was then called to serve on the Supreme Council of India, pushed for the study of English literature in India instead of classical Sanksrit and Arabic literatures. Describing such literature, he says, "To encourage the study of a literature, admitted to be of small intrinsic value, only because that literature inculcated the most serious errors on the most important subjects, is a course hardly reconcilable with reason, with morality, or even with that very neutrality which ought, as we all agree, to be sacredly preserved" (para. 31). Alternatively, he argues that "English is better worth knowing than Sanskrit or Arabic" and calls for efforts to "make natives of this country thoroughly good English scholars" with the aim of fashioning "a class of persons Indian in blood and colour, but English in tastes, in opinions, in morals and in intellect" (para. 34).

Aside from India, Literature education's ideological project was also evident in another country colonized by the British – Singapore. Singapore came under British rule from 1819 to 1963. In 1879, the colonial government specified the chief aims of educating local Chinese in English-medium schools stressing the need to "teach them our system and our language and with it, to instil an admiration for most of what belongs to us" (Nagle, 1928, p. 105). Despite contradictions in colonial policy regarding English education, there was a general tendency to elevate colonial culture and English language rather than the vernacular. This may be observed in one of the oldest schools in Singapore, Raffles Institution, founded by Sir Stamford Raffles, an English colonial administrator famously known as the founder of modern Singapore. Till today, Raffles Institution is regarded as an elite school and its alumni include the former Prime Minister, Lee Kuan Yew, who led the country over three decades. The school functioned to fashion "brown

Englishmen" among locals through instilling English habits of thought (Holden, 2000). Clues may be observed in the English curriculum taught at Raffles Institution in the 1930s. The syllabus of instruction, written by the principal D. W. McLeod (1937), specifies that the primary aim of the Literature curriculum is enjoyment and recommends that teachers refer to Richards' *Practical Criticism* to teach critical appreciation of texts. McLeod outlines a systematic method of reading that includes first having students read the book for themselves then teaching them to trace out main incidents, describe characters and their relationships, examine conflict among characters, and analyze style and linguistic features. Here, we see an example of how colonial authorities employed New Criticism to prioritize aesthetic appreciation while downplaying political criticism of texts. Students, for example, were never encouraged to question the kinds of texts selected for study in the curriculum.

McLeod also speaks about the ultimate end of Literature education: "When students have mastered the mere mechanics of reading they must be initiated into the subtleties of language and thought and imagination, which make for true appreciation" (p. 30). Here, aesthetic appreciation is used as a means to an end with the end being the initiation into English habits of thought and imagination. Akin to the colonization of mind and imagination, aesthetic appreciation would centre on a close study of authors McLeod suggests such as Browning, Keats, Pope, and Shakespeare as well as anthologies of English poets. In this context, Literature education functions as an "ideological state apparatus" (Althusser, 2004) through which English values may be transmitted not via overt teaching of cultural values but via the pedagogy of New Criticism in which its objective approach to aesthetic appreciation serves to mask its ideological intentions.

The politicization of Literature education in postcolonial contexts

What were the responses of colonized subjects to Literature education and its pedagogical focus on aesthetic appreciation? One overt approach was to reject colonial culture through subverting the dominance of English Literature. In Singapore, this became evident following the end of British colonialism. When Singapore gained independence in 1965, the newly formed government initiated the Bilingual Policy the year after. The policy effectively led to the splitting of English education into two subjects – English Language and English Literature. English Language was prioritized as a first language to be studied in all schools and positioned as a lingua franca that would unite its multiethnic population. However, English Literature became a marginal subject given its close ties to colonial culture (Choo, 2014b). The teaching of English Language emphasized proficiency, fluency, accuracy, and effective communication negating aesthetic and cultural engagements with English. Meanwhile, Literature education's marginal position became more evident as observed in the gradually declining enrolment so that by 2012, only 9%

of students who sat for the high-stakes GCE Ordinary level examinations in 2012 took Literature as a full subject (Heng, 2013; see also note 1 in Chapter 1).

Less overt and aggressive ways of subverting the ideological project of Literature education has involved calls to democratize the curriculum. This coincided with the movement of Poststructuralism which came to prominence in the 1960s and 1970s. During this time, Literature departments in the United States introduced philosophers such as Jacques Derrida and Michel Foucault, among others and as literary theory became pervasive in the universities, schools were also pressured to move away from New Criticism's pedagogical focus on the aesthetic features of the text to the exclusion of engaging with its historical contexts and political concerns. If aestheticism in the early twentieth century was reinforced by the pedagogical approach of New Criticism, the politicization of Literature education from the late twentieth century was reinforced by the pedagogical approach of Poststructuralist Criticism.

As opposed to New Criticism, the pedagogy of Poststructuralist Criticism valorizes the constructed and contradictory nature of texts. For New Critics like Richards, literature is viewed as a mode of communication. As he (1929) argues, "What [literature] communicates and how it does so and the worth of what is communicated form the subject-matter of criticism" (p. 10). Conversely, Poststructuralist Criticism attends not to the "what" and "how" of communication but rather, the gaps and contradictions arising from communication. The application of New Criticism involves examining underlying binary oppositions structuring the text's meaning while Poststructuralist criticism and its practice of Deconstruction interrogate and subvert the text's own binary logic. Derrida describes Deconstruction as concerned with resisting closure and one common strategy he employs is to probe into a marginal aspect of the text such as its footnote or casual allusion to dismantle the oppositions unifying the meaning of the work (Eagleton, 1996).

New Criticism's encouragement of a disinterested aesthetic appreciation of texts was now replaced by a politically invested scepticism of texts. But Deconstruction is not merely a critical textual practice; at the heart of this is an ethical demand to attend to the ways language and texts normalize hegemonic systems (Critchley, 2014, p. 1). Poststructuralism and its associated movements of Postcolonialism, Feminism, and Marxism highlight the ways language operates within discourses of power. A critical reading of the binary oppositions framing texts reveals that often, certain values are privileged over others such as occidental over oriental, male over female, first world over third world. In the classroom, students are encouraged to problematize such ideological bias in texts. Like Chinua Achebe (2016), who has accused Joseph Conrad of being a "thoroughgoing racist" (p. 21) for purveying the myth of Africa as "the other world" (p. 15) in *Heart of Darkness*, students are encouraged to examine how the representation of communities in texts normalizes racism, patriarchy, inequality, and other forms of implicit violence.

Poststructuralism's ethical call has become a catalyst to democratizing the Literature curriculum with its push for inclusivity and diversity. The study of Great

Books that was once part of the standard English curriculum in universities in the early twentieth century has increasingly given way to courses on literary theory and Third World literatures which were first introduced to English departments in American universities in the 1960s. The main aim is to give voice to literatures from Africa, Asia, the Caribbean and other parts of the world. Building on the momentum of the multiculturalism movement is Cultural Relevant Pedagogy that gained dominance in the 1990s. African-American scholars such as Gloria Ladson-Billings and Geneva Gay highlight the ways in which school curriculum does not align with the experiences and values of students' own communities especially those from minority and impoverished backgrounds. Ladson-Billings (1994) explores practices and social environments conducive to culturally relevant teaching. Gay (2002) proposes designing curriculum reflecting cultural diversity as well as the culture that students belong to. Increasingly, greater affirmation has been given to the inclusion of immigrant, hip-hop, street, and queer literature, among others in the Literature classroom.

If political advocates for Literature education have won over aesthetes, it has not been met without backlash. The Culture Wars have gained greater visibility with the popularity of Allan Bloom's (1987) *Closing of the American Mind* in which he denounces literary scholars for retreating in their defence of high culture and for devaluing the study of the Great Books of Western thought. Among his allies is Harold Bloom (1994), who has argued that literary criticism "always will be an elitist phenomenon" (p. 16) and advocates reading a poem as a poem with "a stubborn resistance whose single aim is to preserve poetry as fully and purely as possible" (p. 17). He has lambasted Postcolonial, Feminist, Marxist, and other cultural critics whom he calls the School of Resentment accusing them of ushering in an age of mediocrity. Similarly, John Ellis (1997), in *Literature Lost*, has bemoaned the corruption that plagues Literature education. He romanticizes a past when Literature professors could spend much of their time discussing great writers such as Shakespeare and Goethe with students whereas "a concern with exceptional minds and excellence is now dismissed as elitism and many prefer to concern themselves with Madonna videos or gay pornography" (p. 205). Ellis highlights two important dangers about the politicization of Literature education. The first is the danger of tribalism. He argues that race-gender-class scholars, while urging us to celebrate ethnicity, also push people to see themselves as members of an ethnic group. The text is then narrowly interpreted from the lens of "tribal thinking and tribal politics" (p. 112). Related to this is the second danger of resorting to ad hominem arguments. Instead of dealing with the argument or the substantive narrative in the text, Deconstruction pushes the critic to discern its hidden ideology. He argues that such ad hominem tactic "ignores the logic of an argument and counters it by only denouncing the ignoble motives of the opponent" (p. 216).

Rather than rehashing arguments on both sides which may be unproductive in reinforcing and thereby entrenching the binary between aesthetic and political values in Literature education, I propose locating a "third space" (Bhabha, 1994) that mediates these opposing movements. The notion of a third space has been comprehensively theorized by Homi Bhabha and Edward Soja as reflective of attempts to destabilize dualisms in order for new productive conversations to occur between opposing groups. Henri Lefebvre (1991) defines first space as "perceived space" dealing with direct spatial experiences and the second space as "conceived space" dealing with symbolic and normative practices. In the context of the Literature classroom, the first space is the perceived space where students encounter texts and participate in aesthetic readings while the second space is the normative space where students are guided in their interpretation of texts or taught to approach texts using a specific mode of criticism such as New Criticism, Poststructuralist Criticism, among others. The possibility of a third space requires recognition of the limits of these two spaces. In relation to the first space of direct experience, the suggestion that there can be a pure authentic reading of texts is misguided since texts can never be purely received without having already been selected by teachers, school leaders, policymakers, etc. The assumption that students can simply immerse themselves in the world of the text and enjoy the experience of reading naively ignores the fact that a particular world has already been chosen for them to vicariously experience and the fact of selection means that other worlds have been excluded. Hence, teaching literary criticism is an inherently political act. In relation to the second space, the adoption of one particular mode of literary criticism to the exclusion of others presents a single metanarrative of criticism, even in the name of Deconstruction, that limits the varied scope of interpretation. It further assumes that the varied modes of criticism are discrete and discounts their interconnections, for example, the interdependent relationship between textual aesthetics and its political positioning.

The limits of the first and second spaces involving aesthetic encounters with texts and political forms of criticism highlight the need for ethics as the third space mediating aesthetic and political values of Literature education. There are two key characteristics to ethics as third space. First, the third space accommodates binaries by "transforming the categorical and closed logic of either/or to the dialectically open logic of both/and also" (Soja, 2009, p. 52). Here, difference is embraced and the tensions that emerge are viewed as productive platforms for new conceptions of thought. The rejection of totalizing discourses and any finality of knowledge also implies the impetus to constantly push boundaries and negotiate across differences. In relation to Literature education, this would involve first, equipping teachers and students with the repertoire of critical approaches. Given the constraints of curriculum time in schools, this encompasses at minimum introducing both New Criticism and Poststructuralist Criticism over the course of pre-tertiary education. It would also involve attempting to introduce canonical and marginal texts as well as the range of dichotomous pedagogies that enable students to experience texts on one hand while problematizing them on the other and that push them to conduct close readings alongside sociohistorical readings. As Soja (2009) describes, the third space is a "a purposefully tentative and flexible term that attempts to capture what is actually a constantly shifting and changing milieu of ideas, events, appearances and meanings" (p. 50). In this light, teaching is an art in addition to a science and the teacher as artist designs environments that are open and hospitable to new critical methods (Jarvis, 2006). The discerning teacher understands when students need to simply enjoy the reading experience, when to sharpen their analytical understanding of the text's aesthetic qualities, and when to activate students' engagement with political injustices referenced by and reinforced within the text. Over the course of a four-year programme of secondary education, students should have opportunities to experience a full range of critical and affective engagements with texts.

Second, the third space of ethics not only accommodates first and second spaces of aesthetic and political engagements with texts, but it also seeks to expand these engagements. In particular, the kind of ethics I am referring to is not one bounded by communal or nationalistic loyalties; rather, it is a cosmopolitan ethics. In relation to Literature education, this would entail enabling students to recognize the limits of aesthetics and politics in order to push for more committed ethical investments in engaging with others in the world. In essence, the primary objective of Literature education lies not in aesthetic appreciation, enjoyment and analysis. Aesthetics is a means to draw the self out of its own egoistic self-absorption into an ethical accountability with another. Neither is the primary objective one in which aesthetics is used for political ends such as to promote moral norms such as communal and nationalistic values or even "universal" values such as human rights. I propose then that the central task of Literature education is to facilitate cosmopolitan ethical engagements with others in the world. In the second part of this chapter, I discuss key characteristics of a Cosmopolitan Literature curriculum by showing how it is informed by as well as how it extends two precursor curricula models – the World Literature programme and Human Rights Education.

Towards a cosmopolitan Literature curriculum

While most scholars acknowledge that globalization is not a singular condition but a multilayered, overlapping phenomenon lacking in any unified theory (Held, McGrew, Goldblatt, & Perraton, 1999; O'Byrne, 2003), the one commonality has to do with globalization's extraterritorial mobility. This may be observed in the fluidity of capital transactions worldwide leading to the establishment of new markets, the rising influence of neoliberal market flexibility, and the expanding power of a transnational class (factors related to economic globalization); the flexible and rapid exchange of information via digital media pointing to the annulment of temporal-spatial distances (factors related to technological globalization); and the movement of people and groups around the world as knowledge, products, services are exchanged whether this takes the form of tourists, diasporic communities, or asylum seekers (factors related to cultural globalization) (Appadurai, 1996; Bauman, 1998; Berberoglu, 2003; Brown & Lauder, 1996; Kellner, 2002; Scholte, 2005; Tabb, 2009).

These different factors attributed to global mobility has, since the 1990s, led to a cosmopolitan turn in fields such as cultural anthropology, education, international relations, philosophy, and political science. Cosmopolitanism is commonly traced to its use by Diogenes the Cynic in Ancient Greece (404–323 B.C.) who set up his home in the marketplace to demonstrate his rejection of material comfort. Diogenes primarily proclaimed his affinity with humanity and thus rejected the status of a politēs, a citizen, in favour of a *kosmopolitēs*, a citizen of the world (Heater, 2002). However, a better understanding of this concept may be gleaned from Stoic, Socratic, and Confucian philosophers who conceived of cosmopolitanism as "citizen of the universe." Stoic cosmopolitans advocated "treating persons, no matter who or where, as quasi-siblings, whose claims on our care and fair treatment are grounded simply on the fact that we are all human beings" (Long, 2008, p. 51). Taking their cue from Socrates who questioned policies that privileged citizens of the nation-state above its foreigners, Socratic cosmopolitans critiqued parochialism and sought to replace "ordinary politics and its concentrated service of compatriots with extraordinary politics, which is a project to be shared as optimally as possible with all human beings" (Brown, 2006, pp. 550–551).

Similarly, Confucian cosmopolitanism[1] subscribes to the view that the self is embedded in a larger cosmological system and heaven (*tian*) is immanent in nature and human beings. The self aims to live fully but this is not an individualistic, materialistic, or self-seeking endeavour. Rather, it is one in which the self is integrated into an ever-widening circle of human relationships through developing values such as empathy, respect for, and responsibility to others (Tu, 1994). The self learns to be accountable first to his or her family which is the community one is born into and which provides the training grounds for learning to love others. Such love should then extend to others in the community and eventually, to the world at large (Ivanhoe, 2014; Nguyen, 2016). Moral cultivation occurs through practising the virtues of *ren* or cosmopolitan love towards family, community, and the world (Choo, 2020b, see chapter 6). It is education that provides the platform for practising cosmopolitan love in order to counter intolerance and deepen one's commitment to the flourishing of others.

What both Socratic and Confucian conceptions of cosmopolitanism share is the idea of ethics exceeding politics just as the individual as a citizen of the universe is more than a citizen of the material world. Philosophers from both traditions subscribe to "a serious ethical, intellectual and moral commitment to the other" and encourage the "ability to think and act beyond the local" (Elverskog, 2013, p. 10). Today, various scholars have described cosmopolitanism as an orientation demonstrated by a willingness to engage the other (Hannerz, 1990), an attitude that allows one to learn from rather than merely tolerate the other (Hansen, 2011), a normative response to marginalized others hurt by the excesses of globalization (Cheah, 2006), a sensitivity towards empathizing with others (Nussbaum, 1997). The terms orientation, attitude, response, and sensitivity reiterate the sense in which one is directed and turned towards the other. Yet, turning towards the other does not imply a loss of attachment to home as one may have multiple attachments to home and beyond (Robbins, 1998). In this sense, to be cosmopolitan-minded is to participate imaginatively in the creative work of engaging with cultures that pushes towards openness instead of closure and values diversity and ambiguity rather than singularity and purity (Lu, 2000; Mehta, 2000). Thomas Bean and Judith Dunkerly-Bean (2015) highlight the need for more research into the implications of cosmopolitanism for adolescent literacy given that virtual border-crossing has intensified through social media and digital tools. Among key questions are how local adolescent literacy practices can embrace a cosmopolitan orientation and what are the material effects of reconfiguring adolescent literacy practices in the disciplines.

What role can Literature education play in fostering cosmopolitan-mindedness in students? Before we explore the key characteristics of a Cosmopolitan Literature curriculum, I want to highlight two curricula models that are important precursors – the World Literature programme and Human Rights Education. They share close alignment and have informed the evolution of a Cosmopolitan Literature curriculum which also differs and extends from these models. I end with distilling some key characteristics of a Cosmopolitan Literature curriculum.

The World Literature programme

In the first part of this chapter, I described the beginnings of English Literature from the late eighteenth century. Up till the early twentieth century, the Literature curriculum in schools was predominantly centred on British canonical texts. Towards the late 1920s, however, literary texts from other parts of the world were slowly introduced to schools and colleges in the United States while in Britain and her colonies, the tradition of teaching English literature remained dominant. As John Pizer (2006) observes, World Literature as a pedagogical practice and programme of study was almost exclusively a development in the United States even though World Literature as a philosophy was conceptualized by German thinkers particularly Goethe.[2]

A survey of high schools across the United States in 1922 found that America, Britain, Canada, and France were well represented in the literary texts studied but at this point, there were already calls for broader representation from other parts of the world (Bryan, 1922; Koch, 1922). Factors precipitating the popularity of World Literature in schools were the abolishing of a standardized college-entrance reading list centred on classical works of English literature (Applebee, 1974) as well as the introduction of American literature which provided the possibility for educators to imagine the inclusion of other world literatures for study irrespective of the length of their historical literary tradition.[3]

Early World Literature courses tended to be organized around historical and geographical markers. One example is the Lincoln School World Literature curriculum, which has been described as "the first experiment in teaching world literature to high school pupils" (Stolper, 1935, p. 480) and was comprehensively discussed in the *English Journal* and *Teachers College Record*. In this course, the teacher started by placing a large outline of a map of the world on the front wall of the classroom. Next to the map were two huge charts, one with its heading composed of the names of various countries such as America, Greece, and Persia and the other with its heading organized according to distinct periods such as the eighteenth, nineteenth, and twentieth centuries. Throughout the year, students read a wide range of literature in English (including translated texts) from around the world and completed the charts by filling in titles of books for each country and period studied. The front wall was gradually transformed into a giant notepad as handwritten notes and pictures vividly displaying key places and events within these geographical regions were pasted around the map. Following this, the teacher engaged students in making observations about common stereotypes associated with particular groups such as that between Jew and money-lender, Chinese and laundry-men, Italian and bootblack. As students articulated these in discussions, the teacher encouraged them to consider where these biased impressions were derived from, how particular texts contributed to such stereotypes and to compare and contrast depictions of cultures across texts. Throughout, the teacher sought to trouble students' thinking, to lead them to recognize their own assumptions, and to encourage them to raise further questions.

There is an immense sense of pride as the teacher of this American high school in 1927 recounts the implementation of a new curriculum designed to teach literary perspective to students (Stolper, 1928). This Lincoln School World Literature curriculum challenges the predominance of British canonical texts typically studied in English Literature courses at the time and reflects a desire to expand the boundaries of cultural engagement given the teacher's rationalization that "with the development of transportation and communication; with the extraordinary spread of literacy and ease of print; with the growing economic interdependence of one race on another, one country on another, we have become so inextricably bound together, one people with another, that we must have the fullest understanding of each other in every way, or find ourselves doing our own selves a hurt" (Stolper, 1928, p. 392).

The 1920s thus marks an important focal point in the emergence of a cosmopolitan ethos in the teaching of literature occurring primarily through the subject of World Literature. At the same time, in this early World Literature curriculum model, the study of other cultures is determined along national boundaries. In the Lincoln School's World Literature classroom, the map on the wall may convey a visual sense of an inclusive space although paradoxically, it is organized according to lines and markers distinguishing the territory of the United States from Canada, Britain from Ireland, China from Mongolia, etc. Correspondingly, in the first four decades of the twentieth century, the most common approach to designing a World Literature curriculum in schools was teaching students to read across historical time and geographical space.

Another common practice was to teach the great masterpieces according to historical periods such as the classics of the eighteenth century followed by the nineteenth century (Axson, 1906; Koch, 1922; Meader, 1899; Shepherd, 1937).[4] In colleges, World Literature courses implemented from the late 1920s centred on "Great Books" representative of civilizations.[5] For example, the first comprehensive syllabus for World Literature proposed by University of Chicago professor, Richard Moulton, was organized according to what he terms literary bibles beginning with the Bible, followed by Greek and Roman literature, and the literature of Dante, Goethe, Milton, and Shakespeare (Moulton, 1911). Early world literary anthologies developed for such courses were similarly designed to introduce representative texts of particular civilizations such as Greece, Rome, India, China, and the Near-East (Alberson, 1989; Neilson, 1947). In short, the early World Literature programme is premised on the notion of bounded territoriality, which assumes that identities of individuals, cultures, nation-states are fixed, determinable, and discrete.

This tradition continued on to the 1960s when Commonwealth Literature, Third World Literature, among others were introduced to colleges throughout the United States partly in response to rising numbers of immigrants. Area Studies was also established at the beginning of the Cold War to focus on better understanding foreign nations. While these courses were important attempts at decentring a Eurocentric literary tradition, one limitation was its counter-canonical emphasis. In the 1960s, when Third World Literature was introduced as a course in English departments, its primary aim was to construct a counter-canon that displayed civilizational differences. For example, documents of an African past were used as testimonies of African-American heritage as opposed to Dante, Chaucer, and Milton, hallmarks of Western civilization. Not only did such attempts bolster the West versus the rest binary thereby reinforcing colonialism as the dominant frame of reference, the interpretation of minority cultures occurred within national boundaries.

By the late twentieth century, prominent literary scholars called for a rethinking of World Literature focusing not merely on text selection but pedagogy grounded on comparative criticism. In *How to Read World Literature*, David Damrosch (2018) stresses the importance of reading around the tradition to get a sense of its coordinates such as the writers' characteristic form, style, and methods. He also suggests getting acquainted with other art forms associated with the culture and that readers should have at least a rudimentary knowledge of the language so as not to be dependent on translators. Going further, readers can then compare various aesthetic approaches across cultures. This is also reflected in one of the anthologies he was lead editor of – *The Longman Anthology of World Literature* (Damrosch & Pike, 2008). The anthology is organized according to three categories – Regional Divisions, Crosscurrents, and Resonances. In Regional Divisions, distinctive literary traditions such as Greek, Roman, and Indian are examined. In Crosscurrents, a major issue serves as a launchpad to exploring how literary texts across cultures represent this. The aim is not only to show how a common issue is addressed differently but also to highlight interconnectedness across cultures. Finally, in Resonances, intertextual studies are the focus and the section highlights works in response to those from other centuries or regions such as modern reuses of the Ramayana epic. The editors acknowledge that "[w]orks of world literature engage in a double conversation: with their culture of origin and with the varied contexts into which they travel away from home" (Damrosch & Pike, 2008, p. xvii). Likewise, Sarah Lawall (1994) argues that World Literature should move beyond textual exemplarity to infusing cross-cultural pedagogical approaches. She suggests positioning the foreign text to activate a process of "othering" in which readers are invited to compare their beliefs and systems of reality with divergent ones thus leading to greater self-reflexivity.

The World Literature programme has carved a significant role for Literature education in the overall project of developing global citizenship awareness. While early iterations of the programme have provided a useful starting point to appreciating other cultures, latter shifts that embrace more fluid and interconnected perspectives of culture are more aligned with a Cosmopolitan Literature curriculum. Such a curriculum extends the study of texts beyond a single author or culture to foregrounding pedagogies of comparison and interruption in order to encourage students to imagine new forms of belonging that are multiple rather than monolithic. Such a curriculum would thus counter any fixity of values while recognizing how the intermixing of cultures has occurred continually throughout history. In this light, a Cosmopolitan Literature curriculum subscribes to a differentiated perspective of ethics recognizing both dynamic intersections and commonalities across cultures without also negating differences among them (Dallmayr, 2003).

Human Rights Education

Another curriculum model that has informed the emergence of a Cosmopolitan Literature curriculum is Human Rights Education (HRE). The Universal Declaration of Human Rights was adopted by the United Nations (UN) General Assembly in 1948 and recognizes that "All human beings are born free and equal in dignity and rights. They are endowed with reason and conscience and should act towards one another in a spirit of brotherhood" (United Nations, 2011, Article 1). It has grounded contemporary international rights law by envisioning the rights of individuals as no longer residing solely within the jurisdiction of the nation-state. This is in contrast to the Treaty of Westphalia in 1648 following the end of religious wars in Europe. In the Westphalian order, rights were solely a national issue and within the sovereignty of the nation-state. Such a perspective shifted following the atrocities of the Second World War that were crucial to cementing recognition of the importance of natural or human rights as opposed to citizenship rights.

Universal human rights potentially offer a powerful basis in calls for education reform. They have been utilized to claim the right to education for marginalized groups such as women, the disabled and intellectually impaired, refugees, and other groups facing social and political discrimination. Scholars have also proposed infusing human rights in curriculum and pedagogy such as by examining human rights in relation to socially and politically sensitive issues such as religious freedom, immigration, gender discrimination, etc. (Osler, 2016), applying critical pedagogies to promote compassion, solidarity, and dialogue among conflict nations (Zembylas, 2017), and empowering students to be engaged and active cosmopolitan citizens (Menintjes, 1997; Osler & Starkey, 2018).

It was only after the Cold War in the early 1990s that HRE gained momentum particularly following the 1993 United Nations World Conference on Human Rights in Vienna. The conference led to calls for governments to include human rights, humanitarian law, democracy, and rule of law as subjects in the curricula of all learning institutions (United Nations, 1993). It further spotlighted the important role of education for fostering understanding, tolerance, and peace in the world and called on "all States and institutions to include human rights, humanitarian law, democracy and rule of law as subjects in the curricula of all learning institutions in formal and non-formal settings" (para. 79).

One significant proposal for a follow-up of the conference was the "proclamation of a United Nations decade for Human Rights Education" (para. 99) that lasted from 1995 to 2004. The end of this decade saw the establishment of the UN World Programme for Human Rights Education in 2005 which "seeks to promote a common understanding of basic principles and methodologies of Human Rights Education, to provide a concrete framework for action and to strengthen partnerships and cooperation from the international level down to the grass roots" (United Nations Human Rights Office of the High Commissioner, 2006, p. 2). Another significant move was the adoption of the UN Declaration on Human Rights Education and Training, by the UN General Assembly in 2011 (Bajaj, 2017). Article 2 of the Declaration defines HRE (United Nations, 2011) as follows:

1 Human Rights Education and training comprises all educational, training, information, awareness-raising, and learning activities aimed at promoting universal respect for and observance of all human rights and fundamental freedoms and thus contributing to, inter alia, the prevention of human rights violations and abuses by providing persons with knowledge, skills, and understanding and developing their attitudes and behaviours, to empower them to contribute to the building and promotion of a universal culture of human rights.
2 Human Rights Education and training encompasses education:

   a About human rights, which includes providing knowledge and understanding of human rights norms and principles, the values that underpin them and the mechanisms for their protection;
   b Through human rights, which includes learning and teaching in a way that respects the rights of both educators and learners;
   c For human rights, which includes empowering persons to enjoy and exercise their rights and to respect and uphold the rights of others. (p. 3)

The Declaration also advocates HRE as a lifelong process that concerns society at all levels from preschool and primary school through to secondary and higher education. The UN, along with a number of NGOs particularly Amnesty International and Oxfam, has played a key role in catalyzing the global spread of HRE. Two important concepts have undergirded approaches to HRE – conscientization and justice.

First, the notion of conscientization as conceptualized by Paulo Freire (1970) refers to the deepening of the attitude of awareness of historical and social conditions of oppression (p. 85). HRE models informed by conscientization have been termed "transformative Human Rights Education" in that they seek to raise awareness about inequality and prompt reflection and action to overcome forms of subordination and oppression (Bajaj, 2017). Second, the notion of justice informing HRE approaches is built on the recognition that human rights represent an internationally recognized language of justice. HRE frameworks are justice-oriented as informed by John Rawl's (1971) theory of distributive justice that examines the ways political and economic structures reproduce systemic injustice as well as Nancy Fraser's (2008) analytic framework that proposes examinations of justice taking into account redistribution, recognition and representation. Cultural and symbolic forms of representation can, for example, contribute to the misrecognition and non-recognition of individuals or groups which could influence the redistribution of socioeconomic goods. Thus, justice-oriented HRE encourages examinations of injustice at the macro-level of sociopolitical and economic systems and at the micro-level of lived culture, identity, and lived experiences (Gibson & Grant, 2017).

HRE intersects with peace education, Holocaust education, environmental education, among others but the distinguishing feature is that principles of the Universal Declaration of Human Rights remain central to its programme (Tibbitts, 2002). In categorizing HRE models, Felicia Tibbitts (2017) has highlighted three typical models. The first is the values and awareness/socialization model. This model is typically found in schools and colleges and is targeted at students. It is content oriented and focused on acquainting students with such topics as the history of the UN, theory of human rights, human rights violations in past history, among others. Learning may be didactic or involve participatory pedagogies aimed at building knowledge about and understanding of human rights. The second is the accountability/professional development model. In education, this model is focused on formal (preservice training) and nonformal (inservice training). Here,

> HRE is carried out with the explicit aim of developing the motivation and capacities of members of professional groups to fulfil their responsibilities in ways that are consistent with human rights values (i.e. they do not violate human rights) and/or that actively promote the application of human rights norms in codes of conduct, professional standards and local laws.
>
> *(pp. 87–88).*

Teaching tends to be skills-oriented and aimed at promoting criticality, agency, and activism among learners such as teachers. The third model is activism/transformation model. This is usually carried out in nonformal education sectors by civil society or nongovernmental organizations. It may involve various programmes such as the training of human rights workers or the empowering of marginalized populations such as women, underprivileged groups, refugees, persons with disabilities, etc. The aim is to equip these groups to take action to reduce human rights violations and to apply human rights discourses meaningfully to effect long-term social change.

Both the Universal Declaration of Human Rights and HRE support a cosmopolitan vision of human belonging in which respect for human rights is central to a just and peaceful world (Osler & Starkey, 2010; Reardon, 2002). The Declaration, for example, references Kantian Enlightenment cosmopolitanism that promotes an idealized human fraternity bound by shared universal values (Osler & Starkey, 2010). The main critique of HRE, however, has to do with its top down imposition of universal values discounting an understanding of specific cultural traditions (Ignatieff, 2001). For example, human rights have been used by Western powers to intervene politically in less economically advanced countries (Badiou, 2002).

While the HRE model endorses a universalistic vision of belonging, a cosmopolitan curriculum embraces a situated ethics that recognizes the ways belonging to home and world can occur concurrently and via a multiplicity of specific contexts and locations (Calhoun, 2002). Thus, terms such as "rooted cosmopolitanism" (Beck, 2003), "cosmopolitan patriot" (Appiah, 1997), and "vernacular cosmopolitanism" (Bhabha, 1996) capture more complex and diverse visions of belonging. Forms of belonging occur organically through lived experiences and it is this "everyday cosmopolitanism" (Hull, Stornaiuolo, & Sahni, 2010) that involves processes of negotiation as individuals deliberate about competing and conflicting ethical values.

What this means is that a Cosmopolitan Literature curriculum would approach human rights as ethical claims to be subjected to public reasoning. Nobel prize-winning economist Amartya Sen (2004) describes human rights as articulations of ethical demands that should be subjected to scrutiny and debate: "The universality of human rights relates to the idea of survivability in unobstructed discussion – open to participation by persons across national boundaries" (p. 320). In developing a Cosmopolitan Literature curriculum, teachers may support situated discussions of ethics emphasizing a more ground-up dialogic approach to discussions about belonging in the world as opposed to a top-down hegemonic approach determined by the application of universalistic, rights-based instruments. This cosmopolitan conceptualization of ethics resists the extremes of nationalism and imperialism, ethnocentrism, and universalism while supporting "ethical glocalism," or engagement with the local and the global (Tomlinson, 1999).

Cosmopolitan Literature curriculum

Let us return to the earlier notion of ethics as third space inclusive of and extending the first two spaces of aesthetics and politics. In tandem with this, a Cosmopolitan Literature curriculum also functions as that third space incorporating but going beyond aspects of the World Literature programme and Human Rights Education. Summarizing what has been discussed in this chapter, I propose three key guidelines to organizing a Cosmopolitan Literature curriculum.

Guideline 1. Introduce a range of critical pedagogies that support aesthetic, political, and ethical engagements with literature

As mentioned previously, ethical engagements should not discount aesthetic and political forms of engagements. For many centuries, the Literature curriculum in high schools has been overly focused on aesthetics via New Criticism while politics and ethics via Poststructuralist Criticism and Ethical Criticism, respectively, were given less attention. One reason could be the emphasis given to New Criticism in high-stakes national examinations. Ideally, over the course of secondary education, students would have opportunities to learn and apply a range of critical approaches including at the very least these three – New Criticism, Poststructuralist Criticism, and Ethical Criticism. As Ethical Criticism is a newer approach to criticism compared to the first two, attention will be given to how this can be practised in the classroom in the following chapter. In essence, a Cosmopolitan Literature curriculum is organized to promote critical engagements with aesthetics, politics, and ethics through the study of literature.

Guideline 2. Organize curriculum around cross-cultural themes or issues rather than studies of a single text or culture

The organization of early World Literature programmes tended to revolve around selected key texts or cultures resulting in students applying interpretive lenses oriented along national boundaries. The study of one text at a time leads to an emphasis on aesthetic appreciation with particular attention paid to genre and style. If aesthetic appreciation is the first interpretive task that students perform when they encounter a text, then ethical engagement should follow with the recognition that students' immersive experiences cannot remain within the realm of the fictional. Fictional encounters with others in literature are stepping stones to expanding the imagination's capacity to relate to foreign and marginal others in the real world. Not only does exposure to literatures from around the world (including translated texts) foster a sense of curiosity about another, a pedagogy of comparison enables students to attain a differentiated perspective of ethics so that they recognize commonalities, crossings, and mixings of cultures despite their differences. Cosmopolitan ethics extends aesthetics by reframing the curriculum around themes or issues that are conducive to transnational explorations. Such explorations go beyond merely internationalizing the curriculum to integrating dynamic explorations of the global and local as well as the plurality of identities and affinities characteristic of a cosmopolitan outlook (Harper, Bean, & Dunkerly, 2010).

One example may be observed in Karen Downing's (2002) World Literature curriculum she introduced at her high school that was organized around four key themes – Search for Meaning, Injustice, Romantic Love, and Border Crossings. Students study a range of diverse texts from different cultures. For example, under the theme "Search for Meaning," they read excerpts from the Bible, Sunjata, Gilgamesh, Analects of Confucius, and Siddharta. They discuss injustice through works exploring Stalinist repression, apartheid in South Africa, and the Holocaust. They examine romantic love through works by French, Canadian, Chilean, Mexican, Lebanese, and Jewish authors from a mix of genres. The last theme in the unit challenges students to look at transnational authors whose works investigate the struggles of living between two or more cultures. In sum, a Cosmopolitan Literature curriculum would make comparison conducive by organizing it around (1) themes such as gender roles, war and origin stories; (2) philosophical concepts such as power, the nature of good and evil, and the purpose of suffering; and (3) contemporary global issues such as climate change, modern-day slavery, inequality.

Guideline 3. Organize curriculum around human rights and justice but also encourage interrogations and forging of cross-cultural friendships

Ethical Criticism includes and extends Poststructuralist Criticism by engaging with questions about violence and injustice through texts as well as exploring the application of justice-oriented discourses in literary and real-world scenarios. In the following chapter, I explore further the normative and analytical dimensions of Ethical Criticism. One common example of a normative approach to Literature education is to organize the curriculum around human rights which provides a useful lens to critical readings of values in texts. For example, when reading *To Kill a Mockingbird* by Harper Lee, students can use the Universal Declaration of Human Rights to raise questions about specific rights to Blacks that are infringed on and the different rights accorded to Whites versus Black communities depicted in the text. Teachers can also get students to analyze the Universal Declaration of Human Rights as a normative lens. That is, literary texts can be used to challenge human rights. In particular, we can question:

1. The universality of rights

- Do these rights apply in all countries and communities or only in specific contexts? Why?
- Do these rights apply in all circumstances or only in specific circumstances? Why?
- Do these rights apply to all groups of people or specific groups? Why?

2. The significance of rights

- Are these rights important and significant or secondary? To whom and why?
- What economic or political benefits would these rights contribute to?
- How does the significance of rights to one community affect another group?

3. The end of rights

- What ultimate ethical values ground these rights?
- Who would benefit from these rights? Who would be disadvantaged from these rights?
- Who is responsible for securing these rights and what benefit might they have in doing so?

Aside from interrogating normative moral codes such as the Universal Declaration of Human Rights, a Cosmopolitan Literature curriculum would also push students to understand the interrelation between universal and situated ethics. This could occur by introducing transnational literacy in the classroom that trains students to disrupt narratives that reproduce stereotypes of cultures or that perpetuate forms of cultural superiority. Such transnational literacy seeks to expand the imagination's capacity to see how master narratives of nation, class, gender mask the subjectivity, and complex humanity of the other (Purcell, 2020; Spivak, 2012).

Transnational literacy also entails examining the ways one group affects and is affected by another and the role that economic, technological, and political globalization plays in creating these interconnections. The Cosmopolitan Literature curriculum need not be organized to merely validate antagonistic, Poststructuralist interrogations of global injustices. It may also provide space for constructive encounters. Using the metaphor of books as friends, Wayne Booth (1980) argues that all stories "claim to offer something to us that will add to our lives, and they are thus like the would-be friends we meet in real life" (p. 8). The text as friend provides an invitation for the reader to encounter another and witness the world from the perspective of the author and his or her characters. In this sense, the Literature classroom can be a hospitable space where teachers invite "friends" (fictional or real e.g. authors or speakers) whose culture students may not be familiar with or whom students may have misconceptions about arising from misrepresentations by the media and elsewhere. In designing her World Literature course, Downing (2002) shares that it is organized as a survey course but its aim is to expose students to writers, and one might add, voices, that students may not encounter otherwise.

In conclusion, I have sought in this chapter to problematize the binary between aesthetics and politics by suggesting that while these remain important, they are insufficient. Ethics is the necessary third dimension or third space to Literature education. Ethical engagement with text is not only inclusive and indeed dependent on aesthetic and political engagements, it also pushes towards a more invested commitment to engaging with diverse others. To re-envision the Literature curriculum from a cosmopolitan orientation is to reclaim the primacy of the other and hence, to take seriously the importance of cultivating an imagination hospitable to the other.

In the preface to the twenty-fifth anniversary edition of *Masks of conquest*, Viswanathan (2014) writes, "Perhaps the most significant effect of Postcolonialism – with all its shortcomings, blind spots, and metropolitan evasions – is that the curricular study of English can no longer be studied innocently or inattentively to the deeper contexts of imperialism, transnationalism, and globalization in which the discipline first articulated its mission" (p. xi). Indeed, a return to Literature education as pure appreciation of aesthetic beauty, supported by the pedagogy of New Criticism or organized around the close study of the Western canon as typical of early World Literature programmes, is no longer tenable. Around the world, such aesthetic and Eurocentric models of Literature education have encountered pushback particularly from postcolonial countries. Various chapters in a recently edited volume on *Literature education in the Asia-Pacific* (Loh, Choo, & Beavis, 2018) highlight a shift away from a Western-centric curriculum dominated by the pedagogy of New Criticism in many formerly colonized countries. Some examples are the introduction of critical place-based pedagogy in Singapore, re-evaluations of literary criteria used to evaluate regional literature that is not dependent on Western yardsticks in Philippines, and the use of reader-response and constructivist pedagogies that encourage active, creative meaning-making rather than passive readings of texts in Vietnam and Malaysia.

Additionally, a Cosmopolitan Literature curriculum subscribes to a cosmopolitan ethics that is paradoxically anti-metanarrative. That is, even as cosmopolitanism itself is a metanarrative, it works to challenge existing metanarratives such as nation, truth, and beauty. It also works to problematize universalistic moral codes such as the Universal Declaration of Human Rights and endorses both differentiated and situated perspectives to ethics. In sum, a Cosmopolitan Literature curriculum recognizes the necessary alliance of New Criticism and Poststructuralist Criticism. Engaging with the text's metaphors, characterization, and other stylistic techniques would enable students to immerse themselves in this world, to feel and live in wonder as they experience another lived reality. Engaging in questions about the background of these "friends" and their intentions would also empower students to be discerning about ideological values in texts. Going further, deeper ethical engagements would mean asking how one can be responsible and accountable to another to help others flourish in the world. In this way a Cosmopolitan Literature curriculum performs that vital role of preparing students to think critically and ethically as they learn to inquire into and live with diverse others in a global age.

Notes

1 For distinctions between Stoic and Confucian cosmopolitanism, see Chen (2016). See Delanty (2011) on European and Eastern varieties of cosmopolitanism.
2 Many scholars consider Goethe as the first to articulate World Literature's broad parameters as a vehicle for an international exchange of ideas even though he was not the first to use the term (Damrosch, 2003; Lawall, 1994).
3 As American literature became incorporated into schools, it correlated with the introduction of world literature. Carter (1948) provides an example of an early curriculum in which American literature was taught alongside world literature.
4 There is no definitive history of how the subject World Literature emerged in schools. My analysis is based on case studies of World Literature curricula in schools described

from 1900 to 1930 in two important journals – *English Journal* and *The School Review*. See also Pizer (2006) and Damrosch (2009) for a historical and contemporary overview of World Literature education.

5 The fact that World Literature courses involved the study of texts translated into English became a point of contention that eventually distinguished World Literature and Comparative Literature college courses with the former designed as broad survey courses catered to undergraduate students and the latter involving the study of works in the original catered to graduate students (Pizer, 2006).

4

TEXTS

Applying Ethical Criticism to interpreting literature

Some years ago, in the fall of 2011, eight graduate students and their professor convened around a table, as was the usual custom, to discuss the literary text in focus for that week. The course, part of the English and Comparative Literature programme, took place inside an Italian Renaissance-styled building. The weight of history in this Ivy League campus must have been at odds with the topic of discussion that day which centred on such concepts as extraterritoriality and transnational culture affecting the emergence of new literary styles in a global age. One such exemplary text was Kazuo Ishiguro's (2000) *When We were Orphans* which students dissected, analyzing the novel's representation of Shanghai as an international settlement in the 1930s along with its cosmopolitan style of unreliable narration and cultural mixing. As the discussion centred on the aesthetics of the text, the historical backdrop of the second Sino-Japanese war was simply glossed over particularly when students discussed a major climactic moment in the novel. Here, attention was drawn to the psychology of a displaced protagonist frantically searching for his parents whose disappearance, he believed, was connected to the onset of the war. By prioritizing the aesthetic representation of an unreliable fictional narrator, the ethical representation of its historical context, namely, the widespread massacre of the Chinese by the Japanese during the Second World War, was overlooked. Considering the fact that the book was targeted at Western readers more aware of the Jewish Holocaust than what has been termed the Asian Holocaust (Chang, 1997), the author then seemed complicit in the larger, political trivializing of this atrocity in the Western imagination.

As I participated in the class that fall, I raised the concern about the ethics of writers in adequately representing global trauma and holocausts as well as the ethics of readers in critiquing the representation of history in texts. I do not recall the response from the professor or my peers at the time, perhaps because attention soon reverted to uncovering the aesthetics of the text. What I do recall, however, is my own realization of a particular gap in literary discourse, both in schools and university, that led to a shift in the direction my research was to take in the years following my initiation into graduate school. Why, for example, were students well equipped with the language, terminology, and close reading skills that enabled them to critique aesthetic representation rather than ethical representation in texts? Why, when discussing politics in texts utilizing postcolonial, feminist, and other theories, were concepts related to moral philosophy such as virtue ethics largely excluded? Why was literary criticism rarely connected to practical ethics such as the ethics of torture and why was such an association met with fears of politicizing Literature that could potentially lead to censorship of texts deemed "unethical" or to using literature for moral indoctrination? These and other questions foregrounded a need to deepen understanding of the role of ethics in the teaching of literature.

The turn to cosmopolitan ethics and Ethical Criticism

Since the late twentieth century, scholars have noted the emergence of an ethical turn in literary studies that became evident in universities when Poststructuralism, which was then a fashionable form of literary criticism privileging ambiguity and disruption of stable meanings in textual interpretation, began to be viewed with scepticism. As Gregory (2010) argues, a crucial turning point was the revelation that Paul de Man, the renowned advocate of Deconstruction, wrote anti-Semitic articles for pro-Nazi newspapers thus casting doubt on Poststructuralism's claim that ethics has no place in literary criticism, which de Man had strongly defended in his writings. After the 9/11 terrorist attacks at the turn of the twenty-first century, Poststructuralism's discourse of subversion and scepticism came to be seen as profoundly deficient in a climate of fear and tragedy (Gregory, 2010). This paved the way for the reintroduction of ethical considerations in literary theory.

In the late 1980s, various books and journal articles offered compelling arguments for the affinity between literature and ethics. Among them were two seminal works – Wayne Booth's (1988) *The Company We Keep: An Ethics of Fiction* and Martha Nussbaum's (1990) *Love's Knowledge: Essays on Philosophy and Literature.* In the 2000s, a number of edited volumes were published featuring major scholars in literary studies and philosophy such as *The Turn to Ethics* (Garber, Hanssen, & Walkowitz, 2000), *Mapping the Ethical Turn* (Davis & Womack, 2001), and *Ethics, Literature, Theory* (George, 2005).

Prominent literary scholars such as Judith Butler (2000) advocated for a return to ethics, that does not discount the politics of the text. Derrida's (2001, 2002) earlier interest in Deconstruction shifted to questions about ethics and hospitality towards marginalized others. Terry Eagleton's (2009) discussions about literature as ideology evolved to exploring ethical traces in the ideas of Western continental thinkers. Gayatri Spivak (2012) proposed that an aesthetic education (including Literature education) should fundamentally test the limits of the imagination's attempts to know and perceive otherness. Many of these scholars, working in fields such as Poststructuralism, Postcolonialism, and gender studies, now shared an affinity with Levinas (discussed in chapter 2), who proposed ethics as first philosophy that prioritizes ethics before instrumental, aesthetic, and other aims.

The turn to ethics has never been more timely, given the intensification of global interconnectedness that has resulted in time-space compression (Bauman, 1998), "flat" network societies (Castells, 2010), and mobilized "flexible citizens," such as refugees, asylum seekers, and cosmopolitan travellers who move fluidly across borders (Ong, 1999). More significantly, awareness of global risks such as terrorism, fundamentalism, and xenophobia in our everyday consciousness has led to a pressing need for educators to consider how to powerfully cultivate hospitality towards multiple and marginalized others in the world. Literature education plays a fundamental role in equipping students with a knowledge of the world and key dispositions with which to empathize and relate to diverse others. Various scholars have discussed the role of Literature education in developing students as cosmopolitans that essentially entails critical engagement with an ethics of living in an interconnected, global age (Choo, 2013, 2016; Donald, 2007; Jollimore & Barrios, 2006; Nussbaum, 1997). The ethical turn may be seen as Literature education's response to the exigencies of globalization.

Yet, despite growing interest in ethics among literary scholars, theorizations of Ethical Criticism are predominantly observed among scholars working in university settings rather than at high schools, where contemporary literary theory, including Ethical Criticism, is rarely employed in Literature classrooms (Appleman, 2009). In what follows, I argue that cosmopolitan Ethical Criticism should be a core feature of Literature pedagogy in schools because of its potential for developing students as global ethical thinkers. I begin by distinguishing cosmopolitan Ethical Criticism from two other disciplinary practices – aesthetic criticism and didactic Ethical Criticism. I then describe what cosmopolitan Ethical Criticism looks like in practice by applying this to interpreting a selected literary text.

Cosmopolitan Ethical Criticism in theory

Ethical Criticism was a central aspect of literary discourse in Ancient Greece, and discussions about ethical significance typically constituted the start and end points of literary commentary (Gregory, 2010). The idea that the arts could exist for their own sake, with little practical relevance to social reality, was inconceivable because they were regarded as means to provoke ethical reflection and political discussion about civic matters. Two different approaches to the study of literature emerged during this time – the Aristotelian and Platonic views.

The Aristotelian view is that good literature, such as the works of Euripides, Homer, and Sophocles, can promote ethical reflection and cultivate moral virtue by, for example, taming emotions (Carr, 2014). Aristotle (350 BCE/1970) claims that "poetry is a more philosophical and serious business than history; for poetry speaks more of universals, history of particulars" (§1.9, p. 33). It is not that poetry (and literature more broadly) is dislocated from time and place, but the kind of thinking it provokes is more akin to philosophical reflection and such philosophical reflection is necessary for the cultivation of ethical character (Halwani, 1998).

The Aristotelian perspective may be seen as a precursor to cosmopolitan Ethical Criticism. While cosmopolitanism is a complex and contested term with multiple and often conflicting configurations, such as old and new, moderate and strong, universal and hybrid (see Hansen, 2010; Lu, 2000), the one commonality among definitions is that a cosmopolitan orientation is one that shares an existential concern about what it means to live with others in the world (Tagore, 2008) and is correspondingly characterized by an intentional willingness to invest in the other. If Aristotelian ethics revolves around the broad and inclusive question, "How should a human being live?" then Ethical Criticism from a cosmopolitan perspective does not respond to this question through the parochial lens of one's culture or from a dominant culture's perspective but instead aims at inclusivity and hospitable openness towards cultural difference. Literary works are perceived as entry points to rich dialogic inquiry into how one can live fully in relation to diverse others in the world.

In contrast to the Aristotelian perspective, the Platonic view is that bad poetry can deceive young minds. Plato perceives poets as imitators of truth who are not specialists in what they write about and who manipulate people's emotions. Plato believes that emotional discipline is necessary and can be developed through education, which should teach students to be critical of aesthetic craft. At the same time, Plato (375 BCE/1968) recognizes the power of exemplary poetry as a platform for moral training and argues that only the kind of poetry that involves "hymns to gods or celebration[s] of good men should be admitted into a city" (p. 290). In this sense, the Platonic perspective can be seen as a precursor to aesthetic criticism, which stresses a disinterested approach to the critical appreciation of language and exemplary texts, and it has also influenced a form of didactic Ethical Criticism, which involves the utilization of great works of literature for instruction about the moral values of a dominant culture.

When Literature education was institutionalized as part of the formal school curriculum in eighteenth-century England, an iteration of the Platonic approach became popular, with literary criticism being specifically tied to the practices of aesthetic criticism and didactic Ethical Criticism. These practices sought to civilize the masses by encouraging an appreciation of exemplary literature and by conveying bourgeois values of "Englishness" through these works (Doyle, 1989). Not surprisingly, the end of colonialism effectively heightened cynicism towards such grand narratives, including the notion that universal moral principles could be derived from literature. In the late twentieth century, it became increasingly difficult for Literature education to sustain any vision of a singular, universal moral–religious value system as religious and cultural pluralism became even more pervasive. Thus, aesthetic criticism and didactic Ethical Criticism were increasingly viewed with scepticism and an alternative was found in cosmopolitan Ethical Criticism. As highlighted in the previous chapter, a Cosmopolitan Literature curriculum endorses both differentiated and situated perspectives to ethics as opposed to universalistic impositions of ethics. It follows then that the teaching of critical interpretation supports an inquiry and dialogic approach to ethics that equips students to actively question values they read in texts and in the world and that empowers them to construct values that meaningfully allow them to live with and engage with diverse others in the world.

Essentially, Ethical Criticism is a critical hermeneutical approach to reading texts that analyzes the representation and construction of ethical values, how processes of othering and marginalization occur in specific social and geopolitical contexts and how texts can offer entry points to engaging with ethical issues in the community and the world. Ethical Criticism involves aesthetic–political–ethical analysis of texts, readers, and others in an interactional process as depicted in Figure 4.1.

1 **Texts** – Students apply Ethical Criticism in the first instance through their interactions with texts in a variety of modes – oral, written, visual, multi-modal, etc. Here, students engage with the aesthetics of texts but apply Ethical Criticism to analyzing values and beliefs of societies, the depiction of character virtues, and the representation of themes, etc.
2 **Readers** – In the public space of the classroom, students' interactions with texts are never isolated but operate with a community of other readers. The teacher facilitates the development of an interpretive community through designing opportunities for students to question, dialogue, debate, and co-create meaning. These experiences allow students to adapt and negotiate ideas that may be different from their own. Where possible, teachers can also design such dialogic experiences across schools to enable their students to interact with others from different socioeconomic backgrounds or from different cultures via literary discussions.
3 **Others** – Typically, in the Literature classroom, discourse is confined to the transaction between texts and readers. Discussion centres on the fictional lifeworld of the text with little connection to the real world it references or that which the author inhabits. An important aspect of Ethical Criticism is the practical connections to others that students make beyond the text. These connections occur via connecting literary explorations to other cultural texts, to their society, to the world, and to philosophical theories about justice, humanity, suffering, and the nature of evil, etc. It is through these connections that students fundamentally engage with larger questions about what it means

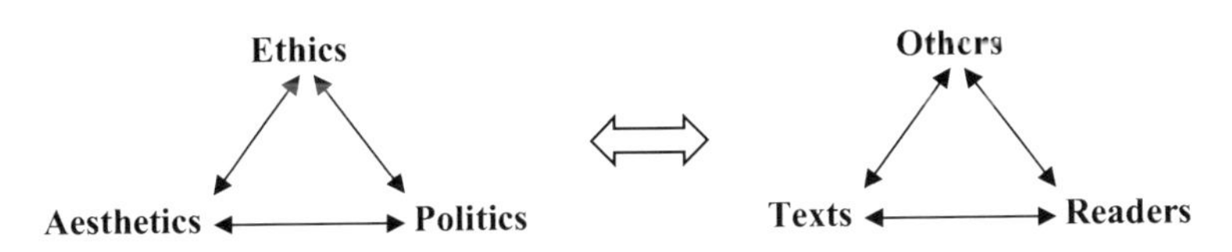

FIGURE 4.1 Dimensions of Ethical Criticism and the interconnections with texts, readers, and others

to be a human being and how we should live in relation to others who have different values, beliefs, and practices. Going further, teachers can make use of students' social and virtual "affinity spaces" to connect with youths from other cultures, even conflicting ones, to find common allegiances towards peace building and other just causes. Such opportunities facilitate the shift from ethical passivity to what Arjun Appadurai (2013) terms an "ethics of possibility" (p. 295) that involves ways of thinking, imagining, feeling, and acting collectively to counter social and global injustices.

Cosmopolitan Ethical Criticism in practice

How can cosmopolitan Ethical Criticism push the boundaries of aesthetic criticism further so that critical appreciation of the text leads to deeper engagement with its ethical concerns? At the same time, how can cosmopolitan Ethical Criticism ensure that the literary text does not become a platform for didactic teaching of moral values? The application of cosmopolitan Ethical Criticism can occur through five ethical lenses to reading texts that are related to descriptive ethics, normative ethics, analytical ethics, practical ethics, and virtue ethics.

In what follows, I demonstrate how these five ethical lenses can be applied using the example of the poem "Self-help for Fellow Refugees" by Li-Young Lee (2008). Access to the poem can be found here: https://poetrysociety.org/features/red-white-blue/li-young-lee. Note that these approaches to cosmopolitan Ethical Criticism do not negate or supplant aesthetic appreciation of texts but instead can extend and build upon aesthetic readings.

1. Descriptive ethics

Descriptive ethics refers to describing the moral norms and values of a community or society depicted in the text. This is perhaps the most basic entry point to reading any text. The method used is empirical involving objective observations of human behaviour or societal values. That is, psychologists, anthropologists, or social scientists may apply a scientific approach to observe and come to conclusions about human behaviour or societal values.

In the Literature class, teachers may apply descriptive ethics when asking students to make observations about the values and ideologies of a particular society or community (Thiroux, 2001). The following questions can serve as a guide:

1.1 Describe groups/communities

- Who are the individuals and communities that comprise the fictional world of the text?
- What is the main source of tension between these individuals or communities in the fictional world of the text?

1.2 Describe expected standards of behaviour

- What are the implicit or explicit standards of behaviour expected of people in this community?
- What happens if these are not adhered to?

1.3 Describe underlying values

- What values or beliefs inform these explicit and implicit moral standards?
- Why are these values significant to particular communities in the text?
- What historical, philosophical, moral, or other reasons are used to justify these values and expected standards of behaviour?

In Lee's poem, "Self-help for Fellow Refugees," two communities and their norms are described. The first is the country the persona was born into. There is an obvious intermixing of the secular and spiritual where bells are used for entertainment as well as to celebrate the birthdays of gods (Lines 3–6). The fusion of nature, social world, and spiritual realm reflects the underlying quasi-cosmological worldview of Daoism. This is in stark contrast to the hard-hitting reality of the country the persona ventures to, presumably as a refugee in the United States given that persona finds affinity with this group as suggested in the title.

The key tension is the foreigner's difference which is perceived negatively rather than as a cause for appreciation or celebration and thus, difference becomes a threat to established values. Explicit standards of behaviour are not described; rather, it is the implicit standards that are the focus. The persona advises refugees not to draw attention to one's foreignness by dressing in "plain clothes" (line 7) and to "try not to talk to loud" (line 9). This suggests that there is an unstated expectation of conformity and a subscription to conditional hospitality[1] in which the foreigner must assimilate, as opposed to integrate, into the other culture. The justification is based on the view that one should not be a burden to citizens of the host country (lines 34–36). This includes explicitly articulating the burden of one's history and culture to others as some citizens may hold the view that they should neither need to be responsible for present and past sufferings of refugees nor should they feel a need to defend these foreigners' claims to justice or invest in bettering their lives.

2. Normative ethics

The subtitle of Michael Sandel's (2009) well-known book *Justice* is "What's the right thing to do?" Likewise, normative ethics is premised on what one ought to do in certain situations. This approach centres on the reader's response in judging whether an action/behaviour is morally right or wrong. As we read the text, we critique characters and make judgements about their behaviour. At the same time, our judgements are not value-neutral but are influenced by what Gregory (2010) describes as the power of invitation inherent in literary texts. These are invitations to shared feelings with characters, shared beliefs about moral or immoral behaviour, and shared judgements about ethical concerns. Texts are culturally constructed artefacts, always in contact with other texts. Ethical invitations to explore occur through a complex web of intersecting narratives, histories, and cultures that expand students' understanding of the world. As Freire (1985) emphasizes, reading the word and reading the world are interconnected: "Every act of reading words implies a previous reading of the world and a subsequent rereading of the world" (p. 18). Unlike didactic moral engagement which assumes that texts have fixed moral lessons exerted by the author's intentionality that can be downloaded into the minds of impressionable readers, Ethical Criticism proposes an active form of critical reading. Rather than a passive sponge, the reader does not absorb a story but dynamically interprets and reimagines it through engagements and negotiations with other selves, real and fictional.

In the Literature class, teachers may apply normative ethics when pushing students to respond and make judgements through taking up what Gregory (2010) describes as three key ethical invitations of texts:

2.1 Invitations to feeling

This involves the way the texts invite readers to connect emotionally with their content and characters. Sample questions include:

- What significant events have affected characters in the text and how do they respond?
- How does the text stir your empathy for these characters and what are your feelings about them as you learn of their experiences?

2.2 Invitations to shared beliefs

This involves exploring beliefs the text depends on or assumptions that are imbued in the text. Sample questions include:

- What beliefs about human nature or the world does the text assume you might subscribe to?
- How does the text invite you to share these beliefs through the presentation of characters and events?

2.3 Invitations to ethical judgement

This involves judging the presentation of values in the text as well as the expression of the author's own values. Sample questions include:

- What values (individual, community, organizational, national, global) are presented in the text?
- To what extent do you subscribe to these values? Why or why not?

In Lee's poem, "Self-help for Fellow Refugees," we are invited to empathize with the persona who provides a glimpse of his violent past. The tranquillity of home has been destroyed by conflict e.g. "armed men" beating and taking away his father (lines 10–11) and "noise of guns in the streets" (line 62). He describes his country as "twice erased" (line 22) referring to the literal annihilation of his family and people by war as well as the learned obliteration of his history by avoiding such conversations in this land of asylum. On one level, the poem provides the guise of dishing out advice to fellow refugees. On another level, the persona paradoxically articulates his history and the factors that have led him to arrive in the United States. In this way, there is an underlying invitation to the reader to share this common ideal of home as a place where one is fully accepted, where one's history is validated and recognized as a significant part of identity formation.

At the level of the text, the primary value explored is alienation. The title sets up the poem as an advisory for newly arrived refugees presumably from the perspective of one who has lived through these experiences. The idea of "self-help" already suggests that one should not seek help from others; one has only oneself to depend on. This is followed by many stanzas that follow with the advice about how one should learn to disconnect oneself from others – "try not to talk too loud" (line 9), "you're standing too far way" (line 27), "you're standing too close" (line 33), "not let another carry the burden of your nostalgia or hope" (line 36). The use of parallelism in lines 44–46 "Get used to seeing while not seeing,/ Get busy remembering/while forgetting" connote the process of erasure in that one must get used to becoming invisible – to no longer see one's burdens and struggles as significant and to remember that one's past is of no importance in this land where cultural and historical difference may be viewed with disdain or hostility. Thus, the advice culminates in the last two stanzas that while thinking and reflecting on one's identity is good, "living is better" because it ensures one survives despite erasure. Of all the lines in the poem, the last stanza's first line stands out as it is the only line with one word – "Alone" (line 69). At the authorial level, it is the alienation and lack of social and political effort in integrating refugees and recognizing their voices that is the author's main critique. In order for us to judge the treatment of refuges and sympathize with their sense of alienation, there is an assumption that readers hold a shared belief about the importance of social belonging and home.

3. *Analytical ethics*

Analytical ethics is concerned with the analysis of normative claims by questioning the basis of values and moral norms (Willmott, 1998). At a generic level, we can analyze ethics in a text by considering the position of the protagonist and what race, gender, class, or other group a person represents, and what vested interest this person may have. We can examine what grounds the values propagated by the author through the text, who determines this and whether such values are situated or universal. We can also consider what social, historical, political, and economic circumstances have given rise to such values and practices.

More specifically, we can use the language of ethics to analyze ethics in the text. Most textbooks on ethics typically begin by contrasting two major schools of thought – Consequentialism and Deontology. Broadly, Consequentialists subscribe to the view that decisions about right or wrong should be determined by consequences or outcomes. Logically, one would then select that which would lead to good outcomes. One popular branch of consequentialism is utilitarianism of which there are three main versions (Baggini & Fosl, 2007):

1 **Classical utilitarianism** subscribes to the view that an act is right if it promotes the greatest happiness for the greatest number. Classical utilitarians include Jeremy Bentham and John Stuart Mill who focus on maximizing good outcomes for the greatest number.
2 **Welfare utilitarianism** subscribes to the view that an act is right in so far as it promotes the welfare and well-being of the greatest number.
3 **Preference utilitarianism** subscribes to the view that an act is right if it allows the greatest number to live according to their preferences.

Interestingly, many works of literature, particularly in the genre of dystopia, warn against the dangers of utilitarian thinking. Some examples are Margaret Atwood's *The Handmaid's Tale*, short stories such as Ursula Le Guin's "The Ones Who Walk Away From Omelas," Shirley Jackson's "The Lottery," Haruki Murakami's "The Elephant Vanishes," the popular young adult fiction *The Hunger Games* by Suzanne Collins and the Japanese cult film "Battle Royale" directed by Kinji Fukasaku. In many of these stories, a minority of individuals is dehumanized and made to suffer various forms of injustice such as imprisonment or a death game to ensure the survival and continued happiness of the majority.

The second approach to ethics, often used to contrast with utilitarianism, is deontology. Deontologists argue that what one ought to do should not be determined by the consequences of actions but by adherence to moral principles. In other words, one should act according to moral codes rather than perform a cost–benefit analysis to determine good outcomes. Since the Second World War, a deontological or rights-based approach to ethics is best exemplified by Human Rights which gained traction following the endorsement of the Universal Declaration of Human Rights (UDHR) in 1948. The UDHR provides a common language of justice and has led to widespread translation (into more than 300 languages) and cultural adaptation (such as the Universal Islamic Declaration of Human Rights in 1981, the African Charter on Human and People's Rights in 1981, and the Asian Human Rights Charter in 1998) (Gibson & Grant, 2017). All this points to its authority as a global ideology.

Deontologists may view universal principles as stemming from God such as the Ten Commandments. This divine command form of deontology subscribes to the view that everyone should adhere to moral laws from God. This may be less practical in a globalized world where conflicting beliefs about the divine exist. Other deontologists subscribe to the view that universal moral laws are determined by reason. The most well-known advocate of such a view is Kant (1785/1995) who sought to identify universal principles that would govern right action. Such universal moral codes must be governed by the condition of universality and the supreme universal law to treat another as an end rather than a means. Some may argue that moral codes are specific to cultural and historical contexts and therefore can never be universalized. However, in one sense, Kant's imperative to treat others as an end finds resonance in major belief systems across time in the form of the golden rule:

- **Buddhism:** "Look where you will, there is nothing dearer to man than himself; therefore, as it is the same thing that is dear to you and to others, hurt not others with what pains yourself." – from the Buddhist Canon, *Udanavarga*, Book 5.18 (Rockhill, 1883, p. 27).
- **Christianity:** "So in everything, do to others what you would have them do to you, for this sums up the Law and the Prophets." – from the Bible, Matthew, 7.12 (New International Version, 2005, p. 1082).
- **Confucianism:** "Do not impose on others what you yourself do not want [others to impose on you]." – from the Analects, §15.24 (Confucius, 500 BCE/2014, p. 259).
- **Hinduism:** "One should not direct towards someone else what is unpleasant to oneself: this is the moral duty in summarized form; the other proceeds from desire." – from Mahabharata, *Udyoga Parvan*, Book 5, §39.57 (Bakker, 2013, p. 44).
- **Humanism:** "Treat others as we would want them to treat us in their position; do not treat others in ways we would not want to be treated ourselves in their position." – from British Humanist Association (2010, p. 25).
- **Islam:** "None of you believes until he loves for his brother what he loves for himself!" – from Sahih al-Bukhari: A collection of Hadith by the Prophet Muhammad, Book 2, Hadith 7 (Homerin, 2008, p. 102).

Beyond the golden rule, moral codes that are universalized contain the danger of being used as an ideological tool to oppress other communities and nations. Numerous literary works have examined the dangers of deontology particularly if moral codes are imposed by totalitarian regimes. Some examples are *The Scarlet Letter* by Nathaniel Hawthorne that exposes the limits and oppression of puritan moral codes and *Animal Farm* by George Orwell that highlights the danger when universal principles are decided by an elite minority to advance their own power and dominance.

In discussions of literature, we can apply both generic questions and utilitarian and deontological concepts to analyzing ethics in texts. The following questions can serve as a guide:

3.1 Analyzing ethical values

- Are there examples of bias or stereotypes in the text?
- Whose voices and perspectives are dominant in the text? Whose voices are absent or less dominant? How might this affect the representation of ethical issues?
- What values does the author hold and to what extent is this representative of a particular race, gender, class, or other group?

3.2 Analyzing texts using Utilitarian concepts

- What outcomes or consequences are valued and who benefits?
- Do the outcomes justify the means? Why or why not?

3.3 Analyzing texts using Deontological concepts

- What moral codes and norms are applied in the text and by whom? What context-specific or universal values are used to justify these?
- To what extent do these norms and values benefit all people? Who are disadvantaged and why?

Lee's poem, "Self-help for Fellow Refugees," describes the alienation of refugees as a consequence of a utilitarian norm that affects the treatment of refugees to presumably ensure the security and sustainability of dominant values held by the majority in the host country. The repetition of "if" in the beginning lines of the first four and sixth stanzas point to the conditions imposed on the foreigner seeking refuge in the United States. The utilitarian and instrumental treatment of the foreigner is observed in that one is valued only in terms of outcomes – what one can contribute to the country's economy while not being a burden to its citizens. This utilitarian treatment leads to the objectification of the other. Thus, the stark irony in stanza 3 that if one should meet another in this foreign land and see an "open sky" and "some promise of a new beginning" (lines 24–25), this idea that one's difference can be accepted and one can live with the promise of flourishing and of fair treatment in this new land, is but an illusion. The run-on-lines end with the stark reality that "it probably means/you're standing too far away" (lines 26–27) highlighting the inability to perceive the disconnect between hope for a utopia and the realities of marginalization.

To counter this form of utilitarian thinking, one can instead adopt a deontological stance by grounding the treatment of all people on a recognition of their inherent dignity and worth. Suppose we begin with the assumption that a country's success should not be measured by economic growth and correspondingly, the contribution of individuals to its economic stability and prosperity; rather, a country's success should be based on the way it supports the development of human well-being. The latter perspective, termed Human Capabilities approach, may be traced to the ideas of Aristotle, Adam Smith, and Karl Marx and, since the late twentieth century, by Amartya Sen and Martha Nussbaum. Unlike a Human Capital approach which reductively employs economic utilitarianism to justify the treatment of others such as refugees, a Human Capabilities approach seeks to promote the capacity of all individuals to live fully which entails the provision of opportunities that enable an individual to pursue that which one values, the freedom to choose among real opportunities provided, and the empowering of an individual's agency to script one's own life (Choo, 2017b; Sen, 2008).

4. Practical ethics

The questions asked in our analysis of ethics in texts are stepping-stones towards uncovering bias, stereotypes, silences, and gaps in texts. In many ways, this was the core project of Poststructuralist Criticism which sought to interrogate ethics in texts and contemporary discourses (Critchley, 2014). However, its privileging of politics eroded the possibility of deep investedness in developing relations and ethical obligations to the other. Thus, analytical ethics, operating at a cognitive level, is insufficient and should be supplemented by practical ethics. As discussed in chapter 2, the philosopher Levinas emphasizes the point that ethics is not purely primal, instinctual, or affective because ethics is inherently intersubjective, closely intertwined with politics since the other is never just a singular entity but always situated. At the same time, this interrogation of politics is not the ultimate end; rather, it is a means to promoting the full flourishing of human beings in the world. In this sense, Levinasian ethics fills the void of Poststructuralist Criticism's sceptical reading of texts by connecting critique with praxis.

In short, practical ethics refers to the application of ethics to practical issues (Singer, 2011). Its roots may be traced to Aristotle who distinguishes *episteme* (knowledge) and *techne* (craft) from *phronesis* or practical wisdom. As opposed to training in productive skills, *phronesis* involves deliberation about everyday ethical dilemmas oftentimes involving negotiations between extreme actions. Since the 1970s, the field of Practical Ethics has gained traction and Hugh LaFollette (2003) identifies four key features distinctive of current discussions in the field: (1) the emergence of sub-fields that explicitly discuss ethics in relation to medicine, business, environment, etc., (2) a diminishing role for bare intuitions e.g. inherited moral beliefs, (3) a heightened concern for and reliance on empirical data, and (4) a more robust relation between ethical theorizing and practical ethical discussion.

Given that ethical issues are complex, ambiguous, and open to multiple perspectives, ethical deliberation and negotiation is fundamental to practical ethics. Such negotiations involve integrating theoretical ideals and practical realities, universal principles and context-specific situations.

In the Literature class, descriptive, normative, and analytical ethics essentially centre on critical readings of text including the text's ideological values and the implied author's intentions. Practical ethics shifts the focus beyond the text. The text is not a self-contained unit; rather, it is a culturally constructed artefact existing within a specific time and space. Literary analysis cannot therefore remain confined to the world of the text or the transactions among text, reader, and author. In relation to practical ethics, the key word is connections. Namely, we are interested in the multiple connections that have been and can be made between the text and other texts, society and the world. In this way, students also learn to see how the literary text can serve as an entry point to understanding the real world. As they engage in ethical dilemmas in the text, they also compare these to similar ethical dilemmas in the world and observe how these are deliberated in fictional and real worlds. The following questions can serve as a guide:

4.1 Connections to texts

- What intertextual connections are implicitly or explicitly made in the text and how does this extend your understanding of the ethical issues explored?
- How do the ethical issues explored in the text compare with similar issues explored in texts from other cultures?

4.2 Connections to society

- How do ethical issues and injustices explored in the text connect with your own society?
- How are you and members of your society complicit in the injustices and marginalization of others?

4.3 Connections to world

- How do ethical issues and injustices explored in the text connect with similar issues in the world either in the past or present?
- How have non-governmental or other groups sought to address these injustices and to what extent have their efforts been successful?
- What forms of action can be taken at the individual, community, state, and transnational levels to address these injustices and what might the effects of these actions be?

In Lee's poem, "Self-help for Fellow Refugees" the phrase "kingdom of heaven" (line 65) is a clear reference to this concept in the Bible. In several passages of the New Testament, discussions about how to enter the kingdom of heaven or what this looks like are described. This notion of a specific future and eternal kingdom is less evident in Eastern philosophy. For example, in Confucianism, it is the mandate of heaven that is discussed and in Buddhism, man enters the state of nirvana following a cycle of rebirth. The intertextual reference to the kingdom of heaven functions to ironically critique "Christian" America that appears to have failed to follow God's call to love the widow, orphans, foreigners, etc. This recalls increasing public cynicism towards the continued refrain that "thoughts and prayers" are with those killed by acts of terrorism or gun violence or with immigrant children separated from their mothers. Thus, the persona undercuts this guise of religiosity by suggesting more attention be paid to improving the conditions and treatment of minorities and refugees because "heaven on earth is better" (line 66).

Lee's depiction of alienation confronting refugees as they try to assimilate to a foreign culture can be compared to numerous literary texts such as the graphic novel *The Arrival* by Shaun Tan. Perhaps the key difference is that in Tan's graphic novel, the foreigner arrives in another land in search of better job opportunities. The alienation is visually exaggerated through the depiction of mysterious landscapes and creatures. The protagonist, however, finds comfort in listening to the histories of fellow immigrants. Likewise, Ken Liu's (2012) award-winning short story "The Paper Menagerie" (the story can be found at this site: https://io9.gizmodo.com/read-ken-lius-amazing-story-that-swept-the-hugo-nebula-5958919) takes us through the effects of alienation as a woman from China, selected for marriage via a catalogue, learns to adjust to life in America. Gradually, her own son, caught between two cultures, increasingly distances himself from her and her culture. Another story for comparison is Yann Matel's (2011) "The Moon Above His Head" (the story can be found at this site: www.salon.com/writer/yann_martel). The protagonist learns of a man who fell into the septic tank twice and suspects this was done deliberately. He investigates and learns that the man has fled the civil war in Mogadishu to seek asylum in Canada. The asylum seeker explains the reasons for his actions but similar effects of exile including psychological alienation and the desperation to hold on to memory are observed.

Broadly, students can shift from deep reading of a central text to wide reading by comparing the different challenges faced by refugees, asylum seekers, foreign workers, and other immigrants. They can consider how non-governmental organizations and governments define these different groups and the differential treatment accorded to them. Wide reading can also lead to research as students examine policies, news articles, and other artefacts that discuss the extent to which citizens and the state in their own country support these groups. This can be compared with immigrant policies in other countries.

5. *Virtue ethics*

Finally, another school of thought that has garnered significant attention of late is virtue ethics. Like deontologists, virtue ethicists subscribe to a non-consequentialist view of ethics. However, where they differ is that while deontologists tend to focus on duty or obligation to others based on moral principles, virtue ethicists are interested in the agent's character and the virtues that make up his or her character (Van Hooft, 2014). Perhaps it is Aristotle who has provided the earliest, most influential and systematic theorization of virtues. For Aristotle (350 B.C.E./1985), it is *eudaimonia* or human flourishing that is the highest good or ultimate end of all human endeavour and which is a property of an entire life not something achieved for the moment. Though human flourishing may be affected by luck or fortune, the central condition is that it is a process supported by the habitual exercising of virtues as we relate to others. The normative ethical question of what one ought to do is then not determined by outcomes or universal laws but virtues that Aristotle categorizes as intellectual (such as comprehension and intelligence) and moral virtues (such as temperance and generosity).

In the Literature classroom, descriptive, normative, analytical, and practical ethics can provide a useful lens to discussing ethics in texts and a launchpad to engaging with ethics in the world. At the same time, the reading of ethics should also be coupled with an ethics of reading. That is, how do teachers empower students as agents with particular ethical dispositions to engage with texts?

Virtue ethics and the cultivation of values in the Literature classroom will be elaborated at length in chapter 6. In general, we can expand on Aristotle's categorization of virtues by focusing on cultivating two key dispositions as students engage in Literature discussions. The first category encompasses intellectual or critical values. Literary engagement evidently involves hermeneutical strategies and critical values of questioning, discernment, and deliberation as students learn to synthesize and evaluate ideas, unpack ideological values in texts, and engage with ethical reasoning as they discuss ethical dilemmas and issues in texts.

The second category encompasses ethical values. Literary discussions occur in the public space of the classroom where reading operates not as an individualistic, private affair but as a social and public form of engagement. Here, teachers can cultivate ethical values such as empathy, hospitality, and responsibility for others. These ethical values are practised through the reinforcement of habits such as learning to listen and to respect the opinions of others.

Broadly, these critical-ethical values are aimed at developing cosmopolitan dispositions. Through Literature, teachers can seek to expand students' worldview by fostering their curiosity about and investedness in other cultures, by developing empathy for those hurt by violence and injustices, and by cultivating an openness to difference. In Table 4.1, I provide a summary list of the five ethical lens to reading texts.

Approaching aesthetics from the angle of ethics

Literature is perhaps the only subject in the school curriculum that can empower students to simultaneously think empathetically as they vicariously experience lived realities of individuals affected by social and global injustices, historically as they delve into sociopolitical contexts around the text, and philosophically as they negotiate diverse and conflicting ethical values. The kind of passive aesthetic criticism that continues to dominate Literature pedagogy results in distanced and disconnected readings of texts, stripping away Literature's power to develop a cosmopolitan orientation to the world.

Ethical readings of texts need not negate aesthetic appreciation. Conversely, we can add an ethical layer to our aesthetic analysis of texts. Typically, aesthetic

TABLE 4.1 Five ethical lenses to reading texts

Ethical Lens	*Focus*	*Typology of Questions*
Descriptive Ethics	Reading Ethics in Texts	1.1 Describe groups/communities • Who are the individuals and communities that comprise the fictional world of the text? • What is the main source of tension between these individuals or communities in the fictional world of the text? 1.2 Describe expected standards of behaviour • What are the implicit or explicit standards of behaviour expected of people in this community? • What happens if these are not adhered to? 1.3 Describe underlying values • What values or beliefs inform these explicit and implicit moral standards? • Why are these values significant to particular communities in the text? • What historical, philosophical, moral or other reasons are used to justify these values and expected standards of behaviour?
Normative Ethics	Responding to Ethics in Texts	2.1 Invitations to feeling • What significant events have affected characters in the text and how do they respond? • How does the text stir your empathy for these characters and what are your feelings about them as you learn of their experiences? 2.2 Invitations to shared beliefs • What beliefs about human nature or the world does the text assume you might subscribe to? • How does the text invite you to share these beliefs through the presentation of characters and events? 2.3 Invitations to ethical judgement • What values (individual, community, organizational, national, global) are presented in the text? • To what extent do you subscribe to these values? Why or why not?
Analytical Ethics	Analyzing Ethics in Texts	3.1 Analyzing ethical values • Are there examples of bias or stereotypes in the text? • Whose voices and perspectives are dominant in the text? Whose voices are absent or less dominant? How might this affect the representation of ethical issues? • What values does the author hold and to what extent is this representative of a particular race, gender, class, or other group? 3.2 Analyzing texts using Utilitarian concepts • What outcomes or consequences are valued and who benefits? • Do the outcomes justify the means? Why or why not?

(Continued)

TABLE 4.1 (Continued)

Ethical Lens	*Focus*	*Typology of Questions*
		3.3 Analyzing texts using Deontological concepts • What moral codes and norms are applied in the text and by whom? What context-specific or universal values are used to justify these? • To what extent do these norms and values benefit all people? Who are disadvantaged and why?
Practical Ethics	Connecting Ethics in Texts to Real-world Concerns	4.1 Connections to texts • What intertextual connections are implicitly or explicitly made in the text and how does this extend your understanding of the ethical issues explored? • How do the ethical issues explored in the text compare with similar issues explored in texts from other cultures? 4.2 Connections to society • How do ethical issues and injustices explored in the text connect with your own society? • How are you and members of your society complicit in the injustices and marginalization of others? 4.3 Connections to world • How do ethical issues and injustices explored in the text connect with similar issues in the world either in the past or present? • How have non-governmental or other groups sought to addresses these injustices and to what extent have their efforts been successful? • What forms of action can be taken at the individual, community, state, and transnational levels to address these injustices and what might the effects of these actions be?
Virtue Ethics	Reflecting on the ethics of reading	5.1 Critical values • Questioning – to value the opportunity to question ideas, traditions, and values. • Discernment – to value critical analysis and evaluation of ideas. • Deliberation – to value dialogue, debate, and discussion with others. 5.2 Ethical Values • Empathy – to value a deep and engaged understanding of others by putting oneself in the shoes of others. • Hospitality – to value different values and practices of others through openness to others and willingness to suspend judgement. • Responsibility – to value another to the extent of feeling a sense of responsibility and accountability for him/her. * *This list is not exhaustive*

appreciation revolves around the analysis of plot, character, setting, style, and theme. For each of these five areas, we can consider adding an ethical angle.

1. Examining ethical dilemmas in plot

Typically, analysis of plot involves examining how the story is structured and sequenced, identifying key events and how events develop at various points leading to a climax and resolution. A vital component in plot is conflict or tension. Without this, there is nothing to hook the reader or cause the story to progress. Students may identify tension by discussing how situations are complicated by flawed or mistaken intentions. To deepen their understanding of plot, students can also identify the ethical dilemma and analyze the underlying philosophical concept the author is exploring.

For example, the following is an excerpt from a well-known short story, "The Ones Who Walk Away from Omelas" by Ursula Le Guin (2015):

> In a basement under one of the beautiful public buildings of Omelas, or perhaps in the cellar of one of its spacious private homes, there is a room. It has one locked door, and no window. . . . The room is about three paces long and two wide: a mere broom closet or disused tool room. In the room a child is sitting. . . . They all know it is there, all the people of Omelas. Some of them have come to see it, others are content merely to know it is there. They all know that it has to be there. Some of them understand why, and some do not, but they all understand that their happiness, the beauty of their city, the tenderness of their friendships, the health of their children, the wisdom of their scholars, the skill of their makers, even the abundance of their harvest and the kindly weathers of their skies, depend wholly on this child's abominable misery.
>
> *(p. 254)*

The story begins with a description of the idyllic city and its joyful inhabitants but later transits to describing its dark secret. A little child, malnourished, neglected, and living in decrepit conditions, is kept in the basement in order for the city's prosperity to be appreciated. As students read the story, they can consider how the author sets up the ethical dilemma. An ethical dilemma involves choosing between two or more options. Each option is equally conflicting and has undesirable consequences. For example, in relation to this short story, we could phrase the ethical dilemma as follows:

- Option 1: Suffering must be witnessed. This may necessitate violence towards a minority for the sake of other peoples' happiness.
- Option 2: Suffering should not be witnessed. This, however, could potentially result in forgetting the effects of suffering resulting in violence towards others.

The fact that an ethical dilemma sets up equally contentious options opens room for debate in the classroom. Students should then aim to unpack the underlying philosophical issue at stake. In this case, the philosophical problem here is utilitarianism and the practicality and consequences of maximizing happiness for the majority at the expense of the minority. Students can discuss the problem of infringing the dignity and rights of a minority (option 1) as well as the limits of universal human rights in securing a community's future (option 2).

2. Examining ethical borders in setting

Aside from plot, another common aspect of literary analysis concerns setting. In analyzing setting, students are typically asked to pay attention to how time and place affects events and characters in the story. Students may also draw connections between fictional setting and historical setting such as how Harper Lee's (1960) *To Kill a Mockingbird* set in 1930s America reflects the American Civil Rights movement of the 1960s when she wrote the book. Analysis of setting provides opportunities for understanding broader sociohistorical contexts informing the story.

At the same time, students can also apply an ethical lens to analyzing setting by interrogating spatial borders and their ethical implications. Notions of border thinking and border pedagogy were conceptualized at least two decades ago. For example, Walter Mignolo (2000) argues that border thinking was a necessary intervention to decentre hermeneutical and epistemological discourses perpetuated by Western colonialism and neoliberal imperialism. Such border thinking needed to occur, he says, from the perspective of the subaltern and is reflective of "other thinking." Border ethics involves an inquiry into the world through the eyes of the other in which one learns to be "epistemically disobedient" by critically reframing the geopolitical situatedness of knowledge (Mignolo, 2013, p. 137). Similarly, Henry Giroux's (1988a) notion of border pedagogy envisions students engaging as border crossers to counter texts and memory constructed around coordinates of difference and power.

Today, the permeation of global risks into everyday realities has led to the erection of physical, political, and cultural walls that have become the zeitgeist of our century (Brown, 2010). Walls define territorial spaces; they provide an image of security in containing and defending those on the inside from foreign intrusion. Yet, the fundamental effect of walling is in normalizing othering. Ethical readings of borders can helpfully sensitize students to how injustice is normalized through spatial markings. Three key questions can serve as a launchpad for discussions.

First, where are the borders and how do they demarcate the "us" versus "them"? The aim is to sensitize students to spatial, political, and discursive boundaries and those with the power to mark them. For example, in the excerpt of Le Guin's short story, one notes how the binary between the rich and poor is set up: "In a basement under one of the beautiful public buildings of Omelas, or perhaps in the cellar of one of its spacious private homes, there is a room." The outcast, like many foreign workers in advanced economies, is hidden away, rendered invisible which makes his dehumanization less visible.

Second, how have boundaries shifted and what values have changed as a result? In reflecting on the collapse of morality in Nazi Germany, Hannah Arendt (2003) observes the reversion of morality to its etymological roots denoting custom or manners. She observes how easily a set of moral values may be exchanged for another, like how table manners can be quickly substituted. This fluidity of moral values is observed in how, during times of crisis, cosmopolitan and humanist values are easily discarded in favour of tribal and fundamentalist beliefs. Critical analysis should identify instances when institutional and symbolic forms of violence become normalized for the preservation of a group in power. For example, in the short story, students can explore how the suffering of the boy is institutionalized and made acceptable and more importantly, discuss who has the power in determining this. To what extent are the rest of the citizens complicit in normalizing such violence?

Finally, in what ways can we unbound the imagination and re-envision cosmopolitan possibilities? The imagination is an expandable faculty of mind that is also bounded by prejudices formed by historical and media stereotypes. Le Guin's story ends with a description of a minority who cannot accept the city's dependence on the boy's suffering. They leave Omelas alone and "walk ahead into the darkness." The idea of a cosmopolitan fraternity here seems like a myth or illusion. It is perhaps here that both teacher and students can contribute alternative narratives and real-life examples that might provide a more hopeful possibility of cosmopolitan communities of justice. One that comes to mind is the City of Refuge that Derrida (2001) describes in his book, *On Cosmopolitanism and Forgiveness*. Cities of refuge operate outside state agendas and are thus equipped with a greater degree of sovereignty capable of protecting the asylum-seeker or outcast. One example is the International Parliament of Writers' institution of the Cities of Asylum to defend the lives of writers fleeing from totalitarian threats (Boudou, 2019). Such cities are free cities governed by principles of hospitality towards others.

3. *Evaluating virtue in characters*

One of the most common question in Literature assessments requires students to discuss their impression of characters or compare two or more characters in the text. Oftentimes, students will identify evidence from different aspects of the text to justify their opinion of a character. On a superficial level, students may highlight character traits that seem obvious. For example, in Achebe's (2001) *Things Fall Apart*, Okonkwo can be described as machoistic in the way he is often consumed with displaying acts of aggression towards his children and wives. Going further, character analysis requires students to examine underlying motivations governing behaviour. This could involve examining the background of the character, his or her history, prior experiences and values as well as observing patterns of behaviour across the text. On further analysis, Okonkwo's drive to prove his manliness has much to do with the repulsion he feels towards his father who he deems weak and incompetent.

To add an ethical layer, we can apply the concept of virtue to evaluating characters. Aristotle describes virtue as a state, condition, or disposition induced by habits (Kraut, 2018). Virtues also result "in the types of action which manifest human excellence" (MacIntyre, 1998, p. 80). In essence, virtues are akin to habitual dispositions that one acquires through learning and experiences (Koslowski, 2001). For Aristotle, one key indicator of virtue is to examine the way an individual negotiates various kinds of conflict in his or her life. Virtue, according to Aristotle (350 B.C.E./1985), "is a mean between two vices, one of excess and one of deficiency" (§1107a, p. 44). Popularly known as the golden mean, the virtuous person is one who deliberates and seeks balance between extremes. Thus, bravery is the mean between cowardice and being overly cautious versus acting rashly and being too over-confident. Generosity is the mean between being self-centred by hoarding pleasures for oneself or by being stingy versus being overly giving to the point of being wasteful. The significance for character evaluation is that the way a character deliberates and the decisions that are made provide a glimpse into a character's personality. One should note, however, that this is not determined by one instance but over the course of many choices made. Over time, this may foreground an underlying value system that guides the individual's behaviour.

Our evaluation of virtue can occur at three levels – text, author, and reader. At the level of the text, we evaluate characters in the text by paying attention to three aspects:

- How has a character acquired particular dispositions over the long term? This ensures that students do not make judgements about a character solely by looking at one or two incidents in the text. Instead, they need to synthesize their observations of the character throughout the narrative. Note that addressing this question may apply better to novels than short stories or poems.
- How does a character learn and grow through various experiences and conflicts in the text? Virtue is acquired through learning which is then dependent on a character's desire and openness to learn from mistakes and be better. It is also connected to how a character is influenced by his or her family and wider community.
- How does a character negotiate tensions and ethical dilemmas? Here, the process of negotiation and the character attributes demonstrated through deliberation is more important that the outcome. Students should also consider the motivations and values that influence a character's decisions and behaviour.

At the level of the author, we should consider the character of the author and his or her values that have informed the text. We can ask the following questions:

- What values is the author promoting?
- Which worldview does this align with?

- Why are these values idealized and what are the historical and sociopolitical reasons for their significance?
- What alternative values may be equally valued?

At the level of the reader, we can reflect on the values we, along with our community of readers, impose as we evaluate characters. For example, when we consider a character admirable or reprehensible, what moral yardsticks are we using?

- What values from our own culture are we imposing when we evaluate characters?
- To what extent does this align or conflict with the values of the fictional society or that of the author's?
- In class discussions, what different evaluations of characters have been proposed and to what extent have different moral yardsticks been used?
- How would people from other cultures evaluate these characters differently from us and why?

The inclusion of an ethical angle to character analysis extends our understanding of characters beyond psychological assessments of their behaviour. It also pushes students to provide compelling justifications to judgements about character based on ethical considerations of their growth, underlying motivations, and values. Take for example the young adult novel, *Wonder* by R. J. Palacio (2012), a popular text used by middle school (lower secondary) students as it explores the pertinent topic of bullying. The protagonist, August, has a facial deformity and has been home-schooled until his parents decide he should go to school. In the beginning, he faces rejection and bullying but meets Jack and Summer who become his friends. Just as he begins to open up and trust Jack, he overhears Jack making cruel remarks about his appearance at a Halloween party. At this point, students may focus on this instance and judge Jack as thoughtless, weak, and easily influenced by others. However, if we focus on how flawed characters learn and grow from the mistakes they make, we begin to see virtue in the way they deliberate about, learn, and understand ethical values and base their actions on these. So while Shakespeare's King Lear may be judged for his vanity at the beginning of the play, virtue is found in the moral insight he gains about the nature of authentic love at the end of the play. We can consider then that the quest motif, a common structuring tool in narratives, as a quest not merely centred on the accumulation of knowledge and material goods for the self but as centred on an ethical quest to understand both self and others through deliberations about principles and values.

As the story progresses in *Wonder*, Jack learns to own up for the hurt he has caused and this learning translates to more occasions where he stands up and defends the bullied, i.e. August, even though this comes at a price as he becomes ostracized by his peers. At a metatextual level, the author perpetuates moral values through the voice of the English teacher who regularly dishes out important precepts and these are summarized in the Appendix at the end of the book. One such precept is "When given the choice between being right or being kind, choose kind." Being kind to others is then the primary moral yardstick that the novel sets up for the reader to use in assessing virtue embodied by various characters in the text. Thus, Julian, the bully, would be rated relatively low on the kindness spectrum as compared to Jack. On the other hand, we can also question whether kindness should be the only indicator of virtue. At a metacognitive level, we can compare the criteria used by our own society in evaluating the moral worth of individuals as compared to the criteria proposed in the book. We can conduct thought experiments and consider how we would evaluate characters differently if different virtue criteria were used instead. Essentially, discussions about what constitutes virtue and how we should evaluate characters would sensitize students to the constructedness of ethical values and the way it shapes our reading of people.

4. Analyzing ethical connotations in literary style

Training students to appreciate literary style is a staple in most high school Literature courses. Broadly, we can examine style at three levels – typographical, sonic, and sensory (Turco, 2000). Various literary techniques contribute to each of these elements of style (see Table 4.2).

Some students enjoy spending hours dissecting the text and thinking about how each word or line connotes an underlying meaning or contributes to the larger intention of the text. Others find this so technical that it robs their experience of the text. Whatever the case, practical criticism, or various iterations of this such as "Unseen" analysis,[2] continues to be a vital aspect in most high-stakes Literature examinations. One problem often highlighted in exam markers' reports is the tendency of students to go "technique-hunting." That is, students may focus on identifying and naming literary techniques in texts but seem unable to explain their function or effect. For example, students may point out the metaphors in Ezra Pound's (1913) two-line poem, "In a Station of the Metro," where faces in a crowded

TABLE 4.2 Stylistic elements and common literary techniques

Levels of Style	*Typographical level*	*Sonic level*	*Sensory level*
Definition	This refers to the way the text looks on the page i.e. its spatial prosody. For example, we can examine line arrangement and layout of the text as well as its shape (such as in concrete poetry).	This refers to the sound of the text as conveyed by its rhythm, metre (patterns of stresses and unstresses) and other sound devices.	This refers to figures of speech intended to evoke the sense of taste, touch, sight, smell, and hearing as well as to effect an emotional response.
Common literary techniques	Form, word order, parallelism, repetition, layout, font, visual design, etc.	Alliteration, assonance, consonance, rhyme scheme, metre, pace, onomatopoeia, etc.	Similes, metaphors, personification, symbolism, hyperbole, etc.

subway station are compared to fragile petals, here today and gone tomorrow. The problem with technique hunting is that it does little to show whether a student understands why a technique is used in the first place and what the intended effect is. One common strategy is to remind students to discuss the function and effect of stylistic techniques. At the same time, when students explain the effect of a literary technique, the focus is on the reader. In Pound's poem for example, students may point to how the metaphor comparing faces to an "apparition" and "petals" conveys an almost zen-like reflection about the transience of life evoking a sense of melancholy in the reader. Attention to function and effect in relation to style aligns with New Criticism's position that the text and its effects are the central focus of close reading. Richards (1924/2004) argues that criticism should be based on how it affects particular responses in the reader thereby requiring close attention to the way language functions in the text.

To build on the notion that stylistic techniques are employed purposefully to convey an effect, we can apply an ethical angle to examine how this affects not just the reader but other communities and cultures as well. Here, we attend to the ethical implications of language and its effects on others. Take for example the well-known fairy tale, *Ugly Duckling* by Hans Christian Andersen (1843/2006). In several picture books I have seen, the ugly duckling is portrayed as brown or yellow in colour. It is rejected by the other ducklings and labelled ugly. Later, it turns into a beautiful white swan and gains acceptance in its community. The moral of this story, we are often told, is not to judge a book by its cover.

To apply ethical readings of style, we can pay attention to conceptual associations. That is, we examine how two or more concepts become associated and the resulting connotations that follow. In the *Ugly Duckling* tale, brown or yellow is connected with ugliness whereas white is connected with beauty. This association sets up a binary between those who are "coloured" as opposed to those who exhibit "whiteness" with latter being privileged. Going further, the community appears to be intolerant of those who do not conform to a set colour and appearance and animals must change to be accepted. The story does not set out to critique racism and intolerance in this community conveying the sense that such a perspective is the norm.

In essence, instead of narrowing our analysis of style to discussing the function of form and technique and their effect on the reader, we can consider ethical readings of labels and conceptual associations in the text. Take for example, the operations of figurative language such as metaphor. One of the earliest definitions of metaphor comes from Aristotle (350 BCE/1970) who explains that the metaphor operates by transference and proceeds to list examples of transference: "Metaphor is the application of the name of a thing to something else, working either (a) from genus to species, or (b) from species to genus or (c) from species to species, or (d) by proportion" (p. 57). Centuries later, I. A. Richards (1936) developed a strategy for the close reading of metaphoric language focusing on comparison. The metaphor, he argues, consists of two components – tenor and vehicle. Tenor refers to the subject (concept, object, person, etc.) in the metaphorical phrase while the vehicle modifies the tenor through its associated qualities or ideas. For example, in the first line of Thomas Campion's (1617) poem "There is a Garden in Her Face," the tenor is the face of the subject spoken about in the poem while the vehicle refers to the qualities associated with "garden." Instead of thinking about metaphor as a transfer or shift in verbal meaning, Richards argues that there are also ambiguities, disparities, and tensions as a result of this transference. This dynamic interaction between terms in a metaphor later became the focus of the interaction theory of metaphor (Knowles & Moon, 2006). Max Black (1962) develops Richards' analytical frame by arguing that the tenor and vehicle are not in equivalent relation. In other words, there is a primary subject and a secondary subject in the metaphor resulting in the secondary subject projecting upon the primary subject a set of associated implications:

> In the context of a particular metaphorical statement, the two subjects "interact" in the following ways: (a) the presence of the primary subject incites the hearer to select some of the secondary subject's properties; and (b) invites him to construct a parallel implication-complex that can fit the primary subject; and (c) reciprocally induces parallel changes in the secondary subject.
>
> *(p. 36)*

In other words, our ethical readings of metaphors and other figurative language should attend to the imposition of any association by the secondary term such as the way ugliness is imposed on the colours brown and yellow. Literary language is constructed and laden with associations that may be influenced by cultural perspectives along with its assumptions and prejudices. Any close reading of texts should attend to the aesthetic workings of language along with its conceptual impositions and ethical connotations. The following are some questions we can ask:

Typographical level

- How does the organization, layout, font, and overall design contribute to the intended ideas and meaning of the text?
- What associations between the meaning conveyed by the text and particular concepts are formed as a result of its typography and how does this affect the representation of other communities and their concerns?
- Are these associations valid when cross-referenced with other literary and non-literary texts? What assumptions inform these associations? What alternative associations can we make?

Sonic level

- How do rhythm, metre, and other sound devices contribute to the overall mood of the text and affect the emotions of the reader?

- How is this emotion associated with the issue explored in the text? How does this emotion influence the reader's perspective of other communities and their concerns?
- Is the association between the emotion effected by the sound of the text and its representation of issues and of other communities valid? What assumptions inform these associations? What alternative associations can we make?

Sensory level

- Identify interesting words, metaphors, hyperbole, and other figurative language and discuss what are two or more entities being compared?
- What ideas and associations are imposed on the first term (tenor) by the second term (vehicle)? How does this influence the reader's perception of issues or communities explored in the text?
- What binary opposition is constructed from this comparison and what is privileged in the binary? Is the comparison valid and what assumptions inform this? What alternative comparisons can we make?

Essentially, an ethical reading of textual aesthetics subscribes to the view that all texts are constructed and language is not neutral but value-laden. Thus, we need to critically unpack the values and perspectives underlying the language we use, especially discourses that contribute to feelings and claims about other communities.

5. Inquiring into ethical concepts in themes

In the first nationwide survey of English Literature teachers' beliefs and practices in Singapore secondary schools, it was found that the top themes discussed in class are related to relationships with others, growing up (childhood, adolescence), race and ethnicity, gender discrimination, romance, war, power, modernization, loss (disease, sickness, and death) and bullying (Choo, Yeo, Chua, Palaniappan, Beevi, & Nah, 2020). In discussions of themes, typical questions often require students to focus on how the author presents the theme, issues, and sub-issues related to this, and how the theme is developed in the course of the narrative. For example, John Boyne's (2006) *The Boy in the Striped Pajamas* is one of the more popular young adult novels taught in Singapore secondary schools. The Holocaust story is told from the perspective of a nine-year-old boy who is the son of a high-ranking Nazi and who later befriends a Jewish boy in the concentration camp. Through the story, students may examine the theme of prejudice and how anti-Semitism is expressed through the dehumanization of Jewish prisoners and servants. Another obvious theme is friendship and students can explore how the two German and Jewish boys grow in their understanding of each other and how their loyalty eventually transcends political boundaries.

The addition of an ethical layer would include examining how theme is represented in the text. For example, in *The Boy in the Striped Pajamas*, how is the representation of the Holocaust portrayed compared to other literary texts and non-literary texts including biographies and memoirs? Here, teachers can introduce critical reviews including the Auschwitz Museum's caution about historical inaccuracies in the text (Eaglestone, 2007; McGreevy, 2020). Additionally, ethical explorations of theme would push discussions beyond the text to include considerations of philosophical concepts. For example, in this story, how is prejudice connected to power? What defines power and how is power wielded differently in different cultures and contexts? Similarly, what denotes friendship? How is friendship expressed to different degrees in other cultures?

Hillocks (2016) argues that Literature teachers need to better align literary with philosophical analysis: "Without an understanding of the moral concepts, students will be unable to generate arguments about the texts they read. For these moral concepts become the basis for the warrants that tie the evidence that readers perceive to the judgements they make about characters, groups, and societies, and the writers themselves and their works as wholes" (p. 110). Hillocks then proceeds to recommend that a good part of the curriculum should be devoted to studying ethical or philosophical ideas that provide a framework for the analysis of concepts such as courage, temperance, justice, friendship, generosity, and prudence, etc. This would become the grounds enabling students to judge literary characters, works, and authors. The following is an easy-to-remember framework to guide ethical readings of thematic concepts in texts.

Reading the text

- What are the central themes of the text?
- How do genre, form, and style of the text convey the theme?
- How does the theme develop as the story progresses?

Reading beneath the text

- What ethical or philosophical concepts are related to the theme of the text?
- How is the presentation of these concepts in the text shaped by the author's culture and background?
- Is the theme portrayed positively or negatively and what values from the author or his or her sociohistorical background may determine this?

Reading around the text

- How is the theme presented similarly or differently in other literary and non-literary texts that explore the same concern? Examine this through a range of genres such as memoirs, historical documents, and news articles, etc.

- Explore the philosophical concept related to this theme. Identify and explore the traditions, movements, and debates contributed by key philosophers and thinkers.

Reading against the text

- How are the themes and related philosophical ideas presented in the text perceived differently in other cultures?
- Research critical reviews of the text. What are alternative and critical perspectives to the representation of history, culture, or philosophical ideas in the text?

While most Literature teachers may not have a background in philosophy, a basic understanding of philosophical concepts can enrich classroom discussion and provide deeper understandings of concepts like power, justice, suffering, good, and evil, etc., that are commonly explored in literature. The resources below offer a good introduction to philosophical concepts, theories, and debates that can complement literary analysis:

- Baggini, J., & Fosl, P. S. (2010). *The philosopher's toolkit: A compendium of philosophical concepts and methods*. Malden, MA: Blackwell.
- Baggini, J., & Fosl, P. S. (2007). *The ethical toolkit: A compendium of ethical concepts and methods*. Malden, MA: Blackwell.
- Sandel, M. J. (2009). *Justice: What's the right thing to do?* New York: Farrar, Straus, and Giroux.
- Singer, P. (2011). *Practical ethics*. Cambridge, UK: Cambridge University Press.

In this chapter, I have argued that the privileging of aesthetic criticism in classrooms should be problematized because it contributes to the insularity of the subject, encouraging students to remain immersed in fictional worlds and to venerate the aesthetic power of literary texts. More than ever, the factious climate of our twenty-first century compels educators to empower students to be critical readers of ethical complexities and issues in all forms of discourse. The literary text provides the catalyst for developing "textual power" (Scholes, 1985) that students may transfer the capacity to reading ethics in texts to reading ethics in the world. As Booth (1998) has argued, literature provides a platform for applied ethics because "it is in stories that we learn to think about the 'virtual' cases that echo the cases we will meet when we return to the more disorderly, 'actual' world" (p. 48). Descriptive, normative, and analytical ethics provide important entry points to uncovering underlying value systems inherent in all texts. Extending such explorations with practical and virtue ethics empowers students with the habits of mind to grapple with ethical philosophy and activates their keen sense of obligation to marginalized others in the world.

The practice of cosmopolitan Ethical Criticism that I have proposed ultimately seeks to cultivate a consciousness of "planetarity" (Spivak, 2003) – a recognition of ourselves as part of a collective species in the universe – while destabilizing notions of cultural purity. More specifically, cosmopolitan Ethical Criticism pushes for an inclusive democracy that resists the tyranny of the majority and demands attention to differences in values, perceptions, and beliefs.

Notes

1 In the third article of "Perceptual Peace" entitled, "The Law of World Citizenship Shall Be Limited to Conditions of Universal Hospitality" (§ 358, p. 102), Kant (1795/1963) theorizes cosmopolitan rights extending beyond the individual and nation-state. This is encapsulated in "the right of a stranger not to be treated as an enemy when he arrives in the land of another" (§ 358, p. 102). Later, Derrida (2000) critiques Kantian hospitality as a form of conditional hospitality premised on the right of temporary rather than permanent visitation and imposition of conditions of conduct by the host country as opposed to what Derrida describes as absolute hospitality or hospitality without limits.

2 "Unseen" analysis refers to the experience in which students must apply practical criticism to critiquing a literary text they would encounter for the first time, typically via a formal assessment, e.g. a test or an exam.

5

PEDAGOGY

Building a critical-ethical community of readers

There is a buzz of excitement as a group of students enters the classroom. This is a grade 8 (equivalent to secondary two)[1] Language Arts class in an affluent neighbourhood in New York state. Their teacher, Karen (pseudonym), had previously given them a reading list centred on the theme of Tolerance with recommended books such as *Malcolm X: By Any Means Necessary* by Walter Dean Myers, *The Skin I'm In* by Sharon Flake, and *The Color Purple* by Alice Walker. They had been asked to work in teams to produce a creative interpretation of one or more of these texts and today is the day of their presentation. I have been invited to watch the students' presentations and give feedback together with their peers. In the weeks leading up to the presentation, Karen conducted a series of lessons centred on the questions of who are we and why differences matter.

I watch as one group presents their project in the format of a video they had scripted and filmed while another presents theirs in the format of Saturday Night Live, a popular variety talk show. During the feedback session, students comment mainly about the innovative reinterpretations of the books such as the varied use of different camera shots, clever incorporation of background music, and innovative use of green screen. Indeed, the students demonstrate much enthusiasm for their projects but what strikes me is the disjuncture between their creative and humorous reimaginings of the text and the serious ethical issues these texts explore. Their presentations are based on young adult novels such as *Speak* by Laurie Anderson, *You Don't Know Me* by David Klass, and *Give a Boy a Gun* by Todd Strasser, among others. These novels deal with various forms of violence including physical and sexual abuse and gun violence. For example in *Speak*, the protagonist is raped at a party and is left traumatized and later ostracized by her friends. Only one student observes, "I thought it [the presentation] was really good and funny, but I think that a lot of our books are not necessarily meant to be funny." A group member replies, "Well, that's why we were doing comedy; it has humour." I also ask the group why they have chosen to present these texts in a comic way to which they reply, "We like the show [Saturday Night Live]; we watch it all the time" and "We all like comedy so we incorporated what we like [to] a project for school."

Perhaps the privileging of students' off-tangent interpretations of these texts is due to the emphasis on reader engagement and responses so that Karen describes her class as "project-oriented." Karen explains that creativity "comes when you have a passion for the project, when you define yourself in your own role" and to her, what differentiates a good project from another is the degree to which students can produce a final product depicting key events in the text in an original way. As such, students' creativity and originality of response trump ethical engagement so that it is the self's interpretive preference and desire for pleasure and entertainment that are validated rather than the experiences of the referent other calling out for justice and empathy. By referent other, I refer to the fictional other in the text who, as an imagined construct, makes reference and points to real others in the world undergoing similar forms of injustice.

Over the past ten years, I have observed more than 80 classes and interviewed 140 teachers in various countries around the world. Yet, there are two scenes of teaching that continue to stand out in my mind due to the disconnect I observed between literary practice and deep ethical engagement. The first scene has just been described. Let me proceed to describe the second one.

Like the first example, this took place about ten years ago in a school in New York State. I was invited to observe a grade 9 Social Studies class on the topic of "Women in Islam." In this lesson, the teacher, Mary (pseudonym), begins with a lively discussion about the ways the Prophet Muhammad sought to establish equality for women in the seventh century. The conversation then turns to how various political forms of governance, such as that under the Taliban, established more patriarchal norms later on:

Mary: What have we heard about how women were treated under the Taliban in Afghanistan?

Student: Women have a lot less rights, they were not allowed to wear makeup outside.

Mary: Oh let's just go there! I'm going to have to give a bit of context here because we haven't read about Afghanistan and the Taliban and women. So including what she said but adding on to it – they literally bombed girls' schools, banned teaching girls to read, forced women who were professors, teachers, doctors to quit their jobs, made it so that a woman could not leave her home without her husband's permission and if she was out and about, she had to be completely covered – head to toe, no eyes showing either – completely covered. Maybe I should teach the rest of the lesson completely covered – that might have an interesting result.

Mary proceeds to take out a burkha and put it over herself leaving her entire body and face covered. She then says to the class: "It's kinda hot under here; it's also very private like I could make faces at you and you won't be able see it." A number of students laugh with one remarking that she looks "scary." Mary explains the different parts of the burkha and how it is worn differently in Middle Eastern countries such as Iraq and Egypt. Returning the focus to Afghanistan, she reiterates that women "had to be completely covered . . . they were not allowed to show their hands, so they had to be totally inside of it no matter how hot it was."

The lesson I observed exemplifies Said's (1979) argument of the West's stereotyping of the orient as a place of exotic beings and strange experiences and the tendency to construct oriental studies to examine and measure oriental culture through the lens of the West. In Mary's lesson, discussions of women in Islam begin not with attempting to help students understand Islamic beliefs about women and their relationships in the family and society but with assessing how free women are as compared with the West. Thus, Prophet Muhammad is praised because he promoted equal rights for women but the Taliban is critiqued as oppressive. Mary, a white American woman, paces around in her burkha making observations of her discomfort to her class made up of a majority of white students from one of the wealthiest towns in the East Coast. At one point, a student remarks, "You look like you should be carrying a scythe or something." In the minds of students then, Mary's wearing of the burkha serves to caricature and demonize the orient as backward and uncivilized reinforcing the ideological superiority of American liberalism.

Both these scenes of teaching highlight for me the significance of a pedagogy of ethics. The first scene of teaching reiterates how textual analysis and reader response, while important, should be subsumed under ethical engagement as priority. If ethics is first philosophy, this would mean designing projects and implementing strategies that would involve appreciating the text and its linguistic nuances as well as activating the reader's creative interpretations and active responses to text. These, however, would be directed ultimately at pushing students to understand issues from the perspective of the other and going further, to develop a greater sense of responsibility for and commitment to another. The second scene of teaching also highlights the need for a pedagogy of ethics that problematizes implicit forms of cultural colonization and imperialism especially when such discourses are masked as a form of moral education about other cultures. Thus, such a pedagogy of ethics must complement Ethical Criticism discussed in the last chapter in which underlying value systems informing texts, authors, readers, teachers, and society are analyzed and literary engagement serves to push students beyond the parochialism of the fictional world and beyond the egoism of reader towards the formation of an exilic imagination. Such an imagination does not entail the negation of home; rather, it is a conscious attempt to see, think and feel imaginatively from a lens outside one's own.

In his musings on exile, Said (2002) observes that in a secular and contingent world, homes are always provisional and seeing the entire world as a foreign land opens new possibilities for the imagination. As he argues, "most people are principally aware of one culture, one setting, one home; exiles are aware of at least two and this plurality of vision gives rise to an awareness of simultaneous dimensions" (p. 148). Given the rise of global mobility resulting in the virtual or physical movement of people and groups around the world as knowledge, products, services are exchanged, schools increasingly need to prepare students to inhabit the orientation of a world citizen which Nussbaum (1997) describes as one living "a kind of exile – from the comfort of local truths, from the warm nestling feeling of loyalties" (p. 11). Teaching students to inhabit an exilic imagination involves encouraging them to perceive other ideological values and belief systems that may be different from their own. The point is to develop rooted cosmopolitans (Appiah, 2006) who retain their connections to their communities while recognizing their affinity with multiple others as part of a larger human fraternity.

Towards a cosmopolitan literature pedagogic framework

Any attempt to transform Literature education needs to take into account not just ways of reading texts but also the pedagogical approaches through which these texts are taught. Prior to the early twentieth century, pedagogy tended to be conceived as a science of teaching, centred on didactics or the processes of learning and the particular content to be learnt (i.e. knowledge and know-how) (Tochon & Munby, 1993). Such views were later challenged by various movements in education, notably the progressive movement inspired by the philosopher John Dewey. Progressive pedagogy is antithetical to reproductive pedagogy. While the latter positions the student as a passive recipient of an already established canon of knowledge, the former emphasizes the student as an active learner whose development is central to the goals of education. Essentially, progressive pedagogy is characterized by the following: developing the child's innate and experiential knowledge in a series of stages (Dewey, 1902), relating knowledge to the real-world (Dewey, 1915), transforming the child's experiences with the physical and social world into an educative exercise, and using knowledge of the past as a means to understanding the present (Dewey, 1938). The rise of progressive education in the early twentieth century also laid the foundation for the shift from pedagogy as a science of learning to pedagogy as both an art and science of learning (Murphy, 2008). Lee Shulman's work on Pedagogical Content Knowledge (PCK) was particularly important in advancing the notion of pedagogy as art. He (1987) defines PCK as follows:

> It represents the blending of content and pedagogy into an understanding of how particular topics, problems, or issues are organized, represented, and adapted to the diverse interests and abilities of learners, and presented for instruction
>
> *(p. 8).*

Pedagogy as art thus involves the creative transformation of subject matter through the intentional use of a range of instructional strategies for specific purposes and within specific contexts (Park & Oliver, 2008). In what follows, I propose a Cosmopolitan Literature Pedagogic Framework to describe a holistic approach to teaching literature grounded on ethics. This framework is encapsulated in Figure 5.1 and is in the form of a spiderweb to denote the web of relations that occurs. Ruth Vinz (2000) uses the metaphor of the spiderweb to describe how teachers need to put stories in dialogue with other stories in the same way that teachers need to appropriate, mix, adapt, and connect the range of conceptual lenses and instructional strategies. Pedagogy as art thus requires teachers to artfully negotiate among the repertoire of knowledge, skills, approaches, and contextual influences.

The centre of the web focuses on the ways teachers facilitate dynamic triadic interactions among texts, readers, and others. Here, the reader transacts with the text including its aesthetic features as well as engage in dialogue and discussions with other readers. These transactions invite ethical engagements with others in both fictional and real worlds. At the heart of these interactions is the ethical call to understand, feel and defend others in the world particularly those hurt by forms of injustice.

The second layer of the web highlights the repertoire of skills that support text-reader-other interactions in the classroom. The list of skills is by no means

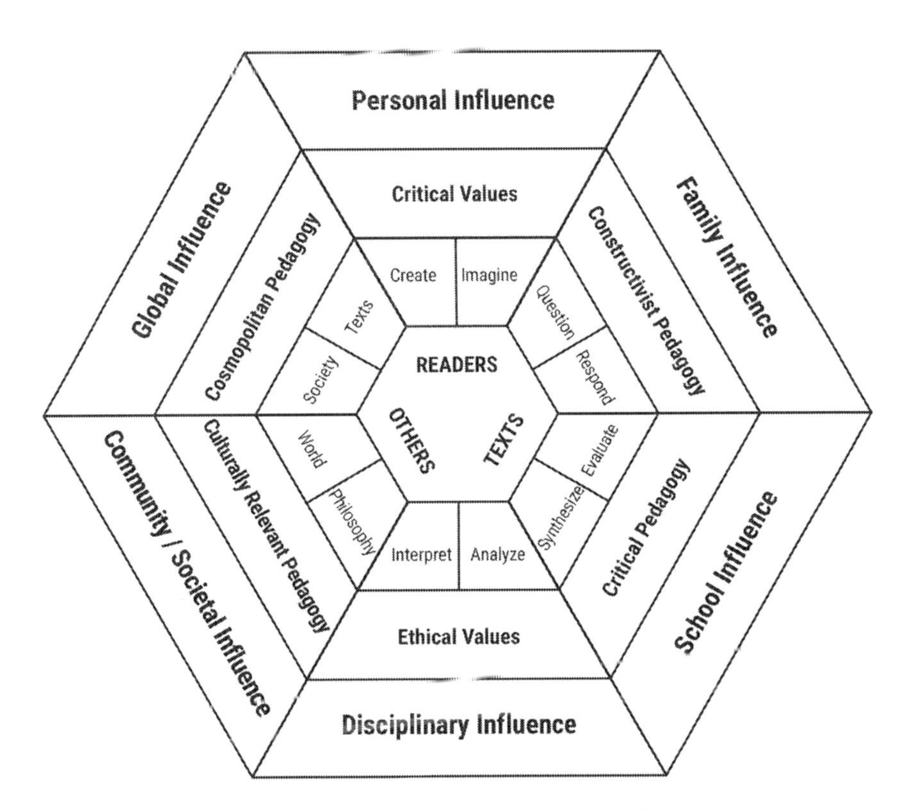

FIGURE 5.1 A Cosmopolitan Literature Pedagogic Framework

exhaustive and is meant to provide an initial sense of the range of skills available. Here, engagement with texts involves teaching students to interpret and analyze content, form and literary techniques. Students also need to synthesize developments in plot and characters. Further critical text analysis involves analysis of norms and ethics in texts including evaluations of bias and representation in texts. Active reader engagement with text involves providing opportunities for students to respond to texts and connect the text to their own experiences as well as to question, imagine, and reimagine texts from other points of view. Literary engagement also does not have to be centred on passive responses but can involve students as creative producers of meaning and of texts. Finally, as discussed in the previous chapter, pedagogies should also facilitate the movement beyond text to exploring practical ethics in the world. Here, the notion of connections is key as students consider the ways fictional texts invite connections to other texts, to issues in their society and the world and broader ideas in ethical philosophy such as justice, suffering, the nature of good and evil, etc.

The third layer of the web centres on the range of key pedagogies, particularly significant since the mid-twentieth century that can support these text-reader-other interactions in the classroom. Again, this is not an exhaustive list but is meant to highlight influential movements that have informed Literature pedagogy in schools – constructivist pedagogy, critical pedagogy, culturally relevant pedagogy, and cosmopolitan pedagogy.

Constructivist pedagogy centres on enabling students to construct and co-construct knowledge and meaning from experiences. Informed by constructivist learning theories of Jean Piaget, Lev Vygotsky, and John Dewey, this approach subscribes to the view that learning occurs from the experiences of students and that social interaction is fundamental to cognitive development (Lave & Wenger, 1991). Reader-response criticism of the 1970s shared constructivist views of learning as transactional and as students interact with texts, learners, and environments, they also become active producers of meaning (Rosenblatt, 1994).

Critical pedagogy shares the ideals of Poststructuralist thinkers of the 1970s by focusing on "educating students to become active, critical citizens (not simply workers)" (Giroux, 1988b, p. 7). Drawing on the work of Freire, Foucault, Postcolonial and Marxist scholars, critical pedagogues draw attention to how the values of a dominant class are perpetuated through symbolic and cultural capital leading to the continued oppression of subordinate classes. Critical pedagogies seek to empower students to dialogue about and critique discourses of power and ideology, class distinctions, and systemic inequities in education.

Culturally Relevant pedagogy may be seen as an extension of critical pedagogy. Influenced by the movement of multiculturalism, this approach gained popularity in the 1990s. Ladson-Billings (1995), a key proponent, has argued for a more dynamic and synergistic relationship between home/community culture and school culture. Gay (2002), another important advocate of the movement, proposes three aims for a culturally responsive approach to teaching that involves equipping teachers to:

acquire a knowledge base about ethnic and cultural diversity, design curriculum and implement strategies that are responsive to cultural diversity, and create classroom cultures that are conducive to learning for ethnically diverse students.

In Literature education, I propose that our teachers be empowered with a repertoire of pedagogical approaches particularly the 4 Cs – Constructivist, Critical, Culturally Relevant, and Cosmopolitan pedagogies. As much has already been written about the first three, the next part of this chapter will focus on the less researched practice of cosmopolitan pedagogies. Before we move to this section, it is important to note that pedagogies should not be reduced to mere innovative techniques of teaching; they should be undergirded by critical and ethical values that students develop while learning. This will be covered in greater detail in the next chapter. Further, one should be aware that the application of pedagogies and their connections to critical and ethical values are influenced by broader factors beyond the classroom. These constitute the fourth layer of the pedagogic framework highlighting Literature education's ecosystem encompassing personal, family, school, community, and national influences. Additionally, disciplinary movements such as Poststructuralist Criticism and Ethical Criticism influence the way certain pedagogies become fashionable at particular points in time. Finally, globalization has led to the proliferation of transnational communities facilitated by social media and digital technologies. These contribute to a greater consciousness of ourselves as world citizens.

The four connections facilitated by cosmopolitan pedagogies

Global citizenship movements and discourses around twenty-first century education have turned attention to how education can equip students with the kinds of skills and dispositions that promote global awareness and ethical engagement with diverse others. The philosophical ideas of cosmopolitanism, or citizen of the world, rooted in the ideas of Aristotle, Cynic, Stoic, and Enlightenment philosophers in the West as well as Confucian philosophers and Hindu thinkers in the East have been discussed in the previous chapters. Today, contemporary scholars conceptualize cosmopolitanism as encompassing multiple forms of belonging so that one may be rooted to home while being open to the world (Appiah, 2006; Hansen, 2011). Cosmopolitan pedagogies are centred on developing key ethical dispositions of hospitality and openness in order to engage with multiple and diverse others in an age of global interconnectedness (Choo, 2018; Nussbaum, 1997; Rizvi, 2009). Ultimately, cosmopolitan pedagogies are aimed at facilitating four key connections as depicted in Figure 5.1 – connections to texts, society, world, and ethical philosophy. In what follows I discuss the specific strategies that can activate these connections drawing upon the work of Literature teachers I have observed from schools in Australia, Singapore, and the United States. Appendix A provides a summary profile of the teachers described in this chapter.

Connections to texts – intertextual strategies

Cosmopolitan pedagogies grounded on the principles of ethics as first philosophy aim to cultivate in students a hospitable openness to the others who may have different histories, values, and beliefs. The desire to connect with others is a first-step to cultivating relations with others. The German philosopher Jürgen Habermas (1984) countered pragmatic and strategic uses of communication by reverting to an inherent intersubjective impulse underlying language. He argues that communicative action occurs "whenever the actions of agents involved are coordinated not through egocentric calculations of success but through acts of reaching understanding" (p. 285). In other words, communicative action is fuelled by the impulse to understand and reach out to the other and this occurs through dialogue rather than imperatives and commands. This resonates with Levinas's (1969) argument that humans are innately relational, called to move beyond themselves and their own subjectivity towards otherness. Language provides the bridge between self and other, for "the essence of language is friendship and hospitality" (p. 305).

One strategy is to encourage students to make intertextual connections to other texts. For example, teachers can encourage comparisons and connections between canonical and contemporary texts. I observed this in Tanya's grade 7 Language Arts class in an independent all-boys school in Singapore. The unit revolves around the study of the classical novel *Animal Farm* by George Orwell. However, this is accompanied by a parallel text, *Shooting Kabul* by N. H. Senzai, which is a relatively new text hardly used in schools. *Shooting Kabul* centres on a family's attempt to gain asylum in the United States as they escape Afghanistan and the Taliban while facing all kinds of discrimination in a post-9/11 climate.

In Tanya's class, there is a clear contrast between the core and supplementary curriculum. The core curriculum is centred on an in-depth analysis of a canonical literary text with the final examination testing students on the analysis of characters and stylistic devices in *Animal Farm* through passage-based and essay-type questions – a format similar to the national examination. Conversely, the parallel text allows Tanya to introduce current issues that students can better relate to. Students are not formally assessed on *Shooting Kabul*. Instead, they are given opportunities to respond to the text through various projects involving creative writing, photography, and use of social media.

Tanya also encourages her students to connect current events such as 9/11 and Islamophobia associated with their study of *Shooting Kabul* with questions related to terrorism in *Animal Farm*. In one discussion, Tanya leads students to consider how migrant communities construct culture in a foreign location. When asked what culture means, one student suggests that it involves "a set of ideas, beliefs, social practices that a certain group of people believes in." Other students talk about culture in terms of accent, language, everyday practices such as greeting another person, and values that are honoured, such as duty to family. As the discussion continues, Tanya leads students to connect culture with the issue of discrimination.

When she asks students to consider similarities between *Animal Farm* and *Shooting Kabul*, she observes that "no one had brought up the idea of discrimination and bias in *Animal Farm* before. It took reading *Shooting Kabul* for students to draw that link." Whereas students had tended to focus on themes concerning power and oppression in discussions of *Animal Farm*, they can now highlight instances of bias towards certain groups and their effects, which then concretizes the ways in which power affects the lives of individuals and communities.

For Tanya, the use of the parallel text is meant to disrupt students' perception of Literature's disconnect from the world. She explains that she chose *Shooting Kabul* after realizing her students were discussing politics in *Animal Farm* in a detached way. Students were seeing little relation between the literary texts they were studying and current political issues reported via the mass media, particularly in relation to terrorism. Tanya had observed that her students were less able to associate *Animal Farm's* satirical comments on the terrorizing effects of communism with political realities due to its allegorical style. Further, the news articles students were reading regularly made reference to 9/11, an event they had little understanding of since most of them were born in 2001.

In one culminating project, students work individually or in groups to select one of ten assignments given to them. One assignment tasks students to conduct research on 9/11, particularly eyewitness accounts, and then to write a story from the point of view of someone living in the United States after the attacks who is either Muslim or South Asian and who may be facing similar forms of prejudice as the protagonist in *Shooting Kabul*. Another assignment tasks students to examine a particular refugee population, such as those in Syria, and consider what prompts them to flee their country, where they go to eventually, and the challenges they face in a foreign environment.

Tanya's strategy of placing contemporary, less familiar young adult texts in conversation with canonical, well-established texts is essentially aimed at helping students connect abstract concepts in the latter with contemporary concerns in the former. In doing so, her curriculum is freed from the clutches of the canonical and encourages more dynamic text-reader-other interactions in the classroom. Here, readers' transactions with text are oriented towards understanding and empathizing with marginalized others through engagement with real-world issues such as terrorism and xenophobia.

Another connections-to-text strategy involves connecting fiction with authentic texts as observed in Kim's grade 8 Literature unit in a mainstream government school in Singapore. The unit is titled, "The Unseen and Unheard" which centres on the lives of migrant workers in Singapore. For Kim, the development of empathy for those who suffer injustices is a key objective informing the design of her lessons. Throughout, she often infuses emotive questions designed to tap into students' feelings of sympathy such as when she shows photographs of living conditions of foreign domestic workers in Singapore and asks, "Look at it – it's literally a shelf bed. There are no mattresses. Can you imagine sleeping on a hard surface like this?" or when she has students read a short story and asks, "Is there something that you find particularly interesting or something that jumps out at you, that you feel for?"

To Kim, empathy is closely aligned with authenticity and thus, she recognizes the importance of drawing students out of their immersion in fictional worlds. This is done by encouraging them to connect fictional text with "authentic" texts depicting actual challenges faced by migrant workers such as memoirs and poems written first hand by foreign workers. These poems, shortlisted from an annual Migrant Workers' Poetry competition, feature the voices of workers from Bangladesh, China, India, Indonesia, and Philippines working in Singapore. They provide glimpses of their lives at home and rich descriptions of their experiences overseas including feelings of alienation and encounters with various forms of unjust treatment. For Kim, using authentic texts helps disrupt negative images of migrant workers on mass media so as "to really let [students] hear their voices instead of one that's stereotypical." The perspective of foreign workers is juxtaposed with news articles describing the views of locals towards foreign workers with headings such as "Why residents want foreign workers to stay away." Kim's lessons frequently interweave fiction and reality. For example, as students read about the physical and emotional toil on foreign workers in the short story "Two Days in a Foreign Land" by Jonathan Tan, they also discuss real accounts of challenges they face such as the burden of repaying huge debts to agents in order to work in Singapore. Kim combines classroom discussions of literary texts with out-of-classroom experiences. For example, in one lesson, she brings students to visit an exhibition featuring photos and reflections written by migrant workers in Singapore. A culminating project requires students to either create a product (poem, skit, or story) based on their research on the experiences of migrant workers in Singapore or conduct an interview with a migrant worker and write a report on this.

The importance of transferring empathy from fictional characters to real-life exemplars is important to Kim who wants students to become more invested in understanding marginalized groups suffering from systemic injustices. At the same time, one limitation is that the profusion of emotive questions can lead to sympathetic rather than empathetic responses which may implicitly reinforce students' own cultural superiority such as when the plight of migrant workers becomes conceived in homogenous, monolithic ways. This suggests the need to continually extend dialogue so that it is inclusive of diverse perspectives allowing students to compare a range of experiences across marginalized groups.

In summary, cosmopolitan pedagogies can encourage intertextual comparisons to foster dialogic conversations through texts including canonical and contemporary literature, fiction, and authentic texts, etc. In the process, students learn to embrace complexity and ambiguity in order to perceive issues from multiple perspectives. While debate is a common pedagogical strategy in Literature lessons, the tendency is that students compete to arrive at a dominant response. Thus, such dialogic connections should build on and extend ideas emerging from debates. By extension, these connections to texts can also encompass varying levels of social distance. Least personal accounts include news articles, documentaries, and reports by non-governmental organizations while more personal accounts include photos, memoirs, and testimonies. These could eventually lead to face-to-face encounters involving first-hand interviews with marginalized individuals.

Connections to texts – strategies of interruption

Cosmopolitan pedagogies that facilitate connections to texts can take two forms. On one level, they may extend and expand understandings of the other. On another level, such connections can also involve strategies of interruption that disrupt singular readings of texts as observed in Keith's grade 11 Literature class in an independent school in Singapore.

Keith explains that he deliberately adopts an intertextual approach to teaching literature because his aim is to have students "think critically and creatively in different contexts and across different contexts [so that they will] get out of the mind-set of thinking in one context." In one lesson, students begin reading the short story "On Discovery" by Asian American writer Maxine Hong Kingston which centres on a male figure who accidentally stumbles upon the Land of Women, is captured, and made to undergo a process of feminization. Following a discussion about how the male character is made female, Keith directs students to the central focus of the lesson. Referring to Shakespeare's *Taming of the Shrew*, students apply the concept of taming a person by comparing how Kate in the Shakespearean play is similar to the male protagonist in Kingston's story in that both are made to conform to society's idealized image of a female object. The intent is to foster new cultural understandings so that students can become aware of how gender identity was perceived in 700 BCE China in which Kingston's story is set as compared to sixteenth-century Italy in which the Shakespearean play is set. Ultimately, Keith aims to have students become more conscious of how certain male chauvinistic ideas and objectifications of women are universal across historical periods and cultures.

In subsequent lessons, Keith continually interrupts his teaching of *Taming of the Shrew* with a series of culturally hybridized texts including those by African American writer Toni Morrison, Caribbean American writer Jamaica Kincaid, Chinese Singaporean writer Stella Kon, and Japanese American writer Kyoko Mori. To Keith, it is important that students be aware of culture as deterritorialized as he explains, "I want my students to be conscious of the fact that they do negotiate across cultural identities and that they are caught in-between cultures." Such a view distinguishes Keith's curriculum from early World Literature curriculum models conditioned by territorial distinctions emphasizing the study of representative texts from around the world while taking little account of cultural mixings (see chapter 3). In Keith's class, consciousness of hybridity is made more prevalent as students, in the process of actively making meaning of the core text, are frequently interrupted and tasked to perform intertextual comparisons. These *in medias res* interruptions surface networks of signification across texts that raise conscious awareness of varied and conflicting cultural values in the world. For example, when Keith asks students to think about the process of effeminizing a man from Kingston's story, students are quick to provide stereotypical judgements commenting about how he turned "dainty" and "subservient." Students begin discussing the role of nature and nurture in defining gender identity and as the unit progresses, they compare different cultural expectations and means of conditioning gender identity through various literary texts around the world. Eventually, this conveys the notion of the world as fragmented rather than whole so that there is no single angle through which gender identity can be conceived. In this sense, intertextuality functions as a form of ethical interruption by guiding students to move beyond their own worldview in judging the other in order to expand their imaginative capacity to perceive multiple value systems in the world.

In a culminating assignment, Keith asks students to "use one of the text extracts to talk about [their] sense of cross-cultural identity." The nature of this question prompts students to reflect on how they feel about being caught in-between cultures. One student remarks, "I do not have a culture that is ready-made and served to me; I have to manually decide what should be mine" while another discusses how the inability to "fit in any neat ethnic pigeonhole" because of her mixed race implies a coexistence between ambiguity and agency in her sense of identity. Here, ethical interruption serves to cultivate students' critical self-reflexivity as they consider how characters deal with various moral ambiguities in the world and as they reflect on how they themselves should navigate cultural plurality. Given the prevalence of global mobility, such a disposition is increasingly pertinent as societies move away from bounded communities to network societies (Castells, 2010) characterized by cosmopolitan openness, extraterritoriality, and fluid interconnections. Consequently, there is a need to repersonalize morality which means situating moral responsibility in the individual and not the nation-state (Bauman, 1993). In education, the impetus is then to equip students with self-reflexive criticality that counters depoliticizations of identity constructions while facilitating a form of critical, reflective openness to value systems encountered in text and world (Delanty, 2006; Hansen, Burdick-Shepherd, Cammarano, & Obelleiro, 2009; Poon, 2010).

Strategies of interruption can involve disrupting a singular cultural perspective; it can also involve intentionally countering stereotypical depictions of the other, as observed in Pamela's grade 10 Literature class in an independent school in Singapore. The central text in the unit is *Frankenstein*. Previously, she had predominantly focused on a close analysis of the text. At this point, she wants to get students to move beyond "SparkNotes kind of responses" and how they are "so used to seeing *Frankenstein* in relation to just a few themes or ideas." As she teaches the text again, she wants to explicitly draw attention to the complexities of "othering" and make this more real to students. She explains that students understand the monster in *Frankenstein* as representing those who are othered, but his foreignness as a creature makes him less relatable to students. Her strategy is to frame the lesson around the concept of representation and ways of seeing. This is to occur in two ways.

First, following the typical analysis of main ideas and character motivations in Frankenstein, she has students work in groups to research a contemporary global issue and discuss how it shapes their understanding of *Frankenstein* and vice versa. Various projects touch on how issues related to the environment, discrimination against gay and lesbian communities, and terrorism connect to the novel. One group proceeds to examine how rumours of other countries' involvement in nuclear research provides the motivation for superpower countries to invest in nuclear power, in the same way that Victor Frankenstein's perception of other scientists' promising scientific breakthroughs spurs him to create life in order to get ahead. Another group discusses the Arab-Israeli conflict, in particular how attention to Palestine is often focused on its terror organizations rather than the territory or its people, which is similar to the way the creature in *Frankenstein* is judged by his appearance rather than his personality.

Next, Pamela guides students to think about the ways in which the perception of marginalized individuals is constructed through the introduction of a short story, "The Moon Above His Head" by Yann Martel, which describes the sense of alienation faced by a Somali-Canadian named Hashi, who gains asylum but loses his family. Pamela provides a series of guiding questions that centres on how each character is interpreted by others. At one point in the discussion, students analyze how Hashi is portrayed in the local newspapers and why the reporter has to introduce him as a Somali-Canadian.

Student A: [His nationality is mentioned] because the most distinguishable thing about a person is skin colour, just like how Chinese people differentiate others by shades of colour.

Student B: But the point is that the media bothered to highlight the nationality so specifically. Why Somali-Canadian? It's not relevant to the story but they bothered to highlight this.

Student C: The identity of the person has to be part of the story. It's part of how they want to introduce the person.

Student D: But automatically you have immediate negative connotations when you hear [that he's] Somali-Canadian. You think of refugees and all that.

Student E: I think mentioning that is meant to emphasize differences to show he is not a true-blue Canadian. He's a naturalized citizen. It seems to me there's segregation because even though they are Canadians, they are Somali-Canadians.

As observed in the discussion, some students wrestle with whether media representations of the marginalized figure are part of the norm of objective reportage, while others question the ethical implications of such a norm itself and whether public acceptance of such reporting implicitly naturalizes xenophobia. As Pamela reflects in an interview, this is one of the more uncomfortable moments in the discussion because of the struggle in thinking about how particular stereotypes of the marginalized other become socially accepted through apparently "factual" techniques of representation. The discussion transits to students thinking about the framing of the story itself and how the author utilizes the narrator, himself a writer, to guide readers on how Hashi, as a representative of the asylum seeker and alienated foreigner, should be perceived. Several students point out how both author and narrator continue to objectify Hashi as his life is utilized by those in privileged positions to educate readers even as they claim to empathize with him. Their insights echo Spivak's (1988) argument in her seminal essay "Can the Subaltern Speak?" on the question of who can adequately speak on behalf of those who do not possess the linguistic, economic, or other resources to represent themselves and whether even sympathetic acts of representing the other as victimized reinscribe their subordinate position.

Towards the end of the unit, Pamela challenges students to think about what they have come to expect in representations of the other in public discourse. She tells them,

> Just because it is the norm [to write about the other in ways we have come to expect], is it ethical? Is there a better way to frame an issue? Here, we are questioning how the [news] article chose to represent the incident and how the narrator chose to represent to us his interpretation or reading of the article, and at the same time, we also question ourselves as readers of stories. I'm asking you to look at perspectives and question your perspectives and how they actually emerge in moments of openness.

Students then return to *Frankenstein* and examine pairs of characters in the text, looking at how one character sees another, how the reader's perception of both is shaped, and whether there are gaps in the interpretation of the other.

In Pamela's unit, a shift occurs as students examine how the other is constructed by those who control the power of discourse, utilizing subtle techniques that reinforce essentialized depictions to influence how the other is read by those in more privileged positions, including the students themselves. Consequently, students' imagined interpretations of the other take on a critical reflexive dimension that Gerard Delanty (2006) argues is activated whenever new relations among self, other, and the world emerge in moments of openness. As Spivak (2012) argues, aesthetic education should fundamentally provide "the training of an imagination for epistemological performance" (p. 101), which involves more intentional interrogations of the way knowledge of self, others, and the world is constructed, performed, and interpreted and the varying power positions of the multiple actors involved in representing and being represented. Given that the imagination may fuel nationalism, she explains that part of this training must involve expanding the imagination's capacity to perceive others. Ultimately, Pamela aims to foster three-dimensional ways of seeing the foreign other by interrupting superficial, consumptive style of tourist-like seeing. This involves continual destablizing of stereotypical interpretations of the other formed from mass media images, which catalyzes a deeper desire to understand the other as a human being caught up in evolving, complex, and intersecting histories.

In summary, two key principles of interruption can serve as a guide. The first is to recognize "The Danger of the Single Story" which is the title of a well-known TED Talk by Chimamanda Adichie. As Adichie (2009) explains, "power is the ability not just to tell the story of another person, but to make it the definitive story of that person" (10:03). Disruptions of the single story can occur by contrasting an issue explored from one cultural perspective with another from a different culture. For example, in my own class, I have had students first identify images of asylum seekers commonly found in the mass media. These include descriptions of asylum seekers as faceless, stigmatized, and victims of abuse. While such accounts may contain some degree of truth, they also represent a single story of asylum seekers. I then have students interrupt this one-dimensional image of the asylum seeker using Adichie's (2010) short story "The American Embassy" that portrays the asylum seeker as one who is empowered, an agent determining her own destiny and whose goal transcends mere self-preservation.

The second principle is to identify and counter existing stereotypes occurring in public spaces, e.g. mass media and social media. Teachers can introduce literary texts to counter such stereotypes. For example, the spread of COVID-19 has resulted in forms of discrimination towards Asians occurring even at the highest levels of office such as when United States President Donald Trump employed the term "China virus" or when a White House official described the virus as "Kung Flu." Instead of avoiding explicit discussions about racism, teachers can introduce texts such as the award-winning graphic novel, *American Born Chinese* by Gene Luen Yang (2006) which employs postmodern techniques and unreliable narration to foreground the effects of overt and casual racism.

Connections to society – strategies that foreground glocalism

The reality of our cosmopolitan age is that the nation can no longer be conceived as bounded and identity as monolithic. Local spaces have become increasingly globalized so that one may have multiple affinities to physical and virtual communities near and distant. The two dominant features of contemporary globalization are mobility and mutability. Both these concepts are essentially tied to place and the ways it has become contingent in defining an individual's sense of identity (Livingston, 2001). As students make ethical connections between the text they study and the reality of their own lives, there is also a need to encourage global connections by problematizing notions of cultural authenticity, ancestry, and the fixation of identity to a particular place in time.

In a unit on the theme of identity, Shanti has her grade 9 Language Arts class, in an independent school in Singapore, discuss identity and change in physical spaces. In this unit, she begins by juxtaposing images of old Singapore, such as the National Stadium, public housing, and playgrounds, with images of modern Singapore. "In the course of rapid development, urbanization, modernization," she asks the class, "is there something that we are leaving behind, forgetting?" To explore this question, students work in groups to examine various artefacts, from critical articles lamenting the commercialization of Chinatown to articles about the state's attempts to preserve culture to poems by writers reflecting on Singapore's changing landscape. Both literary and non-literary texts serve to broaden students' perspective on the issue, with the former providing a more philosophically reflective response and the latter providing historical and informed arguments. Shanti then facilitates a discussion about the effects of mutability on the sense of identity and belonging. For example, when one student shares how the constantly changing landscape in Singapore results in the dilution of a distinctively Singaporean culture, another student points out that such romanticizing of history is an attempt to return to an essentialized past which is itself a myth. Shanti then pushes the class to consider the inevitability of change and how identity can instead be thought of as imagined, constructed, always in the process of being constituted and transformed.

Similarly in Cheryl's grade 8 Literature unit, the focus is on the infusion of global injustices in everyday local spaces. Cheryl teaches in a mainstream government school in Singapore and in this unit, her aim is to sensitize students to the condition of glocalism which refers to the idea that global forces do not exist as discrete, external phenomena but interpenetrate everyday realities and are interpreted through the lens of the local (Roudometof, 2016). Glocalism is akin to thick, rooted, everyday cosmopolitanism and reveals micro-global processes occurring in reality.

Cheryl's unit is titled, "The Place of Memory." Over ten weeks, students explore short stories and documentaries with the key aim of examining "the identities people take on or identities people reject and how that's tied to place of birth or the culture that one comes from." One story, "The Move" by Wena Poon, describes an old lady's struggle to find belonging as she relocates to a newly upgraded housing estate. Another story, "The Paper Menagerie" by Ken Liu, explores how global interconnectedness has facilitated the commodification of individuals such as when a Chinese bride is conveniently purchased by an American via a catalogue. The central ideas in these texts encourage students to perceive the different ways everyday micro-injustices may be tied to larger global forces operating within local spaces whether this occurs as individuals adjust to the state's broader agenda to develop a utopian global city as explored in Poon's story or as individuals encounter intercultural conflicts arising when foreigners are pressured to integrate into local spaces as depicted in Liu's story. Part of the impetus for designing this unit stems from Cheryl's view that students in general are "self-centred" and tend to feel "so secure and so safe that they think the future will always be the same."

In summary, these examples highlight two principles for how teachers can activate students' connections to society. First, it begins with recognizing that literary study cannot remain enclosed within the world of the text and students should be encouraged to see how the issues explored connect with their immediate communities. Second, connections to society entail a dynamic, open-ended exploration based on a view that culture is "always in the state of becoming as a result of interactions of various kinds, rather than something that is entirely inherited within clearly definable boundaries and norms" (Rizvi, 2009, p. 264). Kwame Anthony Appiah (2018) has observed that at the core of identity, whether this is determined by race, class, gender, country, etc., is the assumption there is a deep similarity that binds a group of individuals together and this has tended to erode human solidarity leading to divisions and war. Given that the notion of an authentic culture is a myth since cultures have historically intersected with others, Rizvi (2009) argues that our focus should be on the ways cultural practices become separated from their "homes" and how cultures adapt, appropriate other cultures, and are converted into new forms. One example that comes to mind is taken from the widely acclaimed book *Golden Arches East: McDonalds in East Asia* edited by James Watson (1997) that describes the impact of McDonalds on local cultures in East Asia. For example, during the mid-1990s, high school students in Hong Kong began to use McDonalds' restaurants as after-school social clubs. Watson observes how these youths, who would pack themselves into booths, consume burgers and fries while gossiping about school life, were unconsciously internalizing American culture and mannerisms. Thus, in making connections to society in the classroom, teachers can facilitate critical studies about how local experiences are affected by neoliberal capitalist practices and how these may infringe on the rights and dignity of citizens and foreigners dwelling in local spaces as well as how local traditions are informed by other cultures and how they in turn contribute to cultures in the making.

Connections to the world – strategies that centre on global issues

Cosmopolitan pedagogies facilitate not only the interrogation of national cultures but also world cultures particularly tied to narratives of imperialism and ideologies of global capitalism. To facilitate such critical analysis of the world, a basic approach would involve rethinking the design of the curriculum. Typically, the Literature curriculum is designed around texts that students are to demonstrate aesthetic appreciation of. An alternative approach is to anchor the curriculum around ethical questions especially related to transnational and global themes pertinent to our world.

One example is Helen's grade 10 Language Arts unit on Charles Dickens's *A Tale of Two Cities* which she teaches in a public school in New York State. She explains that the focus had previously been entirely text-based and designed to address specific Common Core State Standards. Some of the key aims included having students analyze how complex characters develop over the course of a text and how an author's choices concerning how to structure a text, order events within it, and manipulate time create such effects as mystery, tension, or surprise. Helen has since decided to redesign her curriculum to align it more closely with her school's efforts to globalize the curriculum. She explains that her school's reform efforts have liberated her from sticking to traditional ways of teaching that emphasized aesthetic appreciation so that she is now able to connect her unit plan to more contemporary global concerns as well as encourage deeper levels of empathy and social activism among her students. The major shift is that her unit is no longer centred solely on a close reading of the aesthetic features of the text but is instead built around questions related to practical ethics, in this case, issues of poverty and social equality. The key questions driving her unit are:

- Can one person make a difference in society? Think about: What qualities enable a person to make a difference? What forces work against this person? What drives individuals to struggle to overcome powerful social institutions or conditions?
- How do issues of poverty that people struggle with today compare to what the French and English experienced in the eighteenth century? How has our attitude towards poverty changed or remained the same since then? What remedies, if any, are offered today?
- How do authors use elements of style and characterization to create social commentary?

In weekly class blogs, students continue to write critical commentaries on specific chapters focusing on the aesthetics of the text – its plot, character, style, themes, and authorial choices. However, class activities and discussions are more explicitly directed towards the politics of a particular time and their ethical implications. For example, in the first lesson, Helen directs students to think about the first sentence of the novel – "It was the best of times; it was the worst of times." She asks students to split a page in half with the title "best of times" on one side and "worst of times" on the other. She instructs:

> I would like you to think about things that are going on in the world, in your community, in the school, that fall into both categories. Where do you see in our country or in the world issues of disparity in the sense that Dickens uses this language in his own text – situations where, for some people, it's the best of times, but for other people in the same scenario, it's the worst of times?

Her students raise a wide range of issues highlighting social inequality. In the following week's lessons, Helen has the students focus more specifically on education and read a news article describing the dismal state of some public schools in New Jersey. For some students, the comparison between those schools and their own well-resourced school brings to light unjust state policies and also makes them more aware of their own privilege. Such discussions add to a theme running through all of Helen's lessons: the role of social commentary. She points out that, like the social reformer Frederick Douglass, Charles Dickens also wrote about conditions "where justice is denied, where poverty is enforced, where ignorance prevails, and where anyone class is made to feel that society is an organized conspiracy to oppress, rob and degrade them." She tells her students that when they analyze Dickens's story, they need to consider his role as a social commentator as well as a fiction writer.

For their culminating project, Helen tells her students, "We have been discussing Dickens's role as a social critic and, in particular, his concerns and advocacy for the poor and disenfranchised in the nineteenth century. How do his concerns about poverty and/or income inequality resonate in America today?" In preparation for this project, students read a range of contemporary social critiques published in The Economist, Reuters, and Newsweek that deal with poverty in America. In one lesson, students compare these articles and rank them according to how persuasive and credible they are. In the process, they identify who they think are some of the better social commentators in America today and compare them with Charles Dickens in how they approach and treat the topic of poverty. One student selects a particular piece because the author's prose style "sound[ed] like what Dickens would sound like in this era." Another student argues that a different text is better because of the ways it follows Dickens's shifting descriptions of discontent to depictions of uprising, thereby arousing readers' sense of activism.

By building her curriculum around ethical questions and issues, Helen gives students the opportunity to connect fiction with the real world, literary with non-literary texts. At the same time, she does not undervalue the importance of aesthetic appreciation, as is evident in the ways students, in their blogs, continue to perform traditional close analysis of the text. However, what becomes clear is that aesthetics must serve ethical ends, as exemplified in the genre of social commentary. Even as students deconstruct the style and structure of both literary novel and opinion pieces, they are consciously evaluating the extent to which these are effective in conveying the author's social justice agenda. Helen's example illustrates how aesthetic analysis need not be compromised for the sake of ethical discourse. By focusing on the aesthetics of social commentary, Helen pushes students to see how the formal features of text connect to its ethical concerns.

Likewise, Brenda's grade 8 curriculum that has been implemented in a mainstream government school in Singapore includes a ten-week unit centred on the topic of modern-day slavery. To introduce this topic, Brenda divides students into groups and gives them a variety of travel brochures to destinations such as Cambodia, Thailand, and Sri Lanka. She asks them to imagine a scenario in which they are given $2,000 to travel to a destination of their choice and then to pick a destination and list reasons why they want to travel there. Later, students enthusiastically discuss where they hope to go and their reasons range from shopping to tasting different cuisines to exploring other cultures. Brenda asks, "Why do people travel? And who are the different travellers? Some of the standard ones are tourists or businessmen, but I want you to think a little further." Students name travel bloggers who write for a living, musicians who perform, missionaries or university students on exchange programmes. After about three minutes, Brenda interjects, "There is one group that you seem to have left out." She proceeds to inform them about a group of people who do not travel by choice and then screens a documentary about individuals from Cambodia, Laos, and Thailand who are all victims of human trafficking.

Later, students indicate in their reflections that they had not known this was taking place in neighbouring countries. When one student expresses regret "because we did not look [at] this matter carefully," Brenda tells the class that she likes how this student has used the pronoun "we" because it suggests that "we are all, in a way, responsible for what is happening to those people." The idea of being responsible for the oppression of others is raised in Brenda's subsequent lessons such as when students analyze the poem "My Mother, Who Came from China, Where She Never Saw Snow" by Laureen Mar which describes the everyday life of a sweatshop labourer. Students analyze the poem's word choice, hyperbole, and rhetorical questions, among other techniques, and discuss how these are used to evoke sympathy in the reader. Brenda then tasks students to apply these techniques to designing an anti-slavery poster. The culminating assignment in this unit requires students to identify a group affected by slavery and write a speech defending its rights. Students' projects bring to light a variety of human rights injustices ranging from underpaid domestic workers in Singapore to bonded labourers in West Bengal, India, and sex trafficking in Myanmar, as well as exploitation of prison labour by multinational corporations.

The examples of Helen and Brenda highlight that one key principle informing a cosmopolitan pedagogy is to develop units of study around practical ethics tied to real-world global issues. One useful starting point is the United Nations 2030 sustainable development goals that seek to address global challenges such as poverty, inequality, climate change, environmental degradation, peace, and justice (United Nations, 2015). One or more of these 17 goals could serve as the anchor theme for the unit plan (consisting of a series of lessons tied a topic). The goal would be to facilitate cosmopolitan consciousness, specifically related to the ways current issues affect others, particularly the persecuted and marginalized around the world. In addition to a central literary text for study, students could be encouraged to read other literary and non-literary texts to complicate their investigations into questions around global injustices.

Connections to philosophy – strategies to explore justice

Thus far, I have been describing the various ways cosmopolitan pedagogies can foster connections to other texts, society, and the world. Going further, teachers can also encourage connections to ethical philosophy. The entrenched practices of close reading have meant that insufficient time has been allocated to students to explore ethical issues including current global challenges. Thus, it is necessary to guard against instances when ethical engagement becomes a mere after-thought to rigorous aesthetic criticism. While the latter encourages students to adopt a passive, distanced attitude in their critique of texts, the former pushes towards an other-oriented active engagement. Such active engagements have been observed in the work of two teachers who made an intentional effort to foreground justice and human rights in teaching literature.

Emily's grade 7 Language Arts class in a specialized independent school in Singapore involves a unit anchored on explorations of justice. The theme is "Myths and Legends" and students study four translated short stories and plays that deal with Ancient Greek, Malay, and Native American cultures. The aim of the unit is to have students appreciate diverse cultures. As Emily explains, "I see literature as a tool or a way of seeing . . . to me, texts are worlds, world views, an insight to a different way of life, different belief systems, different cultural values." Emily uses the literary text as a launchpad for ethical explorations into foreign cultures and the ways justice is enacted in such cultures. For example, a series of lessons on one story, "How Coyote stole fire," begins with Emily showing images of Native Americans and asking students to think about how their way of living might be different such as how story-telling often occurs communally. These excursions into Native American culture help students understand why the just distribution of resources, a key theme in the short story, occurs communally as the hero Coyote obtains the help of other animals to steal fire from the fire-beings in order to save man from dying through the cold winters. In the process, students consider the concept of fairness and how basic resources should be distributed so that all groups can thrive in society.

To contrast the restoration of justice at the end of the story, Emily brings up historic instances such as the Indian Removal Act in 1830 and the Trail of Tears involving the forced removal of Native Americans from their land following their colonization. Texts are used to attune students to concepts of justice significant to Native American Culture and how these are infringed in history. Later, Emily asks students to compare and contrast the story with the Greek mythology of Prometheus who steals fire from Zeus to help mankind. This is meant to reinforce the distinctiveness of Native American culture. As students progress through the unit, they deepen their understanding of the different forms of justice and how justice is enacted differently in specific contexts.

Aside from justice, another ethical philosophy of global significance is human rights. Over the course of 17 weeks, Anne introduces a unit on human rights to her grade 9 Literature class in an independent school in Perth, Australia. She has students read a range of texts, including an anthology of short stories on human rights and *The Arrival* by Shaun Tan which is a graphic novel about the experience of migration. The class also watches a documentary about Ellis Island and students conduct research on the history of human rights. Anne explains the reason she develops this curriculum:

> They're fourteen-year-old students, so, obviously, everything about them is very self-centred. I want them to know how privileged they are, that they live in a very lucky country, and that human rights is something that they may take for granted. But even on their own doorstep we've got people who don't have their human rights.

Later in the unit, once students have gained a better understanding of human rights, Anne directs their attention to investigating human rights in their own country by having students discuss such questions as: What is the Australian Human Rights

Commission? Why are some people's human rights not protected? How can we better protect human rights in our legal system? To develop their understanding further, Anne asks students to choose a human rights issue they feel is pertinent to Australia. Rather than have students research this issue in a disconnected manner, she introduces guiding questions that pushes them to be critically reflexive about its significance to them and their community:

- Why are human rights important to me? Do I think protecting human rights will make Australia a better place?
- What is my experience of human rights in Australia? Do I know of any human rights problems in Australia?
- Do I live in a community where there are human rights problems – for example, limited access to education or health care? What would make a difference to my community?
- What would be the difference in my life (or others' lives) if human rights were better protected?

She further encourages students' personal engagement with human rights by having students express their thoughts in diary entries in which they have to imagine themselves as a member of a group they have identified as disadvantaged, and then she asks them to prepare a submission to the National Human Rights Consultation Committee in defence of that group. In a culminating project, Anne seeks to strengthen students' sense of responsibility by engaging them in role-play, staging a mock forum and having the students act as representatives arguing the need to protect the rights of the oppressed groups they have studied. Students also have to reflect on the significance of human rights to them personally and how the denial of rights to marginalized groups in their country reflects a denial of human rather than national rights.

Two principles contributing to the application of cosmopolitan pedagogies that we can glean from Emily and Anne are to first foreground ethical philosophy not in an abstract manner but in a practical manner through concepts such as justice and human rights. These can serve as stepping-stones to fostering a sense of cosmopolitan obligation towards affected communities. This sense of cosmopolitan obligation is demonstrated by a commitment to values that reference the global rather than the national and is expressed in the ways individuals organize themselves to take collective action for global ends (Albrow, 1996). Outside of schools, such organic globalization-from-below arises from grassroots movements such as those by feminist, environmentalist, and human rights groups that resist neoliberal, market-driven globalization-from-above (Falk, 1993). Inside schools, collective action may be inhibited by a lack of resources or by state mandates. Yet, schools play a crucial role in developing students' cosmopolitan consciousness and sense of human agency. Cosmopolitan pedagogies can facilitate connections to practical ethics and, in doing so, encourage a form of "new, dirty cosmopolitanism" (Robbins, 2012, p. 44) that connects literary reading to real-world issues of global violence and injustice. Additionally, as observed in Anne's class, classroom spaces can be designed to provide dialogic sites of inquiry through such activities as simulated forums that mirror democratic practices of debate needed for the mobilization of a critically informed public sphere.

Connections to philosophy – strategies to explore ethics and religion

Cosmopolitan pedagogies can serve to facilitate connections to ethical philosophy such as justice and human rights. At the same time, such philosophical excursions can also extend beyond the level of material culture to the extraterritorial or cosmological. The latter encompasses deep-seated belief systems that address questions inherent in all cultures such as why do we exist, how did we come to exist, and for what or for whom do we exist. Sarah and Lin's approaches to teaching highlight attempts to introduce such explorations in the Literature class.

Sarah's grade 12 Advanced Topics course in a public school in New York State revolves around the study of "great world literature." Prior to this unit on Shakespeare's *Hamlet*, students had studied Leo Tolstoy's *The Death of Ivan Ilyich* and Franz Kafka's "The Metamorphosis." In designing the curriculum, her aim is to help her students "recognize that great literature changes the world and . . . literature is about human-to-human interaction." In a class discussion on *Hamlet*, Sarah encourages students to examine Hamlet's state of mind at particular points in the play and to connect this with more deep-seated religious beliefs. For example, as students discuss the logic of Hamlet's famous "To be or not to be" soliloquy, she asks, "Religion was of issue to him in the first soliloquy, but we don't see it here do we?" This generates considerable debate as one student remarks, "Not directly, but if it wasn't for his [religious] beliefs, he would have killed himself already" which is then rebutted by another student, "I don't think he would have committed suicide. Religion has been replaced by something else. The image of the Holy Ghost has been replaced by the image of his father. This has replaced a completely new set of values." Another student intervenes and argues that "the whole fear of death and suicide is driven by purgatory, hell, so a lot of this is – he's afraid of going to hell. That fear comes from religion." As the discussion goes on, students begin to connect Hamlet's psychological motivations with his own religious beliefs and later consider how this may be contextualized within a broader Elizabethan belief system.

Similarly, Lin seeks to push students to engage with values at a cosmological level in her grade 10 Literature class in an independent school in Singapore. Lin describes her curriculum as the study of "global literature" since students engage with, among others, Asian American, American, British, and Singapore literature. The curriculum is interdisciplinary in nature and integrates literature with philosophy and cultural studies. In one lesson, students participate in a Socratic discussion of Mary Shelley's *Frankenstein* and the topic of moral responsibility emerges. One student comments that this is linked to Frankenstein's parental obligation because the "act of creating a monster makes him a father, so he is morally responsible" to which another student adds that because "Frankenstein does not recognize the monster's request for a mate, [it] represents a rejection of his responsibility." Another student elaborates on this point by suggesting that moral responsibility is "like a social contract" or shared accountability which prompts Lin to ask, "How is this linked to the idea of original sin?" and the discussion continues as follows:

Student A: Original sin parallels the pursuit of forbidden knowledge like Adam and Eve eating the forbidden fruit and just like he [Frankenstein] pursued forbidden knowledge.

Student B: The original sin is actually him not taking care of the monster; it was not wrong that he went after his passion.

Student C: For me original sin is the action of creating the monster not pursuing knowledge. The pursuit of knowledge brought him to a stage where he had to make a choice to commit that sin. It was his own hope to create the monster.

As students consider different perspectives about the nature of original sin, in this case whether it is related to the pursuit of forbidden knowledge, the abdication of responsibility towards the other, or the innate desire to be like God, the discussion turns to the question of evil and whether the concept of original sin is birthed from a notion of original good. What is evident in this discussion is that students are not engaging with areas typically associated with literary analysis – plot, character, setting, style, and the intentions of the implied author. Here, literature provides the entry point to discussing philosophical concepts related to sin (religion), moral rights and obligation (normative ethics), God and man (metaphysics), and the limits of science and knowledge (epistemology).

In summary, one key principle teachers can consider applying based on the examples of Sarah and Lin is to facilitate closer connections between literature and ethical/religious thought. This echoes Levinas' arguments concerning ethics as first philosophy and ethics as first theology which suggests a tripartite relationship among ethics, philosophy, and religion. Levinas (1987) emphasizes the need to perceive otherness or alterity in both the historical, material world as well as the extraterritorial cosmos. These two notions beckon us to reimagine Literature education as a space that can accommodate explorations of different conceptions of alterity through integrating philosophical and religious reflections. On the one hand, the literary text can serve as an entry point to considerations of oppression, marginalization, and victimization of the other in the world; on the other hand, the literary text can lead to an exploration of how the other's behaviour is historically determined by his or her philosophical or religious perspectives about divinity.

Curriculum that pushes students to grapple with what it means to be a citizen of the cosmos will be increasingly significant given the rise of fundamentalism and terrorism since the late twentieth century coupled with mounting prejudice in the West towards particular religions such as Islam. Since the advent of modernity, religion has been relegated to the private sphere and, aside from religious schools, discussions falling in this domain have been forbidden in public schools. However, the solution is not keeping such questions out of the classroom but to think of ways to promote democratic, inclusive, and non-threatening explorations of philosophical/religious beliefs systems. Ultimately, such explorations must be grounded on the prioritization of ethics involving a commitment to responsibly engaging the other. While conversion is subject-oriented and seeks to transform the other to the self, responsible engagement is other-oriented and seeks to turn the self towards understanding the other. Cosmopolitan Literature pedagogies can promote powerful spaces in the classroom where hospitality is practised both in action and in the imagination if teachers work to establish an other-oriented culture that encourages in students a commitment towards understanding others, particularly those who are in the minority and those who hold different beliefs from themselves.

Note

1 Grade 8 in schools in America is typically equivalent to secondary two or the second year of secondary school in Singapore. Students generally enter secondary one at 13 years of age.

6

VALUES

Developing ethical character through dispositional routines

Two people enter a laboratory to take part in a study on memory and learning. One is designated a "teacher" and the other a "learner." The learner is brought to a room, asked to sit in a chair with his hands strapped and an electrode attached to his wrist. He is told to learn a list of paired words and if he makes an error, he will receive electric shocks. Meanwhile, the teacher is taken to the experimental room and is tasked to administer both the test and the electric shock. If the learner responds correctly, the teacher will move on to the next item. If the learner answers incorrectly, he will use the shock generator to administer an electric shock. For the first mistake, the learner will receive 15 volts but this will occur with 15 volt increments for each subsequent mistake until the maximum voltage of 450 volts is reached.

Unknown to the teacher who is a genuine subject who has volunteered to participate in the experiment, the learner is an actor who receives no shock at all but who performs varying levels of discomfort each time a shock is administered. Throughout the process, the teacher is told to continue using prompts such as "It is absolutely essential that you continue" or "You have no other choice, you must continue." The experiment only stops if the teacher refuses to go any further or when the maximum of 450 volts is reached.

Described above is one of the most famous and controversial psychological experiments conducted by Stanley Milgram at Yale University between 1961 and 1963. Known as the Milgram experiment, the purpose was to examine an individual's propensity to obey authority and more specifically, "how far the participant will comply with the experimenter's instructions before refusing to carry out the actions required of him" (Milgram, 1974, p. 3). The experiment eventually came to involve more than a thousand participants and was repeated at several universities. More than 50 years later, it continues to be studied and adapted.

Of significance is the finding that 65% of the participants obeyed the orders of the experimenter to the end and delivered the maximum 450 volt shock. This high degree of obedience to authority has been attributed by Milgram to the capacity of individuals to accept the legitimacy of the authority figure, to accept the authority figure's definition of reality, and to the individual's transference of responsibility to the authority figure (Blass, 2009).

Milgram, who was born into a working class Jewish family, had been drawn to understanding the psychology of obedience during the Holocaust (Russell, 2011). Many Nazi criminals tried at Nuremberg sought to evade responsibility by arguing that they were merely following orders. As Milgram (1974) observes, millions of innocent people were systematically slaughtered on a massive scale but this could only occur if large numbers of people followed orders. While the Holocaust is an extreme example, "in lesser degree this type of thing is constantly recurring: ordinary citizens are ordered to destroy other people, and they do so because they consider it their duty to obey orders" (p. 1). Milgram was inspired by Arendt's report of the trial of Adolf Eichmann who was in charge of organizing the mass deportation of Jews to Auschwitz and other extermination camps. Arendt (2006) shared her concept of the "banality of evil" and attributed Eichmann's actions to his "inability to think, namely, to think from the standpoint of somebody else" (p. 49). Essentially, Milgram provided empirical evidence supporting Arendt's claim that ordinary, law abiding citizens have the propensity to carry out acts of violence (Jetten & Mols, 2014).

The Milgram experiments have received a fair number of criticisms particularly its use of deception which has resulted in more stringent ethical protocols in research (Benjamin & Simpson, 2009; De Vos, 2009). Scholars have also criticized the lack of a comprehensive theoretical explanation for why people obey authority, the fact that the findings do not account for a multitude of contextual factors that contribute to blind obedience, and that Milgram's deep fascination with the Holocaust led him to conduct numerous pilot studies to adjust the final experiment procedure to achieve his goals (Benjamin & Simpson, 2009; Burger, 2014; Russell, 2011).

Despite these criticisms, the Milgram experiments continue to be significant in drawing attention to the conditions that promote banal obedience to authority. More recently, Jerry Burger (2009) has sought to partially replicate the Milgram experiments while conforming to stricter ethical guidelines. His experiment, conducted 45 years after Milgram's experiments, has shown that the percentage of obedient participants has not differed significantly from the results of Milgram's experiments even though procedural changes Burger implemented should have made it easier for participants to resist authority (e.g. they were repeatedly told they could leave the study at any time).

In summary, two important factors can be drawn from these obedience to authority studies. The first important factor has to do with perceptions of social identity. Studies show that obedience is closely connected to instances when participants see themselves as sharing a common social identity with the experimenter. This is disrupted when the experimenter becomes too imposing or when participants identify with dissenting voices resulting in disobedience (Reicher & Haslam, 2011). A second important factor relates to Milgram's escalation thesis which has been corroborated by other studies showing that people are more accepting of unethical behaviour when this occurs slowly over time (Burger, 2014; Gino & Bazerman, 2009; Miller, 2014).

What these studies on the dangers of obedience suggest is that situations and authority figures play a crucial role in socializing individuals to follow to the extent that moral values can be undermined in the compulsion to obey. Education is one prime site that conditions students to obey. From a young age, children are socialized into acts of obedience through school rules and routines. Most of these are mundane, ranging from queuing up to get on the school bus, learning to raise hands before speaking in class, learning to write along straight lines in an exercise book and so on. They are also conditioned to respect authority figures such as their teachers, discipline masters, etc. At the same time, if children are also not socialized to think for themselves and to think ethically about others, they may unconsciously learn to conform and obey authority even when authority figures impose unjust rules or actions that affect others negatively.

If explicit and implicit conditioning of students to obey authority is part of the everyday culture of schooling, it is important that educators equally emphasize the importance of ethical resistance. By this, I do not mean we should teach students to rebel against authority because this simplistically assumes all authority is harmful. A complete lack of authority may lead to the decline of systems and structures that support learning and at worst, degenerate into anarchy which reproduces other forms of violence. I use "ethical resistance" to refer to a way of thinking in which individuals learn to reflect on who and why they obey and learn to question the morality governing the actions of others. Milgram (1974) defines obedience as "the dispositional cement that binds men to systems of authority" (p. 1). Similarly, I define ethical resistance as a dispositional attribute that orients individuals to apply cosmopolitan ethical thinking through social routines. Such dispositions are first and foremost ethical because they are concerned not about the self but the self in relation to others. Second, such dispositions toward others are cosmopolitan in nature, not limited to an authority figure, family, community, or nation but extends to include diverse others in the world. Finally, a disposition of ethical resistance is inculcated through what I will describe later as dispositional routines. These are social routines aimed at cementing ethical ways of thinking, feeling, and seeing in the world.

It is my belief that too much attention in education has been paid to knowledge and skills and less so to values and dispositions. This is partly due to the world-wide push among policymakers to develop future-ready citizens with requisite twenty-first century competencies (21CC). Many 21CC models have also been popularized by major transnational organizations such as United Nations Educational, Scientific and Cultural Organization (UNESCO) and World Economic Forum as well as non-profit organizations such as Partnership for Twenty-first Century Learning and Assessment and Teaching of Twenty-first Century Skills. These models posit an idealized vision of the future-ready citizen equipped with requisite skills to compete in the global economy. Such models are grounded on economic rationality where the primary aim of schools is to develop citizens as human capital who can thrive in globalized workplaces and ultimately contribute to the progress of their nation. Twenty-first century competencies are thus akin to commodities to be invested in and measured for economic returns rather than for human development that then promotes a managerial school culture characterized by competition, standardization, and accountability. This utilitarian approach to education also perpetuates the image of the citizen as what Michel Foucault (2008) terms, *homo economicus*, one who is an "entrepreneur of himself, being for himself his own capital, being for himself his own producer, being for himself the source of [his] earnings" (p. 226). The idealized citizen, depicted as an individualistic and autonomous capitalist, rather than part of a collective society, seeks to maximize "utilities" via accumulating future-oriented skills.

While much attention has been paid to *episteme* (knowledge) and *techne* (craft or practice), less emphasis has given to *phronesis* (commonly translated as practical wisdom as determined by character dispositions). In this chapter, I focus specifically on cosmopolitan ethical dispositions drawing on Confucian concepts of humaneness and ritual. I then discuss the kinds of dispositional routines in Literature teaching that can cultivate ethical resistance utilizing examples of classroom practices.

Cosmopolitan ethical dispositions in Confucian thought

Dispositions are long-term or habitual character qualities and these are formed through a variety of social situations – family, school, community, mass media, etc. I have briefly discussed cosmopolitanism as an ethical orientation from the perspective of Western philosophers (chapter 3). The wealth of scholarship on cosmopolitanism as an idealized vision of an ethically grounded education has predominantly stemmed from the West rooted in classical Greek, Hellenistic, and Enlightenment philosophers such as Aristotle, the Stoics, and Kant as well as more contemporary postmodern philosophers such as Derrida and Levinas. Less documented has been the scholarship on cosmopolitanism emerging from philosophers in the East.

In this regard, Chen Yudan (2016) has documented how scholars in China began theorizing Chinese cosmopolitanism from the mid-1990s via the doctrine of "tianxia" or all under heaven. At the turn of the century, several scholars have sought to historicize this doctrine such as Zhao Tingyang (2009), who examined how its enactment 3000 years ago under the Zhou dynasty perpetuated the principle of harmony premised on the inclusion of all peoples and lands leading to peace for many centuries in China. In 2012, a seminal conference at the University of California Santa Cruz brought together scholars mainly from the fields of History and Religion leading to an important edited volume titled, *Cosmopolitanism in China 1600–1950*. In framing the book, the editors, Hu Minghui and Johan Elverskog (2016), explain its underlying premise that cosmopolitanism was operative during the Qing dynasty through the early Republican period and played a crucial role in guiding state relations with minority communities as well as the country's relations with the outside world. Many of the scholars in the volume ground their understanding of Chinese cosmopolitanism on the philosophical ideas of Confucianism. Further, two important works by American scholars, Robert Neville (2012) and Philip Ivanhoe (2014), sought to conceptualize Confucian cosmopolitanism by distinguishing this from Western conceptions of cosmopolitanism. Returning to the question of how we can cultivate cosmopolitan ethical dispositions, I suggest that Confucius offers important insights found in the interconnected concepts of cosmopolitan love (*ren*) and ritual (*li*).

*Cosmopolitan love (*Ren*)*

Confucius has been described as the first person in Chinese history to devote his entire life to teaching, particularly the training of character and to making education available to the common people (Chai & Chai, 1973). No other subject, not even filial piety, preoccupied Confucius and his disciples as much as the concept of 仁 [*ren*]. To understand this concept, we need to first comprehend the Confucian worldview.

Confucianism subscribes to an "anthropocosmic worldview" in which heaven, earth, and human beings are interconnected (Tucker, 1998). While Confucianism has typically been regarded as an ethics rather than a religion in the form of membership to a belief system articulated via institutionalized rituals, dogmas, and theological precepts, it is evident that spirituality is prominent in Confucianism (Chai & Chai, 1973). Its concerns with spirituality is reflected in the view that the self is embedded in a larger cosmological system. Heaven is a creative, sustaining force of the universe that is immanent in nature and human beings. The pervasive nature of heaven implies that the transcendental is immanent within the human being who seeks harmony with heaven and participates in heaven's "organic naturalism" or the ongoing creative process of transformation (Cheng, 1991). This does not lead to the transcending of the self or the projecting of the self onto an absolute transcendental entity but the self's immanent recovery of his or her authentic nature that encompasses an ontological unity with *dao* or the way of heaven (Cheng, 1991).

The Confucian cosmopolitan, more clearly conceptualized as a participant of the cosmos, is paradoxically embodied in concrete rather than abstract realities. This perspective is at odds with Enlightenment cosmopolitanism advocating an abstract universalism. Such a view, popularized in the eighteenth century, notably by Kant, proposed that national differences be minimized in favour of one uniform enlightened culture. In more recent times, this universalistic conception of enlightenment cosmopolitanism has been revived by scholars such as Nussbaum (1997) who advocates being "philosophical exiles from our own ways of life" and giving "that community of humanity our first allegiance" (pp. 58–59). Nussbaum's essential premise is that our primary obligation is not to the family, nation, or state but the moral community of human beings. She argues that our task is to treat all human beings in the same way we treat our fellow city-dwellers or neighbours. Ivanhoe (2014) has provided a comprehensive critique of Nussbaum's universalistic approach to cosmopolitanism. Namely, such a position renders one's obligation to the "world" as an abstract community and hence, it is impractical given that individuals have specific duties to nations they live in such as the paying of taxes.

It is here that Confucian cosmopolitanism offers a more practical alternative, one that recognizes the importance of retaining rootedness to one's family and community while striving to extend this to others in the world. Confucian cosmopolitanism subscribes to the view that even as heaven imbibes all things, the *junzi* or morally exemplary man is the one who seeks to fully realize the way of heaven in his or her life. Confucius is less concerned about spiritual beings or life after death than the moral perfectibility of the individual on earth. The nobility of a person is determined neither by blood nor by an external entity; rather, it occurs through the cultivating of character as the individual demonstrates the disposition of *ren* which has been translated as humaneness, goodness, and benevolence towards his or her family, community, and the world at large. Cultivating *ren* begins with one's family. Confucianism recognizes that we naturally have a greater fidelity to our family and community than to distant others and does not discount the value of such attachments because without first learning how to be filial to one's family, one would not be able to accord this same respect and love to distant others (Ivanhoe, 2014). This is because the family is the first community one is born into and provides the training grounds for developing *ren*. Demonstrated through affectionate sympathy and love for others, *ren* occurs in the most basic way when a child puts the interest of the family before his or her own. However, filial piety reaches its highest virtue when it is then extended to all people (Nguyen, 2016).

Thus, a more appropriate term for *ren* is cosmopolitan love. A key attribute of *ren* is the flourishing of both self and others. As Confucius (500 BCE/2014) says, "a humane person wishes to steady himself, and so he helps others to steady themselves. Because he wishes to reach his goal, he helps others to reach theirs" (6.30, p. 69). In another passage in the *Analects*, the other-oriented nature of *ren* is also evident:

> Fan Ch'h asked about humaneness. The Master said, "Love others." He asked about wisdom. The Master said, "Know others."
>
> *(12.22, p. 193)*

From a Confucian perspective, one's relationship with others should be governed by empathetic reciprocity as highlighted in the negative golden rule, "do not impose on others what you yourself do not want [others to impose on you]" (15.24, p. 259). The relationship between self and other that Confucius envisions is a cosmopolitan love that recognizes rootedness in everyday relations (even ties to family) but which seeks to be expansive, extending beyond the family to others in the world. Such a love transcends the material to the cosmological to denote spiritual communion among the human fraternity.

Ritual (Li)

Essentially, Confucian cosmopolitanism subscribes to an embodied cosmopolitanism in which the individual is one fully rooted in his or her specific location and attuned to the fluctuations and rhythms of the natural world. Such an embodied cosmopolitanism recognizes the importance of fidelity to one's family, community, and the world. But how does one come to inhabit and practice the disposition of *ren*? Because *ren* challenges one to overcome self-centredness, 礼 [*li*] or ritual action is an important catalyst that pushes one to relate to others through rituals of interaction. *Li* performs an important role in training one to behave appropriately and respectfully towards others.

A common stereotype of Confucianism is its perpetuation of conformity through adherence to rigid rules of propriety. However, the purpose of *li* is not the performance of ritual action but the facilitation of moral development. Ritual actions originally involved rites and ceremonies tied to religious observances but its focus shifted from man's relationship to the supernatural to man's relationship with other members in the community and world. At the same time, these ritual actions retain their sacred importance by providing an apparatus for spiritual development through social relations (Hall & Ames, 1987). For Confucius, moral development is determined by everyday actions, consistently performed through rituals. Yet, these ritual actions are not simply rules to be followed. As Ivanhoe (1991) observes, Confucius "did not just want people to act in a certain way, he wanted them to act out of certain dispositions" (p. 57).

In this sense, *li* is inherently aimed at the cultivation of dispositions, primarily, the disposition of *ren* or cosmopolitan love. Individuals demonstrate *ren* through everyday customs, rituals, and practices. Li Chenyang (2007) uses the analogy of a cultural grammar where *li* is akin to basic rules and norms embedded in everyday behaviour and mastery of this facilitates the development of *ren* which is the highest virtue demonstrated by a morally exemplary person or *junzi*. Just as grammar comprises rules inherited from tradition, learning and practising *li* also ensures the continuation of a culture's traditions. At the same time, grammar also changes with time incorporating shifting ways of meaning-making; similarly, *li* is also amenable to adjustments based on changing contexts.

Today, one of the most popular routines discussed in education is the visible thinking routines conceptualized by Project Zero at Harvard University. Drawing on Confucian cosmopolitanism, I propose that routines are primarily aimed not at the development of rational thought but at the cultivation of ethical dispositions. This can occur both progressively and expansively in stages. In terms of progression, Karyn Lai (2006) has proposed a three-stage developmental process. In the first stage, the learner is introduced to various routines directed at appropriate forms of behaviour. Familiarity and continual practice are forms of moral training. In the second stage, the learner reflects on principles from these routines and also explores possible applications and limitations through a process of active inquiry. In the third stage, the learner engages with the principles and ideals in meaningful social relations and *li* no longer functions as constraints on behaviour but becomes an avenue for aesthetic expression of a morally cultivated self.

To disrupt egoism, another useful typology proposed by David Hall and Roger Ames (1987) suggests that the process of becoming an exemplary person entails the gradual dissolution of the distinction between self and other. This occurs first between the self and family followed by the community and then wider world. The purpose of dispositional routines is thus to facilitate person-making, community-making, and world-making processes of moral cultivation.

Perceiving dispositional routines in terms of progressive and expansive stages also addresses the debate among Confucian scholars about whether Confucian ethics subscribes to role ethics in which morality occurs through assigned roles and by implication, the performance of ritual actions through these roles (Rosemont & Ames, 2016) or whether it subscribes to virtue ethics in which morality is tied to an agent's character and dispositions (Angle & Slote, 2013; Sim, 2015; Van Norden, 2007). The progressive and expansive nature of dispositional routines perhaps reconciles both given that moral development occurs through roles and cultural practices that one is born into and yet, these should culminate in the disposition of *ren* or cosmopolitan love that one performs in a multiplicity of relationships at home and in the world.

In summary, one may describe Confucian cosmopolitanism as the pursuit of realizing the way of heaven (*dao*) in one's life by demonstrating cosmopolitan love (*ren*) to others. This becomes habitual as one continually learns to relate to others through dispositional routines (*li*). This is a lifelong educative goal that pushes one to overcome egoism, nepotism, parochialism, ethnocentrism, and chauvinistic nationalism in order to embrace inclusivity through a widening circle of relationships (Tu, 1994).

The values of cosmopolitan love

The disposition of *ren* or cosmopolitan love encompasses both critical and ethical values. Criticality is important because without it, love is blind and driven by impulse and emotion. Further, if cosmopolitan love entails ethical resistance demonstrated in challenging all forms of tyranny such as the imposition of the ego or forms of parochialism and totalitarianism, criticism of existing structures and norms that support injustice is fundamental. Criticality and resistance are targeted not at all forms of authority but primarily at authority that devalues the dignity and worth of another person. This could occur via causal or systemic forms of discrimination and injustice.

At the same time, resistance towards tyranny is not an end in itself. Rather, it is a means to ethics as an end or, more specifically, it is ultimately directed towards ethical commitment, accountability, and responsibility for another person.

If cosmopolitan love were purely based on critical resistance of unjust systems, it would be reduced to logical, pragmatic, and technical strategies of relating to another. While determined by reason, such forms of resistance would lack the kind of passion and conviction and even further, the willingness to engage with another more deeply.

In summary, the disposition of cosmopolitan love entails both critical and ethical values. This is similar to the two kinds of virtues that Aristotle (350 B.C.E./1985) outlines in *Nicomachean Ethics* – moral and intellectual. As mentioned previously, virtues are habitual dispositions that demonstrate human excellence. In the pursuit of a cosmopolitan end in education, human excellence is not centred on the flourishing of the self but the flourishing of self and others. Hence, the cultivation of critical and ethical values is integrally connected with the cultivation of others. Self-other cultivation occurs not privately but via a community of fellow travellers pursuing *dao* or the way of heaven while mutually encouraging one another (Tu, 1994). *Eudaimonia* is then part of a larger project of human flourishing that the individual participates in by learning with and from others.

What specifically are the critical and ethical values that can facilitate the disposition of cosmopolitan love? Though this is by no means exhaustive, I highlight six important values below:

Critical Values

1 Questioning – to value the opportunity to question ideas, traditions, and values.
2 Discernment – to value critical analysis and evaluation of ideas.
3 Deliberation – to value dialogue, debate, and discussion with others.

Ethical Values

4 Empathy – to value a deep and engaged understanding of others by putting oneself in the shoes of others.
5 Hospitality – to value different values and practices of others through openness to others and willingness to suspend judgement.
6 Responsibility – to value another to the extent of feeling a sense of responsibility and accountability for him/her.

Dispositional routines in the teaching of literature

What are some examples of dispositional routines that Literature teachers can encourage to foster critical and ethical values? To be clear, routines are actions practised very often so that it becomes habitual. Routines are part and parcel of acculturating children to adopting the values of a community. Some examples are washing hands before eating or queuing up to buy something. The best routines are simple and easy to replicate. The concept of dispositional routines I am discussing are not aimed at moulding blind obedience to authority figures or structures such as rules. Conversely, we need to continually keep the end in mind. That is, these dispositional routines are ultimately aimed at *ren* or cosmopolitan love for another. In what follows, I highlight some examples of dispositional routines that can cultivate critical and ethical values of cosmopolitan love.

Routines that cultivate critical values

At first glance, the notion of "ethical resistance" may seem at odds with Confucianism which some associate with enforcing obedience to rules and authority. This could be partly due to the perception that education systems in Confucian Heritage Culture countries (China, Japan, South Korea, Taiwan, Hong Kong, Singapore, etc.) place much emphasis on rote-learning, test-taking, and teacher-centric instruction. Various scholars have discussed how these students avoid expressing personal opinions or questioning forms of authority such as the textbook or the teacher (Durkin, 2008; O'Sullivan & Guo, 2011). At the same time, other scholars have drawn attention to how critical thinking is, in actual fact, much emphasized in Confucian philosophy (see Tan, 2015, 2017; Wu, 2018).

In Confucian thought, critical thinking is evident in the way Confucius (500 BCE/2014) constantly encourages his disciples to examine arguments and present counter arguments (*Analects*, 2.9, p. 16) and pushes them to seek out weaknesses even in his own teaching and not engage in baseless opinions (9.4, p. 131). Confucius appears to be against dogmatism and he disdains inflexibility (*Analects*, 14.32, p. 238). He encourages his disciples to ask questions, even about rituals (*Analects*, 3.15, p. 34). More significantly, in Confucian thought, the ultimate goal of such critical thinking is the pursuit of moral rightness. Confucius stresses the principle of remonstrance or duty of someone junior to correct his superior when the latter compromises on moral issues (Andrew & LaFluer, 2014).

Given Literature education's close connections to the variety of critical movements, particularly New Criticism, Reader Response Criticism, and Poststructuralist Criticism, it is not surprising that engaging in critical analysis and reasoning is routine in Literature classrooms. Often, however, the primary focus is on the activity of criticism itself rather than the dispositions that the teacher hopes the student would cultivate. Worldwide, there has been a concerted push to infuse higher-order critical competencies, inquiry-based learning, and the use of thinking routines. Absent from such conceptions is the Confucian connection between critical thinking and ethical dispositions. This means that common routines in the Literature class like analyzing plot, character, setting, and style or critical evaluations of ideology in texts are insufficient. Routines that foster critical dispositions should be directed at developing ethical attunement about the moral rightness of everyday actions of oneself, others, and those in power.

Inductive learning routines

One basic routine that fosters critical dispositions involves inductive learning. Inductive learning focuses on having students observe phenomena as they experience it and then learning to theorize from this. Inductive learning taps on skills of observation as well as synthesis as students must learn to draw on various kinds of evidence in order to derive common patterns and theorize from there. Inductive learning draws from Dewey's (1915, 1938) ideas about developing the active learner through relating his or her experiences with the world and tapping on students' past knowledge to make sense of present experiences.

An inductive learning routine I employ in my preservice Literature methods course at my university allows students to take ownership of the learning process. For example, prior to a session on prosody and how to talk about rhythm and sound in poetry, I have students explore different ways to perform a poem using various musical instruments given to them. Half a group may perform a reading of the poem and the other half will try to add sound and rhythm using shakers, drums, triangles, etc. They figure out different ways to harmonize and vary the beat to bring across the idea of the poem. At the end of the exercise, they try to respond to an essential question displayed on the whiteboard – what contributes to rhythm? Typically, students will highlight various techniques they have applied such as pace, tone, pauses, patterns of stresses, rhyme, choice of words, etc. I then have them apply these techniques to interpreting the effect of rhythm in a given poem. This inductive exercise occurs before we run through the mechanics of metre and sound techniques.

In another example, after I distribute a literary text in the classroom, I give students the opportunity to make any observations they have on the text. I remind them that they are free to comment and to base this on their intuition and observation. For example, their comments can be about what stands out to them, what puzzles them, what the text reminds them of, what doesn't make sense, etc. In this way, I try to create a non-threatening environment where students feel at ease to make initial observations about the text. Although the logical next-step would be for the teacher to then address these questions, my aim is to create an "interpretive community" (Fish, 1980) in which engagement occurs through social situations involving negotiation, discussion, and debate. As the teacher, I then take a step back and allow students to respond to other students' comments and questions. Here, students work in small groups with each student sharing comments or questions they had about the text to which the whole group then collaborates to address. At the end, a presenter from each group then shares the questions and responses. We then identify common ideas across all groups and discuss their implications that inform our understanding of the text.

Inductive learning routines can simply involve the teacher taking a step back and devoting the first segment of the lesson to having students make observations about the text and then trying to interpret the text within a collaborative community. It can also involve more elaborate approaches in which the teacher designs specific situations or tasks e.g. having students watch and read a range of early modern comic texts and then theorizing features of comedy as a genre before embarking on an analysis of a Shakespearean comedy. When inductive learning is routinely employed, students acquire the habit of independent thinking and learn to sharpen their powers of observation which are important precursors to critical analysis.

Questioning routines

Questions are the primary mechanisms through which we understand our world. At its most basic, questions are statements expressed to elicit further information in contrast to propositions or declarative statements. What drives deep critical inquiry are the questions we ask. As Richard Paul and Linda Elder (1996) state, "the key to powerful thinking is powerful questioning. When we ask the right questions, we succeed as a thinker, for questions are the force that powers our thinking" (para. 1).

In education, questioning is one of the most basic and often used techniques that teachers use to provoke thinking. It has been effectively used to motivate students through tapping on their curiosity and challenging them intellectually. The majority of questions Literature teachers ask are likely to be aesthetic in nature. That is, these deal with understanding the craft of the text including its content, form, plot, character, and style. Popular question taxonomies may also be applied to guide analysis. One of the most well-used models for generating critical questions is commonly known as Bloom's Taxonomy (Bloom, Engelhart, Furst, Hill, & Krathwohl, 1956). Lorin Anderson, David Krathwohl, and their team (2001) have revised the model and made several modifications including the inclusion of the "creating" domain. Nonetheless, many educators have applied the original Bloom's taxonomy to generating useful question stems such as in Table 6.1.

One of the key criticisms of Bloom's Taxonomy is that it is too static and hierarchical with a prior category serving as a prerequisite to a latter category. In the revised model, there is a recognition that categories overlap and the original cognitive processes have been renamed as remember, understand, apply, analyze, evaluate, and create (Anderson et al., 2001). Instead of labelling cognitive thought as lower or higher order, these processes are mapped against a knowledge dimension comprising four dimensions – factual, conceptual, procedural, and metacognitive (Krathwohl, 2002). However, this assumes that critical thinking is tied to knowledge. Conversely, we can also map each domain of critical thinking to an ethical dimension using these same terms (see Table 6.2):

- The factual dimension involves questions that deal with ethical values and norms observed in the text.
- The conceptual dimension involves questions that relate to ethical concepts and its underlying philosophy such as the concepts of good and evil, justice, human flourishing etc.
- The procedural dimension involves questions that relate to processes that address injustice and other ethical concerns in society and the world.
- Finally, the metacognitive dimension involves questions that help students become aware of their own thought processes including the logical reasoning they have applied and the values that have influenced their approach to ethics.

TABLE 6.1 Question stems based on Bloom's taxonomy

Description of Cognitive domain (from Bloom et al., 1956)	*Question Stem (adapted from Kugelman, n.d.)*
1. **Knowledge** – this refers to remembering, recognition or recall of facts, trends, classifications, conventions, methods, criteria, theory, etc.	What is . . . ? When did . . . ? Why did . . . ? What do you remember about . . . ? Who was. . . .? How did . . . happen? Can you list . . . ? What is the method . . . ? What is expected of . . . ? What do you know of the theory behind . . . ?
2. **Comprehension** – this refers to understanding, interpretation and extrapolation or making estimates or predictions.	How would you classify the type of . . . ? How would you interpret . . . ? How would you compare/contrast . . . ? How will you state/ rephrase/summarize in your own words . . . ? What is the main idea of . . . ? What evidence support . . . ? Can you explain what is happening . . . ? What do you think will happen . . . ?
3. **Application** – this refers to application of knowledge, facts, principles, procedures, and generalizations to problems or situations.	How would you use/apply . . . ? How would you solve . . . using what you have learned? What approach/method would you use to solve . . . problem? How would you organize . . . to show . . . ? What would result if. . . ? Can you make use of . . . to show. . . ? What would you use or change to arrive at . . . solution?
4. **Analysis** – this and what follows are regarded as more advanced than the previous three skills. It involves analysis of elements, relationships among elements and the organizational principles, techniques, or concepts used to convey meaning.	How is . . . related to . . . ? What is the author's purpose? What ideas are used to justify . . . ? How is . . . distinguished from . . . ? What techniques are used to convey . . . ? How is the text organized and what effect does this have? Whose point of view is conveyed and what is the underlying intention? What assumptions are made . . . ? What assumptions are necessary in order for . . . to occur?
5. **Synthesis** – this refers to the combining elements or parts to form a whole leading to insights about patterns not observed previously or a novel product or solution.	What changes would you make to solve . . . ? How would you improve . . . ? Can you propose an alternative to . . . ? How do would you connect . . . elements to design . . . ? What different functions do . . . contribute to . . . outcome? What new patterns emerge through different ways of connecting . . . ?
6. **Evaluation** – this refers to making judgements or appraisals through the use of criteria, standards or values.	How credible or reliable is the evidence used to support . . . ? Do you agree with the accuracy of the evidence presented? How credible or reliable is information presented? Do you agree with the outcome or conclusions? How would you prove/ disprove of . . . ? Assess the value or importance of . . . ?

TABLE 6.2 Mapping critical thinking against ethical dimensions

Ethical Dimension	*Remember*	*Understand*	*Apply*	*Analyze*	*Evaluate*	*Create*
Factual	Questions that require students to recall what they learnt about the moral norms or values of a community as depicted in the text.	Questions that require students to show understanding of the moral norms or values of a community as depicted in the text.	Questions that require students to apply their understanding of norms or values to the text or from the text to another event.	Questions that require students to analyze a community's underlying beliefs and values as well as the structures that support these.	Questions that require students to evaluate the values of a community and their effect on others as well as to critique the yardstick used to evaluate other cultures.	Questions that require students to create, demonstrate and perform their understanding of ethical values and issues in the text and beyond.
Conceptual	Questions that require students to recall what they learnt about ethical concepts or theories.	Questions that require students to show understanding of ethical concepts or theories.	Questions that require students to apply a concept or theory to deepening their understanding of other communities.	Questions that require students to analyze ethical issues or concepts and their underlying philosophical justifications.	Questions that require students to evaluate ethical issues or concepts, including their underlying assumptions or bias, and their effects on others.	Questions that require students to create, demonstrate, and perform their understanding and analysis of ethical concepts and theories in the text and beyond.

(*Continued*)

TABLE 6.2 (*Continued*)

Ethical Dimension	*Remember*	*Understand*	*Apply*	*Analyze*	*Evaluate*	*Create*
Procedural	Questions that require students to recall what they learnt about the processes of addressing forms of injustice and other ethical concerns.	Questions that require students to show understanding of what they learnt about the processes of addressing forms of injustice and other ethical concerns in various settings.	Questions that require students to apply a particular method or process of addressing forms of injustice and other ethical concerns in specific settings.	Questions that require students to analyze the processes of addressing injustice and other ethical concerns, including policies and actions by government and nongovernmental actors and their underlying justifications.	Questions that require students to evaluate the processes of addressing injustice and other ethical concerns and the effects of policies and actions by government and nongovernmental actors on others.	Questions that require students to create, demonstrate, and perform their understanding and analysis of ethical processes from the text and beyond.
Metacognitive	Questions that tap on awareness of the source and influence of prior knowledge and experience with forms of injustice and other ethical concerns.	Questions that require students to recognize their own thought processes and how they have arrived at an understanding of justice and other ethical concerns.	Questions that require students to apply metacognitive strategies to help make visible the logical structure of their thinking about justice and other ethical concerns.	Questions that require students to analyze their own reasoning, logic, and the underlying values that informs their approach to justice and other ethical concerns.	Questions that require students to evaluate their own reasoning, logic, and the underlying values that informs their approach to justice and other ethical concerns.	Questions that require students to create, demonstrate, and perform an examination of their own reasoning and the values informing their approach to justice and other ethical concerns.

Table 6.2 provides an overview of how critical thinking capacities can connect to these four ethical dimensions. Teachers can use the table to generate a range of different critical questions that can tap on different ethical dimensions. For example, a question such as "In Achebe's *Things Fall Apart*, what was the penalty for Okonkwo's accidental killing of a child?" could classify as a remember-factual question whereas the question "Was sending Okonkwo and his family to exile for seven years a sufficient punishment to fit the crime?" would be an analyze-procedural question. A question such as "Is the death penalty an effective deterrence to drug-related offences?" is an evaluation-conceptual question whereas the question "How did you arrive at determining the appropriate measure to address injustice in this situation" is an analyze-metacognitive question. Of course, such critical questions need not be restricted to the ethical dimension alone but can be connected to knowledge and aesthetic dimensions as well.

The usefulness of such a table is that teachers can become more cognizant about the different types of questions they can ask in relation to differing ethical dimensions. When such questioning routines are consistently encouraged, the classroom transforms into an interpretive community where students are enculturated into habits of questioning, debating, discussing, and dialoguing. They learn to question their society and the world along with their taken-for-granted norms, values, and traditions. In the process, they acquire discernment and as critical-ethical questions become common practice, they become more sensitized to ethical concepts, ways of seeing the world, and different approaches to addressing forms of injustice.

Routines that cultivate ethical values

Ethical values of empathy, responsibility, and hospitality involve routines that deal with perception and socialization. In relation to perceptual routines, these work at expanding ways of seeing, feeling, and thinking about others. Our natural instinctive impulse is to think of and for ourselves and our loved ones and protect their interests. A cosmopolitan perspective seeks to disrupt forms of egoism and parochialism and this is reinforced through routines.

In coining the term "lateral thinking," Edward de Bono (1970) argues that the ability to perceive something from a new or different perspective is an important aspect of creativity. However, perceptual thinking takes a broader understanding beyond mere creation to encompass sensory perceiving. Rudolf Arnheim (1969) provides an account of how, from the time of the Greek philosophers to the present, the senses have always been mistrusted and associated with subjectivity and irrationality. He further describes intuitive cognition as an aspect of perceptual thinking that has been neglected. Intuitive cognition occurs when the observer perceives the totality of interacting components through his or her sensory experience. Thus, the capacity of perspectivizing encompasses the ability to consider an issue from multiple perspectives to the extent of moving beyond one's familiar social environment to consider the reality of distant lives.

Wide reading routines

Routines that seek to foster perceptual dispositions are aimed at resisting parochial perspectives while developing cosmopolitan awareness of other worldviews. Such routines push students to be curious about other cultures and encourage them to expand their understanding of wider sociopolitical and historical contexts.

One example I observed was the use of an independent wide reading routine used by Tom who was a Literature and Language Arts teacher at an international high school in Singapore. At the time of my interview in 2017, Tom taught grades 9, 10, and 12 and his class size ranged from 12 to 20 students from a variety of countries. In every single class, Tom insists that 15 minutes of class time is given to silent reading. Students are free to select any book they want, fiction or non-fiction, from any genre of theme. His aim is to create a culture of independent reading and his motto is to develop "confident, capable, enthusiastic lifelong readers, writers, and thinkers."

Despite the opportunity to free-read, various structures have been put in place to support this culture of reading. First, the classroom is designed so that students are seated in either a horse-shoe structure (for classes of about 20 students) or around a seminar table (for classes of about 12 students). This structure facilitates peer sharing of books, which often follows their silent reading.

Second, along the walls of the classroom are shelves of books. These include both classical and contemporary texts and, more importantly, texts from around the world. Visually, this enhances students' curiosity about other cultures each time they come to class and sit in an environment surrounded by these books. At the same time, Tom reiterates that students should have the freedom to choose the books they want to read because he wants them to enjoy reading.

Third, students are encouraged to set reading goals about the number of books they aim to read each term. Previously, he encouraged students to read about 25 books a year independently but now he encourages students to set their own goals even though this should be more than a book a month. As Tom explains, whether they can reach the goal is irrelevant; the point is to challenge students to read widely as a lifelong habit.

Finally, during the 15 minutes of silent reading, Tom holds individual conferencing with two or three students each time. He has a literary conversation with the students about their book, asking them why the book interests them, what they like about it and he also discusses their reading plans and progress. The purpose is to ensure students are accountable for their reading. Aside from such teacher-student conferences, Tom also encourages a culture of reading by getting students to share about their books as well as through organizing book festivals.

In this example, the repeated routine of independent wide reading is clearly linked to several key dispositions that Tom aims to foster. He wants his students to "have the ability to leave class and say, I have the identity as a reader." Part of having an identity as a reader is the confidence to think independently. Another key disposition is openness to other worldviews. As Tom says, "I want them interacting with a variety of texts from a variety of authors or a variety of places in the world, . . . that allows them to see or get a sense of or empathize with or understand other people's places and cultures, both English speaking and non-English speaking." Although Tom acknowledges that reading widely will not necessarily correlate with students becoming more empathetic, he believes that it encourages openness to other people and will help "students into conversations about the ways in which the different people from different places do different things."

This independent wide reading routine is dependent on the commitment of teachers and schools to dedicate curriculum time to free reading. Oftentimes this is also dependent on a teacher's own vision as observed in Tom's passion to make reading a habitual part of his students' identity. Tom states, "my job as a Literature teacher, is to make sure that this [independent wide reading] is a lifelong pursuit." When made regular and sustained, it can contribute to the development of perceptual dispositions that orient students to become more appreciative of difference. In perceiving other viewpoints, particularly when these involve distant social realities, one necessarily taps into more originary or instinctive empathetic sensibilities.

Listening routines

While perceptual routines are aimed at expanding and deepening our understanding with others, social routines are also important in strengthening connections. Social routines facilitate cosmopolitan dispositions such empathy, hospitality, and responsibility to others.

I observed an example of a social routine in a grade 10 Literature class in a mainstream all-girls government school in Singapore. The teacher, Raya, values the responses of her students. When asked about the most important objectives of teaching literature, she indicates that developing students' personal responses to texts and helping them make connections to their own experiences are the most important. To model this, she routinely tells stories about her life and her family in connection to the issues in the literary text. She then ensures that curriculum time is also given for students to respond to texts and make connections to their own experiences.

The most interesting routine observed was how she seeks to cultivate a culture of respect and openness to other students' responses. This is done by ensuring that students practise the habit of genuinely listening to the responses and opinions of their peers aside from the teacher's. In one lesson, for example, she has students analyze Instagram poems. She had compiled a number of such poems, which are typically short (usually a stanza of less than ten lines that may involve arrangement and accompanying images). In groups of five, each student picks a poem of their liking. They are then asked to talk about the poem for one minute including what they think it means, what they like about it and how it connects to their lives. The rest of the students are asked to listen carefully without writing anything. Raya tells the students,

> in understanding and appreciating literature, you must always give respect to the opinions of others . . . So for the next one minute, the person who is standing, you are going to stay and talk about this poem. The rest of the people, don't write anything. You put your pen down, really listen to what this person is saying, appreciate her opinion, understand what she's trying to say.

After the student has finished, the rest of the students are given 30 seconds to reflect on what she has shared, record what they have learnt, and note down questions they may have.

In the next segment of the lesson, response shifts from impressionistic personal response to close analysis. Raya selects three poems on themes of urban redevelopment that students read previously. She has the poems enlarged and pasted on the walls around the classroom. Students are each given a marker pen and can go to any poem of their choosing. They are given ten minutes to annotate the poem. Raya uses a popular critical thinking framework known as Paul's Wheel of Reasoning encompassing eight dimensions of reasoning – purpose, question, assumptions, point of view, evidence, concepts, interpretation, and implications (Paul & Elder, 1997). Students apply this framework to analyzing the poems paying attention to details like word choice, form, and other stylistic devices. They write their comments around the poem. At the end of ten minutes, students are asked to go to a different poem pasted on the wall. This time, instead of freely annotating on the poem as they did previously, they are tasked to build on comments given by their peers. They can extend the ideas by adding another insight or other evidence. Raya also tells them to give a "star" or "smiley face" next to their peer's comments if they like it.

In these two examples, the activities of getting students to listen carefully to their peers and then noting down or building on their comments, builds a routine that instils respect for the opinions of others. Raya's lessons are also often designed around the questions generated by students. For example, she explains that in teaching a novel, one common strategy she uses is that as she comes across a key segment in the novel, she will get students to generate questions about it. She then compiles these questions into a handout and students will work to address them collaboratively. In this way, students' questions are validated and addressed. This is done before she engages in a discussion with the class so as to take away dependence on the teacher for answers.

The routine of listening to others is an important platform for developing cosmopolitan empathy because it disrupts the tendency to become absorbed in one's own ideas. Raya says, "Because when you listen to somebody else, it also deepens your own thoughts. It's also about listening to your friends. I think I also want them to be able to see quality in somebody else's response because a lot of times students only want to hear what the teacher has to say." She explains that there is a natural tendency for students to only take notes when the teacher is speaking and not when their peers are giving an opinion. She has tried to change this by giving time for students to share and listen to one another as well as by encouraging students to pay attention to what their friends are saying. She does this by affirming students such as when she tells them, "Do you know how important what she just said was? It's so intelligent even I can't say that. I'm going to let her repeat that. I hope you wrote it down because it's really smart."

Bridge-building routines

Ethical values that facilitate hospitality and responsibility to others also involve routines that enhance self and social awareness. In several passages of the *Analects*, Confucius (500 BCE/2014) discusses the importance of mastering oneself by showing restraint, practising self-reflection, and taking steps to know others deeply (*Analects*, 1.10, 1.16, 12.1, 12.22). Unlike the concept of autonomous personhood observed in Western philosophical traditions (see for example Descartes' mind–body dualism), Confucianism subscribes to a relational concept of personal identity in which consciousness is innately other-directed and the self is formed through its interdependent relationship with others. Even the act of self-reflection is not merely confined to self-evaluation but to evaluating how one has served others as exemplified by Zengzi, the youngest of Confucius' disciples who says, "Every day I examine myself on three points. When I worked to benefit someone else, did I do my best? In my relationship with my friends, did I fail to be trustworthy? Did I pass on any knowledge I myself had not put into practice?" (*Analects*, 1.4, p. 3).

One important consideration is how schools can facilitate relational learning and ways to foster deeper commitments to one another. In schools, especially in Asian countries like Singapore, the development of deep friendships is typically not the primary goal of education. More often than not, the concept of friendship is excluded in mission statements or school goals. The phrase "going to school to get an education" implies that education is about attaining knowledge or skills for future use such as a lucrative career. As a result, the classroom is perceived as a space where parents send their children to learn from teacher experts. Those who interfere with such learning are sent out of the classroom to be disciplined or, at worst, expelled. Imagine, however, if the development of friendship were an important goal of education. This would mean that school leaders and teachers should consider how best to develop strong bonds among students and how to create communities of justice locally and globally.

One strategy can entail providing what I term bridge-building opportunities where students collaborate with others on matters of ethical significance. This can involve the use of "artefactual literacy" in which lessons incorporate artefacts that students bring to class and opportunities are given for them to share personal stories connected to these (Dejaynes, 2018, p. 48). When the opportunity to share about oneself to others is regularly incorporated into the curriculum, this can serve to invite other students to witness and understand, in a more authentic way, the experiences of others and, in the process, facilitate relational learning and empathetic listening in the classroom.

Another example was a unit on "Exploring race and identity through poetry" that we co-designed with Literature teachers. Kamini, one of the teachers in a mainstream school in Singapore, had only five students in her grade 10 Literature class. Previously, she had discussions with her class on issues of racism but this was always at a distance. For example, students explored American race relations through literature or the experiences of migrant workers in Singapore. She explains, "We focus so much always on what's happening outside that we don't realize what's happening at home. This [unit] gave them a chance to explore that in detail and realize that actually, there are so many things going on [in society]."

The ten-week unit comprises four key topics. The first series of lessons centres on "who is the other?" and students explore groups that are marginalized through examining literary and non-literary texts articulating the experiences of various minority groups in Singapore. The second series of lessons centres on "How are they othered and why?" and focuses on ways in which various ethnic groups have been stereotyped and discriminated against and the effects of this. The third series of lessons centres on "What are the perspectives of the other?" and students attempt to understand and listen to the perspective of various minority groups in Singapore through reading their poems and exploring their various positive and negative lived experiences in Singapore. Finally, the fourth series of lessons centres on "Negotiating home and belonging" and students have the opportunity to connect issues of race previously discussed with broader understandings of identity and belonging. Students read and compare various translations of poems about Singapore as home from the voices of minority writers and also write their own poem exploring what belonging to Singapore means.

The unit also makes conversations about race and identity part of the routine of Literature lessons. Previously, more focus was given to analyzing the novel and the play in preparation for the high-stakes national examinations. The inclusion of weekly discussions about social justice issues through literary texts has contributed to enhancing Literature's relevance in students' lives. As Kamini says, "In the past, poetry is just done in one lesson and then we go back to set texts; because they had to face [social justice issues] every day, it became a routine and they definitely opened up a bit in terms of talking." The selection of poems is particularly important as they serve as catalysts to building bridges and deepening empathy. Each week, a poem is given that serves as a launchpad for authentic conversations about race and identity. Some examples are "What's It like Being Malay" by Riqi Hanzrudyn or "Letter to Anonymous Policy Maker (RE: 'Others Is Not A Race')" by Melissa de Silva. At the end, students are given the opportunity to write their own poem in English or their own mother tongue language to express their experience of belonging in Singapore, as seen through race/ethnicity or any other aspect of their cultural identity. Through the poems, students explore issues such as how race is only one facet of identity, the effects of patriarchy, navigating cross-cultural, multilingual influences, encounters with racism, and bullying, etc. As students reflect on the unit, they share about how their understanding of their classmates has deepened after hearing and reading about their experiences.

One of the minority students has shared that the conversations "opened my eyes in terms of racism [as] I have been a victim of those jokes [and] I just laughed it off because I didn't want to offend the other party." The conversations allow her to express her discomfort and validate her voice. This allows other students to become more aware of the effects of their words as one student shares,

> I can't deny that I don't make certain off-handed comments or jokes; again, they're very light-hearted and I generally don't mean any harm but it's never really struck me that while someone else is laughing, they might actually be deeply hurt. . . . It's really struck me that maybe even if this person is laughing, they're maybe not laughing with you but they are laughing at themselves.

Bridge-building acquires a more cosmopolitan orientation when students are given the opportunity to collaborate with others on issues of social and global justice. The vision of the moral psychologist-philosopher, Lawrence Kohlberg, is particularly apt. Well known for theorizing the stages of moral development. Kohlberg was critical of the "bag of virtues" approach to moral education in which educators transmit an agreed upon list of socially acceptable Boy Scout-like traits such as loyalty, kindness, bravery, obedience etc. Not only are such virtues arbitrary and relative to prevailing cultural standards, they tend to be communicated in top-down ways which he likens to indoctrination. Kohlberg's (1981) central argument is that "virtue is not many, but one, and its name is justice" (p. 39). As children mature in moral reasoning, they progress from acting based on avoidance of punishment (stage 1) or on instrumentally satisfying their own needs (stages 2) to acting based on interpersonal expectations within social groups and the family (stage 3) or respecting the maintenance of social order in the nation (stage 4). At the highest levels, moral reasoning expands beyond self-interest, community or familial affiliation, and deference to social authority. Rather, actions are based on moral principles such as social contract in which rights and standards have been critically examined and agreed upon in society (stage 5) as well as universal principles of justice and human rights (stage 6). Building on Dewey's ideas of progressive education and the principles of justice espoused by philosophers such as Kant and Rawls, Kohlberg argues that the fundamental aim of education is the moral development of the child and the task of educators is to push students towards higher stages in which they increasingly have to adopt a more cosmopolitan, non-parochial perspective in moral reasoning eventually considering questions about fairness and rights of minorities and other individuals whose values and circumstances may be different from their own.

One way in which educators can push students towards developing deeper cosmopolitan engagements with others is through providing bridge-building opportunities for students to collaborate with other students from different cultures. Glynda Hull and Amy Stornaiuolo (2010) describe the creation of an international social network that allows students from Africa, India, Norway, and the United States to exchange and create digital artefacts. From stories to music, stop-motion videos, animations, and artwork, students engage in critical dialogue about common concerns such as discrimination, school pressures, poverty, and the challenges of media representation. Likewise, Lalitha Vasudevan (2014) describes a theatre-initiative programme for court-involved youths. Through improvisations that reflect daily realities of their lives, youths are pushed to critically engage with their own and one another's stories and then to collectively explore alternative possibilities. The multiple stories elicited from these exercises sensitizes youths to the multiplicity of perspectives.

While it may be impractical for these projects to be conducted every semester, these projects can still be a regular, yearly feature of a school's programme. For example, as one of the co-founders of the Global Learning Alliance (GLA), which was formed in 2012 at Teachers College, Columbia University in New York, my colleagues and I began working with teachers to design intercultural projects. In the last three years, schools in Finland, Singapore, and the United States have included an intercultural project each year in their school programme allowing students to collaborate on various global issues. In the first iteration of the project in 2017, the focus was on the theme of wellness and human well-being.

In the first stages of the project, students share their own community's experiences with wellness using various artefacts (such as advertisements, posters, videos) as well as interviews with their peers. Students from other schools learn about how issues of stress and mental health are similar as well as different across countries. Next, students are put in mixed groups comprising at least one other student from another school. Using an online platform, asynchronous and synchronous meetings are organized allowing students to first define a problem related to human well-being or wellness that they have observed based on what was shared previously. Students have to generate a range of questions and then as a group, decide on a key question to solve or investigate. They then conduct further research and discuss possible ways to address the issue. At the GLA conference held in Helsinki, Finland, in 2018, student representatives presented their group's recommendations before delegates comprising about 65 scholars and educators from over 14 universities and schools in Australia, China, Denmark, Finland, Hong Kong, Singapore, and the United States including the students' own superintendents, principals and teachers. The presentation was especially powerful given the fact that students highlighted to school leaders issues of stress and mental health caused by school culture and policies through research they had conducted with their own peers. This lent authenticity to their research and also empowered them to be agents of change.

Indeed, such intercultural projects where bridge-building projects are directed at transformative change aligns with Kohlberg's (1985) vision of the just community in schools where students are empowered to engage actively in dialogues with peers in their school and beyond on fair solutions to moral issues and injustices they face.

Through this, students would also seek to build just communities in their own school by deliberating with peers and faculty about the kinds of moral norms that would characterize school culture, systems, and policies. The kind of cosmopolitan education Kohlberg envisions entail a respect for students as autonomous agents; a view of the classroom as a space where participatory democracy can be modelled through discussion, reasoning, and argumentation; and where discourse would transcend the learning of instrumental skills to encompassing explorations of how principles of justice can be applied to resolving various ethical dilemmas in society and the world.

To conclude, I have suggested routines that can facilitate critical and ethical values – inductive learning, questioning, wide reading, listening routines, and bridge-building routines. There are indeed many more routines that Literature teachers already employ. The point is not to make Literature education a mechanized experience for students. Rather, there should be a balance between innovative pedagogical strategies and everyday routines. In Chapter 5, I have described some of the innovative pedagogical strategies teachers have used to facilitate ethical interruptions and connections. In this chapter, I focus on the everyday routines that teachers can use to reinforce cosmopolitan character dispositions. Drawing on the integral connection between *ren* (cosmopolitan love) and *li* (rituals) in Confucianism, these routines are aimed at developing altruistic concern for others. In the Literature class, engagement with literary texts from different cultures and perspectives alongside open dialogues with diverse others are important in establishing a greater sense of the self's connection to the world. This is an essential step to developing greater investedness in the flourishing of others in the world.

7

CONCLUSION

Literature education and the hospitable imagination

"I know it is wrong . . . but I will still do it in the future," says one student during a discussion about the offensiveness of racist jokes. Students in this grade ten class are into the sixth week of a Literature unit on "exploring race and identity through poetry." Their teacher, Kamini (described in the previous chapter), has just gotten them to analyze comments made on #NotOKSG, an Instagram account consisting of posts by locals that highlight casual racism in Singapore. Students are then asked to contribute their own perspectives following the template: "It's not okay to . . . Instead try . . ." For example, one student writes, "It's not okay to assume all Chinese people have the Wuhan virus. Instead try to be more educated and informed about current news about the virus." Another student writes, "It's not okay to use racist slurs as a joke. Instead, try understanding that it is offensive and only funny to you and a few others." Kamini then asks the students to share their contributions and a lively discussion on the effects of racism follows.

On listening to the students, I am struck by two ideas. The first is the authenticity of the discussion. Despite the fact that these students have been studying the effects of racism via poetry, graphic novels, news articles over the past six weeks, and other students have highlighted the hurt arising from racist jokes, this student's attitude remains unaffected. Having admitted that she will continue making racist remarks about minorities, she explains that "if it's something that is accepted by the victim, then it's not that wrong" and "it's like our sense of humour in this generation."

The second idea that stands out to me is the fact that any claim that Literature education, particularly one that foregrounds Ethical Criticism and engagement, can enable a student to become more empathetic and more grounded on moral principles, remains hypothetical. While it is possible that this is indeed the case for some students, we also need to be cautious about over-romanticizing ethical visions of literature. To this point, those from the tradition of aestheticism might agree such as Posner (1997) who asserts,

> immersion in literature does not make us better citizens or better people. One might be able to pick out some works of literature that would have such an effect because of the information they convey or the emotional state they induce, but they would constitute a skewed sample of literary works.
>
> *(p. 2)*

Just as no vaccine can guarantee full protection including evolving variants of the virus, so too an ethically grounded education cannot assume to guarantee ethical-mindedness in all students. Why then should educators prioritize ethics in the teaching of literature? I end this book with some final reflections on this question.

To the objection that Literature cannot make a person better, proponents of ethics may argue that while this may be true in some instances, such as in the example given earlier in this chapter, other studies have also shown that reading fiction leads to increased levels of empathy for others (Djikic, Oatley, & Moldoveanu, 2013; Kidd & Castano, 2013). However, my response to the question is to consider the nature of the question itself for such a question, along with the response it hopes to elicit, is framed around a utilitarian logic. That is, the value of literature, and correspondingly Literature education, is measured against instrumental outcomes – to develop more morally-grounded individuals. We should instead premise the value of literature on core principles. Whether or not students attain a greater degree of empathy or care for others then becomes less significant. Just as we know that a vaccine cannot save everyone, this should not stop researchers from developing one because the point is not merely about saving the most lives but about the fundamental principle that all human life is sacred so that even if a vaccine saves only one life, developing it is still worthwhile. Similarly, the value of Literature education should not be determined by practical outcomes but by ethical principles.

Whether this principle is based on the ideals of human flourishing, stemming from the Greek notion of *eudaimonia*, or the Confucian notion of cosmopolitan love, there is that common aspiration akin to what Derrida (2000, 2002) describes as "absolute hospitality." Derrida contrasts this term with the concept of conditional hospitality espoused by Kant (1795/1963) who defines hospitality as "the right of a stranger not to be treated as an enemy when he arrives in the land of another" (§358, p. 102). For Kant, the stranger is, at minimum, not to be regarded with hostility even though the extension of hospitality is on condition of his or her capacity to assimilate to the foreign country. Conversely for Derrida, absolute hospitality is hospitality without limits, without succumbing to the language of difference and without the imposition of categories when one addresses the other –

> absolute hospitality requires that I open up my home and that I give not only to the foreigner (provided with a family name, with the social status of

> being a foreigner etc.), but to the absolute, unknown, anonymous other and that I give place to them, that I let them come, that I let them arrive, and take place in the place I offer them without asking of them either reciprocity (entering into a pact) or even their names.
>
> *(Derrida, 2000, p. 25)*

While absolute hospitality is an impossibility, it is nonetheless an imaginative aspiration that literature offers. One scene that comes to mind is from Emily St. John Mandel's (2014) novel, *Station Eleven*. In this story, a global pandemic has wiped out 99% of the world's population. Cities have been abandoned and basic supplies like water and electricity cut-off. The remaining survivors live alone or in settlements and home has become provisional. Kirsten, one of the main characters, journeys with the travelling symphony towards Seven City Airport in hopes of finding some of her lost companions. They pass through abandoned towns and the groups they meet along the way are mostly tribalist in their thinking, preferring to stick together for safety reasons. The group finally reaches the airport where those who have taken shelter there open its doors to welcome them. But the airport is not emblemic of absolute hospitality. It is the actors of the travelling symphony who journey from place to place staging their plays and playing their music to whoever would welcome them that point to hospitality as an active practice concerned with disrupting barriers between self and others. In this landscape of devastation and emptiness, the symphony's art brings people together, connects them via emotion and memory of the past. Mandel's book is a fitting reminder that in our pandemic age, literature and the arts are as important as medicine and technology. While we rely on the latter to save lives or enhance communication, the former is what makes existence meaningful "because survival is insufficient" (p. 58) as the tagline of the travelling symphony's lead caravan reminds us. The very act of picking a book or watching a performance evokes that innate recognition that one exists not for oneself alone but for the sake of another. Literature orients our imagination to think hospitably by reminding us that other worlds and perspectives exist, by attuning us to see that beauty lies in the complexities of flawed human nature, and by pushing us to care about others, fictional and real.

While the literary text provides that invitational call for us to hospitably expand our imagination to other worlds, it is Literature education that offers the tools to enable students to engage critically and ethically with others. The aspiration for absolute hospitality requires that we take the claims and experiences of others seriously, which means attending to the real-world concerns referenced in the fictional text. It also means not blindly accepting what we are told nor interpreting others through our own frameworks and norms. Throughout the *Analects*, Confucius (500 BCE/2014) reiterates the significance of literature, especially poetry and this is summed up in the following:

> The Master said, "My young friends, why is it that none of you learn the Odes? The Odes can give the spirit an exhortation [*xing*], the mind keener eyes [*guan*]. They can make us better adjusted in a group [*qun*] and more

articulate when voicing a complaint [*yuan*]. They teach you [the humane and the right way] to serve those who are as close to you as your parents and as distant from you as your ruler.

(17.9, p. 286)

Confucius highlights four important functions of literature that correspond well to the teaching of literature.[1] The first function, 興 [*xing*], relates to the idea of awakening the soul so that one begins to take an interest in the world and in the lives of others. For this reason, I began, in the second chapter of this book, by situating the philosophical end of Literature education on ethical attunement. I highlighted the need to recentre Literature education away from its centuries old obsession with aesthetics while recovering its integral concern about ethical relations with others. Ethics as first philosophy in Literature education translates to reframing its objectives and curriculum around cosmopolitan ethical inquiry and engagement.

The second function that Confucius highlights is 観 [*guan*], which relates to the idea of perception. The expansion of the imagination through literary reading is strengthened when our eyes are provided with interpretive lenses to reading language and texts. This would entail introducing aesthetic, political, and Ethical Criticism among other interpretive traditions. The point is to equip students to see that texts are not neutral but constructed artefacts informed by ideologies, values, history, and cultural traditions. Students should then be empowered to employ the repertoire of critical-ethical lenses that would enable them to analyze texts from a multiplicity of perspectives.

The third function is 群 [*qun*], which refers to the idea of socialization. Literary engagement transits from private to public reading in the context of the classroom. When Confucius says that literature "can make us better adjusted in a group," the idea is that not only do we gain access to other experiences and practices of living but we also acquire habits of negotiation and dialogue as we engage in literary discussions. The pedagogies that teachers employ are important in supporting a dialogic interpretive community in the classroom. In this book, I have shown how various teachers have applied pedagogies of interruption as well as pedagogies that allow students to explore global issues, justice, ethics and religion utilizing simulated forums, Socratic questioning, and inquiry-based projects among others. Aside from these innovative pedagogies, everyday pedagogical routines entailing habits of listening to others or strengthening curiosity about other cultures through independent wide reading strategies are important in cultivating cosmopolitan dispositions of openness, empathy, and hospitality toward diverse others in the world.

The final function is 怨 [*yuan*], which has to do with the notion of criticality. Confucius does not elaborate on why literature helps one become more articulate in voicing a complaint and one may wonder how this sentence fits with the following one in which he says that literature teaches one to serve those close and distant including one's ruler. The idea of serving one's ruler may seem antithetical to a critical consciousness, but this should be contextualized as part of Confucius' larger vision of moral governance. In the Confucian worldview, nature and humanity are folded into the divine order, and the ruler is subordinate to *dao* or the way of heaven (Brockover, 2008). As such, the ruler is the one who carries out the mandate of heaven and part of this is to be responsible for and accountable to the welfare of the people. Those under the ruler serve him in order to support this larger goal of human flourishing. Such service necessarily encompasses the need to criticize the ruler when he hampers the well-being of others. Confucius is against blind obedience and advocates the necessity of remonstrance:

> if confronted by reprehensible behaviour on his father's part, a son has no choice but to remonstrate with his father and if confronted by reprehensible behaviour on his ruler's part, a minister has no choice but to remonstrate with his ruler. Hence, remonstrance is the only response to immorality.
>
> *(cited in Rosemont & Ames, 2009, p. 114)*

The role of the scholarly official, *junzi*, was particularly important in advising and rectifying the ruler's behaviour. The purpose was not to attack the ruler or to overthrow the regime but to reiterate moral principles that official policies should be grounded on. Critiquing the ruler often brought the risk of punishment and death, but this was regarded as a moral duty to the ruler and countrymen. Hence, the phrase 諫死 [*jiansi*] or "risking one's life in remonstrance" conveys the importance of maintaining unwavering courage to critique those in power (Andrew & LaFluer, 2014).

In what way can Literature education facilitate criticality? Aside from the obvious point that Literature education is centrally concerned with equipping students with the tools of critical reading via its various traditions such as New Criticism, Reader Response Criticism, Poststructuralist Criticism, Ethical Criticism, etc., Literature education provides the model for a critical public space where citizens can exchange ideas about social and global issues. Habermas (1991) has argued that the formation of a public sphere in Europe occurred around the eighteenth century with the spread of capitalism and the rise of an educated bourgeoisie class who often gathered in salons or coffeehouses to discuss political and economic issues via works of art and literature. In my previous book (Choo, 2013), I discuss the significant role that literary periodicals in England such as the *Tatler* and the *Spectator* played in developing a critical civic space where the public could collectively and actively engage in debate and discussions on sociopolitical issues. In Singapore too, English Literature education began not in the English schools run by British colonialists but with the work of two Singaporeans, Lim Boon Keng and Song Ong Siang, who, on their return to Singapore after completing their studies in England, started the *Straits Chinese Magazine* in the early twentieth century. The first of its kind, this literary periodical included short stories and poetry alongside opinion articles on a range of social and political topics including those that were critical of the colonial government's policies. For example, in one story titled, "The awakening of Oh Seng Hong," a Chinese worker stands up to his British employer by asking for fair wages leading to tragic consequences (Lew, 1898). This is followed by an essay titled, "Chinese problems" that discusses the need for the Chinese to regain a position of power in the face of injustices perpetuated as a result of Western colonization (Tan, 1898). Here, the literary text brings to life the experiences and emotions of individuals struggling in the face of colonial subjugation while the opinion article contextualizes this with an analysis of historical and present conditions of colonialism. Other topics covered in the magazine were more targeted at developing cultural awareness and taste such as articles about adapting Chinese and Western fashion styles, understanding different religions such as Confucianism and Christianity, and appreciating Chinese, Malay, and English poetry. In short, the magazine sought to construct the modern subject as one who is cosmopolitan, enlightened about different cultures and informed about issues in the country and the world. Like literary periodicals that had become fashionable across Europe at the time, these functioned as vehicles through which the public could come together to discuss aspects of politics and culture through literary and non-literary texts. In this way, they offer a glimpse of what Literature education can be – a space where an interpretive community can exercise critical habits of analysis and dialogue alongside ethical engagement about pertinent social issues of the day. The literary text functions as a launchpad as discussions about ethical issues in the fictional world are extended to real world concerns.

The historical role of Literature education in developing a critical citizenry has been somewhat lost today as teachers focus on the skills of aesthetic appreciation to meet the demands of high-stakes examinations where the kind of interpretation that is valued is limited to the stylistic properties of the text and to that which affirms a student's personal response shared on a test paper. In light of growing intolerance we witness around the world today, it is perhaps important to recover Literature education's characteristic role in empowering students to participate in a critical public space. It is crucial to the progress of civic society that when students leave school, they have the skills and dispositions to be active citizens who are invested in the moral progress of communities in their country and beyond.

As I conclude this book at the end of 2020, the World Health Organization (2020) has updated its Coronavirus dashboard reporting that there are more than 55 million cases of the disease with more than a million deaths worldwide. In Europe, a series of terrorist attacks have occurred provoked by anger towards the publishing of political cartoons depicting the Prophet Mohammed which is deemed blasphemous to Muslims. In America, mainstream media have announced results of the presidential elections, but the current President has refused to concede leading to protests particularly by far right and militia groups. In global cities such as Singapore, the pandemic has contributed to a deepening recession that has exacerbated resentment of foreigners among locals who have lost income and jobs. While the future remains bleak, I am reminded of an important quote that may shed light on how humanity can respond in trying times. This is from Confucius (500 BCE/2014) who replies to the following question:

> Zigong asked, "Is there a single word that can serve as the guide to conduct throughout one's life?"

> The Master said, "It is perhaps the word *shu*. Do not impose on others what you yourself do not want [others to impose on you]."
>
> *(15.24, p. 259)*

We may recognize Confucius' words as a version of the golden rule to treat others as we would ourselves. But the principle on which this is based stems from the Chinese character 恕 [*shu*] which is akin to the notion of empathy. The top of the character comprises 女 or Woman and 口 or mouth which conveys the image of a woman listening to the words of another. But these words flow from the 心 or heart as depicted at the bottom part of the character. Essentially, 恕 [*shu*] means listening to the heart of the other (Wu, 2013). This concept fittingly sums up the ethical mission of Literature education.

To teach our children what it means to listen to the heart of another, teachers may begin by simply introducing diverse literature into the classroom. Here, the literary text provides that open invitation to those who would listen to the words of another. Yet, the text alone is insufficient. To truly empathize with another, the pedagogies that teachers employ should push students to take the words of another seriously. This means equipping them to critically deconstruct discursive systems that have led to forms of labelling, marginalization, and injustice done to the other. It also involves pushing students to engage deeply with the other's experiences, history, and values while helping students recognize their own assumptions and the ways they may unconsciously impose their own cultural values in judging others.

As we imagine what it means to live together in a post-pandemic age in which limitations on human contact may be normalized through social distancing laws and the wearing of face masks that inhibits casual speech, educators must make a concerted effort to counterbalance alienation and individualism. The challenge is how we can disrupt parochial mindsets and enable students to forge stronger bonds with diverse others. While physical travel may be compromised, imaginative travel can occur through engagement with narratives. It is here that Literature education offers that platform for ethical encounters with others and pushes the boundaries of hospitality in our attempts to understand and engage with the other. A commitment to Literature education and its ethical call to listen to the heart of another remains vital in our continued quest to secure a harmonious world where all can flourish despite differences.

Note

1 In his notes on this passage, Chin Annping, in his translation of the *Analects* (350 BCE/2014) explains that Confucius states his love for the Odes in several passages of the *Analects* but this passage (17.9, p. 286) sums up his view of its transformative power through the four words – *xing, guan, qun*, and *yuan*.

APPENDIX A

Profile of Teachers

Note: Pseudonyms are used in the place of actual names to respect the confidentiality of the teachers involved in this research.

TABLE A.1 Profile of teachers discussed in the book

Name of teacher (Pseudonym)	*Grade level and Subject*	*Type of School and Country*
Anne	Grade 9, Literature	Independent School, Perth, Australia
Brenda	Grade 8, English Language	Mainstream government school, Singapore
Cheryl	Grade 8, Literature	Mainstream government school, Singapore
Emily	Grade 7, Language Arts	Specialized Independent School, Singapore
Helen	Grade 10, Language Arts	Public school, New York state, United States
Karen	Grade 8, Language Arts	Public school, New York state, United States
Kamini	Grade 10, Literature	Mainstream government school, Singapore
Keith	Grade 11 Literature	Independent School, Singapore
Kim	Grade 8, Literature	Mainstream government school, Singapore
Lin	Grade 10, Literature	Independent School, Singapore
Mary	Grade 9, Social Studies	Public school, New York state, United States
Pamela	Grade 10, Literature	Independent School, Singapore
Raya	Grade 10, Literature	Mainstream government school, Singapore
Shanti	Grade 9, Language Arts	Independent School, Singapore
Sarah	Grade 12, Advanced Topics	Public School, New York state, United States
Tanya	Grade 7, Language Arts	Independent School, Singapore
Tom	Grades 9, 10, 12, Literature and Language Arts	International School, Singapore

BIBLIOGRAPHY

Literary Texts Discussed

Achebe, C. (2001). *Things fall apart*. London: Penguin.

Adichie, C. N. (2010). *The thing around your neck*. New York: Anchor Books.

Andersen, H. C. (2006). Ugly duckling. In *Fairy tales* (T. Nunnally, Trans.). London: Penguin. (Original work published 1843).

Boyne, J. (2006). *The boy in the striped pajamas*. London: Penguin.

Campion, T. (1617). *There is a garden in her face*. Retrieved November 20, 2020 from https://www.poetryfoundation.org/poems/43871/there-is-a-garden-in-her-face

Ishiguro, K. (2000). *When we were orphans*. New York: Vintage.

Le Guin, U. K. (2015). The ones who walk away from Omelas. In *The wind's twelve quarters and the compass rose* (pp. 254–262). London: Orion.

Lee, H. (1960). *To kill a mockingbird*. New York: HarperCollins.

Lee, L.-Y. (2008). Self-help for fellow refugees. In *Behind my eyes* (pp. 16–18). New York: W. W. Norton.

Liu, K. (2012). *The paper menagerie*. Retrieved November 3, 2020, from https://io9.gizmodo.com/read-ken-lius-amazing-story-that-swept-the-hugo-nebula-5958919

Mandel, E. S. J. (2014). *Station eleven*. London: Picador.

Matel, Y. (2011). *The moon above his head*. Retrieved November 3, 2020, from www.salon.com/writer/yann_martel

Palacio, R. J. (2012). *Wonder*. New York: Alfred A. Knopf.

Pound, E. (1913). *In a station of the metro*. Retrieved November 20, 2020 from https://www.poetryfoundation.org/poetrymagazine/poems/12675/in-a-station-of-the-metro

Yang, G. L. (2006). *American Born Chinese*. New York: First Second.

References

Achebe, C. (2016). An image of Africa: Racism in Conrad's *heart of darkness*. *The Massachusetts Review*, *57*(1), 14–27.

Adichie, C. N. (2009). The danger of the single story. *TEDGlobal*. Retrieved November 3, 2020, from www.ted.com/talks/chimamanda_ngozi_adichie_the_danger_of_a_single_story

Alberson, H. (1989). Non-Western literature in the world literature program. In M. Haskell (Ed.), *The teaching of world literature: Proceedings of the conference at the University of Wisconsin* (pp. 45–52). Chapel Hill, NC: University of North Carolina Press.
Albrow, M. (1996). *The global age: State and society beyond modernity*. Palo Alto, CA: Stanford University Press.
Albrow, M., & King, E. (1990). *Globalization, knowledge and society*. Thousand Oaks, CA: Sage.
Alford, C. F. (2002). Emmanuel Levinas and Iris Murdoch: Ethics as exit? *Philosophy and Literature, 26*(1), 24–42.
Allison, H. (2001). *Kant's theory of taste: A reading of the critique of aesthetic judgment*. Cambridge, UK: Cambridge University Press.
Althusser, L. (2004). Ideology and ideological state apparatuses. In J. Rivkin & M. Ryan (Eds.), *Literary theory: An anthology* (2nd ed., pp. 693–702). Malden, MA: Blackwell.
Anderson, L. W., Krathwohl, D. R., Airasian, P. W., Cruikshank, K. A., Mayer, R. E., Pintrich, P. R., . . . Wittrock, M. C. (2001). *A taxonomy for learning, teaching, and assessing: A revision of bloom's taxonomy of educational objectives*. New York: Longman.
Andrew, A., & LaFluer, R. A. (2014). Remonstrance: The moral imperative of the Chinese scholar-official. *Education in Asia, 19*(2), 5–8.
Angle, S., & Slote, M. (Eds.). (2013). *Virtue ethics and Confucianism*. New York: Routledge.
Appadurai, A. (1996). *Modernity at large: Cultural dimensions of globalization*. Minneapolis, MN: University of Minnesota Press.
Appadurai, A. (2013). *The future as cultural fact: Essays on the global condition*. New York: Verso Books.
Appiah, K. A. (1997). Cosmopolitan patriots. *Critical Inquiry, 23*(3), 617–639.
Appiah, K. A. (2006). *Cosmopolitanism: Ethics in a world of strangers*. New York: W. W. Norton.
Appiah, K. A. (2018). *The lies that bind: Rethinking identity*. New York: W. W. Norton.
Applebee, A. (1974). *Tradition and reform in the teaching of English: A history*. Urbana, IL: National Council of Teachers of English.
Appleman, D. (2009). *Critical encounters in high school English: Teaching literary theory to adolescents* (2nd ed.). New York: Teachers College Press.
Arendt, H. (2003). *Responsibility and judgment*. New York: Schocken.
Arendt, H. (2006). *Eichmann in Jerusalem: A report on the banality of evil*. London: Penguin.
Aristotle. (1970). *Poetics* (G. F. Else, Trans.). Ann Arbor, MI: University of Michigan Press. (originally published 350 BCE).
Aristotle. (1985). *Nicomachean ethics* (T. Irwin, Trans.). Indianapolis, IN: Hackett Publishing. (Original work published 350 B.C.E.).
Arnheim, R. (1969). *Visual thinking*. Los Angeles, CA: University of California Press.
Arnold, M. (1993). *Culture and anarchy and other writings* (S. Collini, Ed.). Cambridge, UK: Cambridge University Press. (Original work published 1861).
Axson, S. (1906). The study of the history of English literature. *The School Review, 14*(3), 164–177.
Bacon, A. (Eds.). (1998). *The Newbolt report: The teaching of English in England*. Vermont, VT: Ashgate.
Badiou, A. (2002). *Ethics: An essay on the understanding of evil* (P. Hallward, Trans.). New York: Verso.
Baggini, J., & Fosl, P. S. (2007). *The ethics toolkit: A compendium of ethical concepts and methods*. Malden, MA: Blackwell Publishing.
Baggini, J., & Fosl, P. S. (2010). *The philosopher's toolkit: A compendium of philosophical concepts and methods*. Malden, MA: Blackwell Publishing.
Bajaj, M. (2017). Introduction. In M. Bajaj (Ed.), *Human rights education: Theory, research, praxis* (pp. 10–21). Philadelphia, PA: University of Pennsylvania Press.

Bakker, F. L. (2013). Comparing the golden rule in Hindu and Christian religious texts. *Studies in Religion, 42*(1), 38–58.

Ballinger, G. J. (2003). Bridging the gap between a level and degree: Some observations on managing the transitional stage in the study of English literature. *Arts and Humanities in Higher Education, 2*(1), 99–109.

Bauman, Z. (1993). *Postmodern ethics*. Malden, MA: Blackwell.

Bauman, Z. (1998). *Globalization: The human consequences*. New York: Columbia University Press.

BBC News. (2014, June 3). *How to read a poem consisting only of punctuation*. Retrieved November 3, 2020, from www.bbc.com/news/blogs-magazine-monitor-27680904

Bean, T. W., & Dunkerly-Bean, J. (2015). Expanding conceptions of adolescent literacy research and practice: Cosmopolitan theory in educational contexts. *Australian Journal of Language and Literacy, 38*(1), 46–54.

Beck, U. (2003). Rooted cosmopolitanism: Emerging from a rivalry of distinctions. In U. Beck, N. Sznaider, & R. Winter (Eds.), *Global America? The cultural consequences of globalization* (pp. 15–29). Liverpool, UK: Liverpool University Press.

Beck, U. (2007). The cosmopolitan condition: Why methodological nationalism fails. *Theory, Culture & Society, 24*(7–8), 286–290.

Beck, U. (2014). *Ulrich Beck: Pioneer in cosmopolitan sociology and risk society*. Dordrecht, the Netherlands: Springer.

Benjamin, L. T., & Simpson, J. A. (2009). The power of the situation: The impact of Milgram's obedience studies on personality and social psychology. *American Psychologist, 64*(1), 12–19.

Berberoglu, B. (2003). *Globalization of capital and the nation-state: Imperialism, class struggle, and the state in the age of global capitalism*. London: Rowman & Littlefield.

Bhabha, H. (1994). *Location of culture*. New York: Routledge.

Bhabha, H. (1996). Unsatisfied: Notes on vernacular cosmopolitanism. In L. Garcia-Morena & P. C. Pfeifer (Eds.), *Text and nation* (pp. 191–207). London: Camden House.

Black, M. (1962). *Metaphor*. Ithaca, NY: Cornell University Press.

Blass, T. (2009). From New Haven to Santa Clara: A historical perspective on the Milgram obedience experiments. *American Psychologist, 64*(1), 37–45.

Bloom, A. (1987). *Closing of the American mind: How higher education has failed democracy and impoverished the souls of today's students*. New York: Simon & Schuster.

Bloom, B. S., Engelhart, M. D., Furst, E. J., Hill, W. H., & Krathwohl, D. R. (1956). *Taxonomy of educational objectives: The classification of educational goals. Handbook 1: Cognitive domain*. New York: David McKay.

Bloom, H. (1994). *The Western Canon: The books and school of the ages*. New York: Penguin.

Bluett, J., Cockcroft, S., Harris, A., Hodgson, J., & Snapper, G. (2006). *The future of A-level English*. Sheffield, UK: National Association for the Teaching of English.

Booth, W. C. (1980). The way I loved George Eliot: Friendship with books as a neglected critical metaphor. *The Kenyon Review, 2*(2), 4–27.

Booth, W. C. (1988). *The company we keep: An ethics of fiction*. Berkeley, CA: University of California Press.

Booth, W. C. (1998). The ethics of teaching literature. *College English, 61*(1), 41–55.

Boudou, B. (2019). Hospitality in sanctuary cities. In S. M. Meagher, S. Noll, & J. S. Biehl (Eds.), *The Routledge handbook of philosophy of the city* (pp. 279–290). New York: Routledge.

Bradshaw Foundation. (n.d.). *The art of the Chauvet Cave*. Retrieved November 3, 2020, from www.bradshawfoundation.com/chauvet/

Brauer, L., & Clark, C. T. (2008). The trouble is English: Reframing English studies in secondary schools. *English Education, 40*(4), 293–313.

British Humanist Association. (2010). *Exploring humanism*. London: Author.

Brockover, M. I. (2008). The *Ren Dao* of Confucius: A spiritual account of humanity. In D. Jones (Ed.), *Confucius now: Contemporary encounters with the Analects* (pp. 189–205). Chicago, IL: Open Court.

Brown, E. (2006). Hellenistic cosmopolitanism. In M. L. Gill & P. Pellegrin (Eds.), *A Companion to ancient philosophy* (pp. 550–558). Malden, MA: Blackwell.

Brown, P., & Lauder, H. (1996). Education, globalisation, and economic development. *Journal of Education Policy, 11*(1), 1–25.

Brown, W. (2010). *Walled states, waning sovereignty*. New York: Zone Books.

Bryan, W. F. (1922). Review: An introductory study of world literature. *The School Review, 30*(8), 627–628.

Burger, J. M. (2009). Replicating Milgram: Would people still obey today? *American Psychologist, 64*(1), 1–11.

Burger, J. M. (2014). Situational features in Milgram's experiment that kept his participants shocking. *Journal of Social Issues, 70*(3), 489–500.

Burns, C., Barton, K., & Kerby, S. (2012, July 12). *The state of diversity in today's workforce. Center for American Progress.* Retrieved November 3, 2020, from www.americanprogress.org/issues/economy/reports/2012/07/12/11938/the-state-of-diversity-in-todays-workforce/

Butler, J. (2000). Ethical ambivalence. In M. Garber, B. Hanssen, & R. L. Walkowitz (Eds.), *The turn to ethics* (pp. 15–28). New York: Routledge.

Calhoun, C. (2002). The class consciousness of frequent travellers: Toward a critique of actually existing cosmopolitanism. *South Atlantic Quarterly, 101*(4), 869–897.

Cambridge Assessment International Education. (2015). *Cambridge IGCSE world literature*. Cambridge, UK: Author.

Cambridge Assessment International Education. (2019). *Cambridge IGCSE literature in English syllabus (for exams in 2022)*. Cambridge, UK: Author.

Cambridge Assessment International Education. (2020). *Cambridge IGCSE literature in English paper 1: Poetry and prose (Specimen paper)*. Cambridge, UK: Author.

Carr, D. (2014). Four perspectives on the value of literature for moral and character education. *Journal of Aesthetic Education, 48*(4), 1–16.

Carter, M. (1948). The case for world literature. *The School Review, 56*(7), 415–420.

Casner-Lotto, J., & Barrington, L. (2006). *Are they really ready to work? Employers' perspectives on the basic knowledge and applied skills of new entrants to the 21st century US workforce*. New York: The Conference Board.

Castells, M. (2010). *The rise of the network society* (2nd ed.). Malden, MA: Blackwell.

Chace, W. M. (2009, Autumn). The decline of the English department. *American Scholar*. Retrieved July 10, 2018, from www.theamericanscholar.org/the-decline-of-the-english-department/

Chai, C., & Chai, W. (1973). *Confucianism*. Woodbury, NY: Barron's Educational Series.

Chang, I. (1997). *The rape of Nanking: The forgotten holocaust of world war II*. New York: Basic Books.

Cheah, P. (2006). *Inhuman conditions: On cosmopolitanism and human rights*. Cambridge, MA: Harvard University Press.

Chen, Y. (2016). Two roads to a world community: Comparing stoic and Confucian cosmopolitanism. *Chinese Political Science Review, 1*(2), 322–335.

Cheney, L. V. (1987). *American memory: A report on the humanities in the nation's public schools*. Washington, DC: National Endowment for the Humanities.

Cheng, C. (1991). *New dimensions of Confucian and Neo-Confucian philosophy*. Albany, NY: SUNY Press.

Choo, S. S. (2013). *Reading the world, the globe, and the cosmos: Approaches to teaching literature for the twenty-first century*. New York: Peter Lang.

Choo, S. S. (2014a). Cultivating a hospitable imagination: Re-envisioning the world literature curriculum through a cosmopolitan lens. *Curriculum Inquiry*, *44*(1), 68–89.

Choo, S. S. (2014b). Towards a cosmopolitan vision of English education in Singapore. *Discourse: Studies in the Cultural Politics of Education*, *35*(5), 677–691.

Choo, S. S. (2016). Fostering the hospitable imagination through cosmopolitan pedagogies: Re-envisioning literature education in Singapore. *Research in the Teaching of English*, *50*(4), 400–421.

Choo, S. S. (2017a). Globalizing Literature pedagogy: Applying cosmopolitan ethical criticism to the teaching of literature. *Harvard Educational Review*, *87*(3), 335–356.

Choo, S. S. (2017b). Approaching twenty-first century education from a cosmopolitan perspective. *Journal of Curriculum Studies*, *50*(2), 162–181.

Choo, S. S. (2018). The need for cosmopolitan literacy in a global age: Implications for teaching literature. *Journal of Adolescent and Adult Literacy*, *62*(1), 7–12.

Choo, S. S. (2020a). The cosmopolitan turn in Literature education and its resulting tensions in Singapore schools. *Critical Studies in Education*, *61*(4), 512–527.

Choo, S. S. (2020b). Examining models of twenty-first century education through the lens of Confucian cosmopolitanism. *Asia Pacific Journal of Education*, *40*(1), 20–34.

Choo, S. S. (2021). Expanding the imagination: Mediating the aesthetic-political divide through the third space of ethics in Literature education. *British Journal of Educational Studies*, *69*(1), 65–82.

Choo, S. S., Yeo, D., Chua, B. L., Palaniappan, M., Beevi, I., & Nah, D. (2020). *National survey of literature teachers' beliefs and practices*. Singapore: National Institute of Education.

Cianciolo, A. T., & Sternberg, R. J. (2004). *Intelligence: A brief history*. Malden, MA: Blackwell.

Clottes, J. (2008). *Cave art*. London: Phaidon Press.

Cohen, R. A. (1974). Foreword. In *Otherwise than being of beyond essence* (A. Lingis, Trans., pp. xi–xvi). Pittsburgh, PA: Duquesne University Press.

Cohen, R. A. (2016). Levinas on art and aestheticism: Getting "reality and its shadow" right. *Levinas Studies*, *11*(1), 149–194.

Confucius. (2014). *The analects* (A. Chin, Trans.). New York: Penguin. (Originally published in 500 BCE).

Crignon, P., Simek, N., & Zalloua, Z. (2004). Figuration: Emmanuel Levinas and the image. *Yale French Studies*, *104*, 100–125.

Critchley, S. (2014). *Ethics of deconstruction: Derrida and Levinas*. Edinburgh, UK: Edinburgh University Press.

Curriculum Planning and Development Division. (2013). *Literature in English teaching syllabus 2013: Lower and upper secondary*. Singapore: Ministry of Education.

Curriculum Planning and Development Division. (2018). *Literature in English teaching syllabus 2019*. Singapore: Ministry of Education.

Curtis, P. (2009, April 28). Number taking GCSE in English literature falls. *Guardian*. Retrieved July 10, 2018, from www.guardian.co.uk/education/2009/apr/29/schools-english-literature-gcse-decline

Dallmayr, F. (2003). Cosmopolitanism: Moral and political. *Political Theory*, *31*(3), 421–442.

Damrosch, D. (2003). *What is world literature?* Princeton, NJ: Princeton University Press.

Damrosch, D. (Ed.). (2009). *Teaching world literature*. New York: MLA.

Damrosch, D. (2018). *How to read world literature*. Oxford, UK: Wiley-Blackwell.

Damrosch, D., & Pike, D. L. (2008). *The Longman anthology of world literature (Compact Ed.)*. Upper Saddle River, NJ: Pearson.

Davis, T. F., & Womack, K. (2001). *Mapping the ethical turn: A reader in ethics, culture and literary theory*. Charlottesville, VA: University Press of Virginia.

de Bono, E. (1970). *Lateral thinking: Creativity step by step*. New York: Harper & Row.

de Saussure, F. (1916). *Course in general linguistics* (C. Bally & A. Sechehaye, Eds., R. Harris, Trans.). Chicago, IL: Open Court.

de Vos, J. (2009). Now that you know, how do you feel? The Milgram experiment and psychologization. *Annual Review of Critical Psychology*, 7, 223–246.

Dejaynes, T. (2018). "What makes me who I am?" Using artifacts as cosmopolitan invitations. *English Journal*, *108*(2), 48–54.

Delanty, G. (2006). The cosmopolitan imagination: Critical cosmopolitanism and social theory. *The British Journal of Sociology*, *57*(1), 25–47.

Delanty, G. (2014). Not all is lost in translation: World varieties of cosmopolitanism. *Cultural Sociology*, *8*(4), 374–391.

Department of Statistics. (2016). *General household survey 2015*. Singapore: Ministry of Trade & Industry.

Department of Statistics. (2019). *Population trends, 2019*. Singapore: Ministry of Trade & Industry.

Derrida, J. (2000). *Of hospitality* (R. Bowlby, Trans.). Stanford, CA: Stanford University Press.

Derrida, J. (2001). *On cosmopolitanism and forgiveness*. New York: Routledge.

Derrida, J. (2002). Hospitality. In G. Anidjar (Ed.), *Acts of religion* (pp. 356–420). New York: Routledge.

Derrida, J. (2008). Secrets of European responsibility. In *The gift of death* (D. Willis, Trans., 2nd ed., pp. 3–36). Chicago, IL: University of Chicago Press.

Dewey, J. (1902). *The child and the curriculum*. Chicago, IL: University of Chicago Press.

Dewey, J. (1915). *The school and society*. Chicago, IL: University of Chicago Press.

Dewey, J. (1938). *Experience and education*. New York: Palgrave Macmillan.

Djikic, M., Oatley, K., & Moldoveanu, M. C. (2013). Reading other minds: Effects of literature on empathy. *Scientific Study of Literature*, *3*(1), 28–47.

Donald, J. (2007). Internationalisation, diversity and the humanities curriculum: Cosmopolitanism and multiculturalism revisited. *Journal of Philosophy of Education*, *41*(3), 289–308.

Doukhan, A. (2012). *Emmanuel Levinas: A philosophy of exile*. London: Bloomsbury.

Downing, K. (2002). Travelers, not tourists: A world literature curriculum. *English Journal*, *91*(5), 46–51.

Doyle, B. (1989). *English and Englishness*. London: Routledge.

Dreyfuss, H. L. (1991). *Being in the world: A commentary on Heidegger's being and time*. Cambridge, MA: The MIT Press.

Durkin, K. (2008). The adaptation of East Asian masters students to western norms of critical thinking and argumentation in the UK. *Intercultural Education*, *19*(1), 15–27.

Eaglestone, R. (1997). *Ethical criticism: Reading after Levinas*. Edinburgh, UK: Edinburgh University Press.

Eaglestone, R. (2007, March 23). Boyne's dangerous tale. *The Jewish Chronicle*, p. 50.

Eaglestone, R. (2008). *The holocaust and the postmodern*. Oxford, UK: Oxford University Press.

Eaglestone, R., & McEvoy, S. (1999, November 30). A critical time for English. *The Guardian*. Retrieved July 10, 2018, from www.theguardian.com/education/1999/nov/30/schools.theguardian1

Eagleton, T. (1996). *Literary theory: An introduction* (2nd ed.). Malden, MA: Blackwell.

Eagleton, T. (2009). *The trouble with strangers: A study of ethics*. Malden, MA: Blackwell.

Economic Review Committee, Ministry of Trade and Industry, Singapore. (2003). *Creative industries development strategy*. Singapore: Author.

Ellis, J. M. (1997). *Literature lost: Social agendas and the corruption of the humanities*. New Haven, CT: Yale University Press.

Elverskog, J. (2013). China and the new cosmopolitanism. *Sino-platonic Papers, 233*, 1–30.

European Union. (2020, March 6). *COVID-19: Commission steps up research funding and selects 17 projects in vaccine development, treatment and diagnostics*. Press Release. Retrieved March 27, 2020, from https://ec.europa.eu/commission/presscorner/detail/en/ip_20_386

Falk, R. (1993). The making of global citizenship. In J. Brecher, J. B. Childs, & J. Cutler (Eds.), *Global visions: Beyond the new world order* (pp. 39–52). Boston, MA: South End Press.

Fish, S. (1980). *Is there a text in this class? The authority of interpretive communities*. Cambridge, MA: Harvard University Press.

Fish, S. (2008). Will the humanities save us? *New York Times*. Retrieved November 3, 2020, from http://opinionator.blogs.nytimes.com/2008/01/06/will-the-humanities-save-us/

Foucault, M. (2008). *The birth of biopolitics: Lectures at the Collège de France, 1978–79* (G. Burchell, Trans.). New York: Picador.

Fraser, N. (2008). *Scales of justice: Reimagining political space in a globalizing world*. Cambridge, UK: Polity Press.

Freire, P. (1970). *Pedagogy of the oppressed* (M. B. Ramos, Trans.). New York: Continuum.

Freire, P. (1985). Reading the world and reading the word: An interview with Paulo Freire. *Language Arts, 62*(1), 15–21.

Fricke, H.-J., Gathercole, C., & Skinner, A. (2015). *Monitoring education for global citizenship: A contribution to debate*. Brussels: DEEEP.

Friedman, T. (2007). *The world is flat 3.0: A brief history of the twenty-first century*. New York: Picador.

Garber, M., Hanssen, B., & Walkowitz, R. L. (Eds.). (2000). *The turn to ethics*. New York: Routledge.

Garner, R. (2005, April 19). Scrap English literature A-level, teachers demand. *Independent*, p. 14.

Gay, G. (2002). Preparing for culturally responsive teaching. *Journal of Teacher Education, 53*(2), 106–116.

George, S. K. (2005). *Ethics, literature, theory: An introductory reader*. Lanham, MD: Rowman & Littlefield.

Geulette, M. (2020, March 10). Canada pledges C$275M for coronavirus R&D, adding to global funding rush. *Science Business*. Retrieved March 27, 2020, from https://sciencebusiness.net/news/canada-pledges-c275m-coronavirus-rd-adding-global-funding-rush

Gibson, M. L., & Grant, C. A. (2017). Historicizing critical educational praxis: A human rights framework for justice-oriented teaching. In M. Bajaj (Ed.), *Human rights education: Theory, research, praxis* (pp. 179–197). Philadelphia, PA: University of Pennsylvania Press.

Giddens, A. (1991). *The consequences of modernity*. Cambridge, UK: Polity Press.

Gino, F., & Bazerman, M. H. (2009). When misconduct goes unnoticed: The acceptability of gradual erosion in others' unethical behaviour. *Journal of Experimental Social Psychology, 45*(4), 708–719.

Ginsborg, H. (2013). Kant's aesthetics and teleology. *Stanford Encyclopedia of Philosophy*. Retrieved November 3, 2020, from http://plato.stanford.edu/entries/kant-aesthetics/

Giroux, H. A. (1988a). Border pedagogy in the age of postmodernism. *Journal of Education, 170*(3), 162–181.

Giroux, H. A. (1988b). *Teachers as intellectuals: Toward a critical pedagogy of learning.* Westport, CT: Bergin & Garvey Publishers.

Gregory, M. W. (2010). Redefining ethical criticism: The old vs. The new. *Journal of Literary Theory, 4*(2). Retrieved November 3, 2020, from www.jltonline.de/index.php/articles/article/view/287/879

Habermas, J. (1984). *The theory of communicative action: Vol. 1. Reason and the rationalization of society* (T. McCarthy, Trans.). Boston, MA: Beacon Press.

Habermas, J. (1991). *The structural transformation of the public sphere: An inquiry into a category of bourgeois society* (T. Burger, Trans.). Cambridge, MA: MIT Press.

Hall, D. L., & Ames, R. Y. (1987). *Thinking through Confucius.* New York: SUNY Press.

Halwani, R. (1998). Literary ethics. *Journal of Aesthetic Education, 32*(3), 19–32.

Hannerz, U. (1990). Cosmopolitans and locals in world culture. *Theory, Culture, Society, 7*(2–3), 237–251.

Hansen, D. T. (2010). Chasing butterflies without a net: Interpreting cosmopolitanism. *Studies in Philosophy and Education, 29*(2), 151–166.

Hansen, D. T. (2011). *The teacher and the world: A study of cosmopolitanism as education.* New York: Routledge.

Hansen, D. T., Burdick-Shepherd, S., Cammarano, C., & Obelleiro, G. (2009). Education, values, and valuing in cosmopolitan perspective. *Curriculum Inquiry, 39*(5), 587–612.

Harper, H., Bean, T. W., & Dunkerly, J. (2010). Cosmopolitanism, globalization and the field of adolescent literacy. *Canadian and International Education, 39*(3), 1–13.

Heater, D. (2002). *World citizenship: Cosmopolitan thinking and its opponents.* London: Continuum.

Heidegger, M. (1971a). The origin of the work of art. In *Poetry, language, thought* (A. Hofstadter, Trans., pp. 17–76). New York: HarperCollins. (Original work published 1950).

Heidegger, M. (1971b). . . . Poetically man dwells . . . In *Poetry, language, thought* (A. Hofstadter, Trans., pp. 211–227). New York: HarperCollins. (Original work published 1950).

Held, D., McGrew, A., Goldblatt, D., & Perraton, J. (1999). *Global transformations: Politics, economics and culture.* Stanford, CA: Stanford University Press.

Heng, S. K. (2013, February 7). *Schools offering and annual cohorts taking full Literature at 'O' and 'N(A)' levels.* Parliamentary replies. Singapore: Singapore government.

Hiatt, B. (2018, May 23). Students miss out as some WA high schools drop literature as a subject. *PerthNow.* Retrieved July 10, 2018, from www.perthnow.com.au/news/education/students-miss-out-as-some-wa-high-schools-drop-literature-as-a-subject-ng-b88844222z

Hicks, D. (2003). Thirty years of global education: A reminder of key principles and precedents. *Educational Review, 55*(3), 265–275.

Hillocks, G. (2016). The territory of literature. *English Education, 48*(2), 109–126.

Holden, P. (1999). The great literature debate: Why teach literature in Singapore. In S. H. Chua & W. P. Chin (Eds.), *Localising pedagogy: Teaching literature in Singapore* (pp. 79–89). Singapore: National Institute of Education.

Holden, P. (2000). On the nation's margins: The social place of literature in Singapore. *Sojourn: Journal of Social Issues in Southeast Asia, 15*(1), 30–51.

Homerin, E. (2008). The golden rule in Islam. In J. Neusner & B. D. Chilton (Eds.), *The golden rule: The ethics of reciprocity in world religions* (pp. 99–115). London: Continuum.

Hu, M., & Elverskog, J. (Eds.). (2016). *Cosmopolitanism in China, 1600–1950*. Amherst, NY: Cambria Press.

Hull, G. A., & Stornaiuolo, A. (2010). Literate arts in a global world: Reframing social networking as cosmopolitan practice. *Journal of Adolescent & Adult Literacy, 54*(2), 85–97.

Hull, G. A., Stornaiuolo, A., & Sahni, U. (2010). Cultural citizenship and cosmopolitan practice: Global youth communicate online. *English Education, 42*(4), 331–367.

Ignatieff, M. (2001). *Human rights as politics and idolatry* (A. Gutmann, Ed.). Princeton, NJ: Princeton University Press.

International Association for the Evaluation of Educational Achievement. (2016). *Progress in international reading literacy study*. Washington, DC: Institute of Education Sciences.

International Baccalaureate Organization. (2019). *Diploma programme language a: Literature guide (first assessment 2021)*. Cardiff, Wales: Author.

Ivanhoe, P. J. (1991). Character consequentialism: An early Confucian contribution to contemporary ethical theory. *Journal of Religious Ethics, 19*(1), 55–70.

Ivanhoe, P. J. (2014). Confucian cosmopolitanism. *Journal of Religious Ethics, 42*(1), 22–44.

Jarvis, P. (2006). Teaching: An art or a science (technology)? In P. Jarvis (Ed.), *The theory and practice of teaching* (2nd ed., pp. 16–27). Abingdon, UK: Routledge.

Jenkins, H. (2006). *Confronting the challenges of participatory culture: Media education for the 21st century*. Chicago, IL: MacArthur Foundation.

Jerald, C. D. (2009). *Defining a 21st century education*. Center for Public Education. Retrieved November 3, 2020, from www.cambridgeinternational.org/programmes-and-qualifications/english-literature-0475/past-papers/

Jetten, J., & Mols, F. (2014). 50:50 hindsight: Appreciating anew the contributions of Milgram's obedience experiments. *Journal of Social Issues, 70*(3), 587–602.

Jollimore, T., & Barrios, S. (2006). Creating cosmopolitans: The case for literature. *Studies in the Philosophy of Education, 25*(5), 363–383.

Kamenetsky, C. (1984). *Children's literature in Hitler's Germany*. Athens, OH: Ohio University Press.

Kant, I. (1963). Perpetual peace. In *On history* (L. W. Beck, Ed. & L. W. Beck, R. E. Anchor, & E. L. Fackenheim, Trans., pp. 85–135). New York: Palgrave Macmillan. (Original work published 1795).

Kant, I. (1987). *Critique of judgment* (W. S. Pluhar, Trans.). Indianapolis, IN: Hackett. (Original work published 1790).

Kant, I. (1995). *Foundations of the metaphysics of morals* (2nd ed., L. W. Beck, Trans.). Upper Saddle River, NJ: Prentice-Hall. (Original work published 1785).

Kellner, D. (2002). Theorizing globalization. *Sociological Theory, 20*(3), 285–305.

Kernan, A. (1990). *The death of literature*. New Haven, CT: Yale University Press.

Kidd, D. C., & Castano, E. (2013). Reading literary fiction improves theory of mind. *Science, 342*(6156), 377–380.

Knowles, M., & Moon, R. (2006). *Introducing metaphor*. New York: Routledge.

Koch, H. E. (1922). The value of books recommended for high-school students in widening the geographical horizon. *The School Review, 30*(3), 193–198.

Kohlberg, L. (1981). *The philosophy of moral development: Moral stages and the idea of justice*. New York: Harper & Row.

Kohlberg, L. (1985). Resolving moral conflicts within the just community. In C. G. Harding (Ed.), *Moral dilemmas and ethical reasoning* (pp. 71–97). Piscataway, NJ: Transaction Publishers.

Koslowski, P. (2001). *Principles of ethical economy*. Dordrecht, the Netherlands: Springer.

Krathwohl, D. R. (2002). A revision of bloom's taxonomy: An overview. *Theory into Practice, 41*(4), 212–218.

Kraut, R. (2018). *Aristotle's ethics. Stanford encyclopedia of philosophy*. Retrieved November 3, 2020, from https://plato.stanford.edu/entries/aristotle-ethics/

Kugelman, F. (n.d.). *Bloom's taxonomy cheat sheet*. Retrieved December 9, 2020, from https://www.bloomstaxonomy.org/

Ladson-Billings, G. (1994). *The dream keepers: Successful teachers of African American children*. San Francisco, CA: Jossey-Bass.

Ladson-Billings, G. (1995). Toward a theory of culturally relevant pedagogy. *American Educational Research Journal, 32*(3), 465–491.

LaFollette, H. (2003). *The Oxford handbook of practical ethics*. Oxford, UK: Oxford University Press.

Lai, K. (2006). Li in the "Analects": Training in moral competence and the question of flexibility. *Philosophy East and West, 56*(1), 69–83.

Lave, J., & Wenger, E. (1991). *Situated learning: Legitimate peripheral participation*. Cambridge, UK: Cambridge University Press.

Lawall, S. (1994). Introduction. In S. Lawall (Ed.), *Reading world literature: Theory, history, practice* (pp. 1–64). Austin, TX: University of Texas Press.

Lefebvre, H. (1991). *The production of space* (D. Nicholson-Smith, Trans.). Malden, MA: Blackwell.

Levinas, E. (1969). *Totality and infinity: An essay on exteriority* (A. Lingis, Trans.). Pittsburgh, PA: Duquesne University Press.

Levinas, E. (1974). *Otherwise than being of beyond essence* (A. Lingis, Trans.). Pittsburgh, PA: Duquesne University Press.

Levinas, E. (1987). God and philosophy. In *Collected philosophical papers: Emmanuel Levinas* (A. Lingis, Trans., pp. 153–173). Pittsburgh, PA: Duquesne University Press.

Levinas, E. (1989). Reality and its shadow. In S. Hand (Ed. & Trans.), *The Levinas reader* (pp. 129–143). Oxford: Blackwell.

Levinas, E. (1999). *Alterity & transcendence* (M. B. Smith, Trans.). New York: Columbia University Press.

Levinas, E. (2006). *Humanism of the other* (N. Poller, Trans.). Urbana, IL: University of Illinois Press. (Original work published 1972).

Lew, S. F. (1898). The awakening of oh Seng Hong. *Straits Chinese Magazine, 2*(6), 108–111.

Lewin, T. (2013, October 30). As interest fades in the Humanities, colleges worry. *New York Times*. Retrieved July 10, 2018, from www.nytimes.com/2013/10/31/education/as-interest-fades-in-the-humanities-colleges-worry.html

Li, C. (2007). Li as cultural grammar: On the relation between *li* and *ren* in Confucius' "Analects." *Philosophy East and West, 57*(3), 311–329.

Liew, W. M. (2012). Valuing the value(s) of literature. *Commentary, 21*, 57–71.

Lingis, A. (1974). Introduction. In *Otherwise than being or beyond essence* (A. Lingis, Trans., pp. xvii–xlviii). Pittsburgh, PA: Duquesne University Press.

Livingston, R. E. (2001). Glocal knowledges: Agency and place in literary studies. *PMLA, 116*(1), 145–157.

Loh, C. E. (2013). Singaporean boys constructing global literate selves through the reading practices in and out of school. *Anthropology and Education Quarterly, 44*(1), 38–57.

Loh, C. E., Choo, S., & Beavis, C. (Eds.). (2018). *Literature education in the Asia-Pacific*. Singapore: Routledge.

Long, A. A. (2008). The concept of the cosmopolitan in Greek & Roman thought. *Daedalus, 137*(3), 50–58.

Lu, C. (2000). The one and many faces of cosmopolitanism. *Journal of Political Philosophy, 8*(2), 244–253.

Macaulay, T. B. (1835). *Minute on Indian education.* Retrieved November 3, 2020, from www.columbia.edu/itc/mealac/pritchett/00generallinks/macaulay/txt_minute_education_1835.html

MacIntyre, A. (1998). *A short history of ethics.* Notre Dame, IN: University of Notre Dame Press.

Maslow, A. H. (1943). A theory of human motivation. *Psychological Review, 50*(4), 370–396.

McGreevy, R. (2020, January 5). Avoid John Boyne's Holocaust novel, Auschwitz Museum advises. *Irish Times.* Retrieved November 3, 2020, from www.irishtimes.com/culture/books/avoid-john-boyne-s-holocaust-novel-auschwitz-museum-advises-1.4131194

McLeod, D. W. (1937). *Syllabus of instruction.* Singapore: Raffles Institution.

Meader, E. I. (1899). A high school course in English. *The School Review,* 7(8), 473–477.

Mehta, P. B. (2000). Cosmopolitanism and the circle of reason. *Political Theory, 28*(5), 619–639.

Menintjes, G. (1997). Human rights education as empowerment: Reflections on pedagogy. In G. J. Andreopoulos & R. P. Claude (Eds.), *Human rights education for the twenty-first century* (pp. 51–79). Philadelphia, PA: University of Pennsylvania Press.

Michael, I. (1987). *The teaching of English: From the sixteenth century to 1870.* Cambridge, UK: Cambridge University Press.

Mignolo, W. D. (2000). The many faces of Cosmo-polis: Border thinking and critical cosmopolitanism. *Public Culture, 12*(3), 721–748.

Mignolo, W. D. (2013). Politics of sensing & knowing: On (de)coloniality, border thinking, & epistemic disobedience. *Confero: Essays on Education Philosophy and Politics, 1*(1), 129–150.

Milgram, S. (1974). *Obedience to authority: An experimental view.* New York: HarperCollins.

Miller, A. G. (2014). The explanatory value of Milgram's obedience experiments: A contemporary appraisal. *Journal of Social Issues, 70*(3), 558–573.

Moulton, R. G. (1911). *World Literature and its place in general culture.* New York: Palgrave Macmillan.

Murphy, P. (2008). Defining pedagogy. In K. Hall, P. Murphy, & J. Soler (Eds.), *Pedagogy and practice: Culture and identities* (pp. 28–39). London: Sage.

Nagle, S. J. (1928). *Educational needs of the straits settlements and federated Malay states.* Baltimore, MD: Johns Hopkins University.

National Endowment for the Arts. (2004). *Reading at risk: A survey of literary reading in America.* Washington, DC: National Endowment for the Arts.

National Endowment for the Arts. (2007). *To read or not to read. A question of national consequence.* Washington, DC: National Endowment for the Arts.

National Endowment for the Arts. (2009). *Reading on the rise: A new chapter in American literacy.* Washington, DC: National Endowment for the Arts.

National Library Board. (2017). *2016 National reading habits study: Findings on teenagers.* Singapore: Author.

Neilson, F. (1947). Introductory reading for the great books course. *American Journal of Economics and Sociology,* 7(1), 9–32.

Neville, R. C. (2012). Dimensions of contemporary Confucian cosmopolitanism. *Journal of Chinese Philosophy, 39*(4), 594–613.

New International Version. (2005). *Holy bible.* Grand Rapids, MI: Zondervan.

Nguyen, N. T. (2016). Confucianism and humane education in contemporary Vietnam. *International Communication of Chinese Culture, 3*(4), 645–671.

Nie, Z. (2015). Towards an ethical literary criticism. *Arcadia, 50*(1), 83–101.

Nussbaum, M. C. (1990). *Love's knowledge: Essays on philosophy and literature*. New York: Oxford University Press.

Nussbaum, M. C. (1997). *Cultivating humanity: A classical defence of reform in liberal education*. Cambridge, MA: Harvard University Press.

Nussbaum, M. C. (2010). *Not for profit: Why democracy needs the Humanities*. Princeton, NJ: Princeton University Press.

O'Byrne, D. J. (2003). *The dimensions of global citizenship: Political identity beyond the nation-state*. London: Frank Cass.

Ong, A. (1999). *Flexible citizenship: The cultural logics of transnationality*. Durham, NC: Duke University Press.

Organisation for Economic Co-operation and Development (OECD). (2005). *Definition and selection of key competencies*. Paris: Author.

Organisation for Economic Co-operation and Development (OECD). (2016). *Trade in employment*. Retrieved July 10, 2018, from www.oecd.org/sti/ind/trade-in-employment.htm

Osler, A. (2016). *Human rights and schooling: An ethical framework for teaching for social justice*. New York: Teachers College Press.

Osler, A., & Starkey, A. (2010). *Teachers and human rights education*. London: UCL Institute of Education Press.

Osler, A., & Starkey, A. (2018). Extending the theory and practice of education for cosmopolitan citizenship. *Educational Review, 70*(1), 31–40.

O'Sullivan, M. W., & Guo, L. (2011). Critical thinking and Chinese international students: An East-West dialogue. *Journal of Contemporary Issues in Education, 5*(2), 53–73.

Park, S., & Oliver, S. J. (2008). Revisiting the conceptualisation of pedagogical content knowledge (PCK): PCK as a conceptual tool to understand teachers as professionals. *Research in the Sociology of Education, 38*, 261–284.

Partnership for 21st Century Skills (P21). (2013). *Learning for the 21st century*. Washington, DC: Author.

Paul, R., & Elder, L. (1996). *The critical mind is a questioning mind*. Foundation for Critical Thinking. Retrieved November 3, 2020, from www.criticalthinking.org/pages/the-critical-mind-is-a-questioning-mind/481

Paul, R., & Elder, L. (1997). *The elements of reasoning and the intellectual standards*. Retrieved November 3, 2020, from www.criticalthinking.org/pages/the-elements-of-reasoning-and-the-intellectual-standards/480

Perpezek, A. T. (1995). Transcendence. In A. T. Perpezak (Ed.), *Ethics as first philosophy: The significance of Emmanuel Levinas for philosophy, literature and religion* (pp. 185–192). New York: Routledge.

Pizer, J. (2006). *The idea of world literature: History and pedagogical practice*. Baton Rouge, LA: Louisiana State University Press.

Plato. (1968). *The republic of Plato* (A. Bloom, Trans.). New York: Basic Books. (Originally published in 375 BCE).

Poon, A. M. C. (2010). Constructing the cosmopolitan subject: Teaching secondary school literature in Singapore. *Asia Pacific Journal of Education, 30*(1), 31–41.

Posner, R. A. (1997). Against ethical criticism. *Philosophy and Literature, 21*(1), 1–27.

Posner, R. A. (1998). Against ethical criticism: Part two. *Philosophy and Literature, 22*(2), 394–412.

Purcell, M. E. (2020). Cosmopolitanism as transnational literacy: Putting Spivak to work. *Asia Pacific Journal of Education, 40*(1), 61–73.

Rajaratnam, S. (1972, February 6). *Singapore: Global city*. Singapore: Speech given at the Singapore Press Club.

Rawls, J. (1971). *A theory of justice* (Rev. ed.). Cambridge, MA: Belknap Press.

Reardon, B. A. (2002). Human rights and the global campaign for peace education. *International Review of Education, 48*(3/4), 283–284.

Regents High School Examination. (2020, January). *Regents examination in English language arts*. New York: University of the State of New York.

Reicher, S., & Haslam, A. S. (2011). After shock? Towards a social identity explanation of the Milgram 'obedience' studies. *British Journal of Social Psychology, 50*(1), 163–169.

Richards, I. A. (1929). *Practical criticism: A study of literary judgment*. New York: Harvest Book.

Richards, I. A. (1936). *The philosophy of rhetoric*. Oxford, UK: Oxford University Press.

Richards, I. A. (2004). *Principles of literary criticism*. London: Routledge. (Original work published 1924).

Rizvi, F. (2009). Towards cosmopolitan learning. *Discourse: Studies in the Cultural Politics of Education, 30*, 253–268.

Robbins, B. (1998). Introduction part I: Actually existing cosmopolitanism. In P. Cheah & B. Robbins (Eds.), *Cosmopolitics: Thinking and feeling beyond the nation* (pp. 1–19). Minneapolis, MN: University of Minnesota Press.

Robbins, B. (2012). *Perpetual war: Cosmopolitanism from the viewpoint of violence*. Durham, NC: Duke University Press.

Robertson, R. (1992). *Globalization: Social theory and global culture*. London: Sage.

Rockhill, W. (1883). *Udanavarga: A collection of verses from the Buddhist canon*. London: Trubner & Co., Ludgate Hill.

Rosemont, H., & Ames, R. T. (2009). *The Chinese classic of family reverence*. Honolulu: University of Hawaii Press.

Rosemont, H., & Ames, R. T. (2016). *Confucian role ethics: A moral vision for the 21st century*. Taipei, Taiwan: National Taiwan University Press.

Rosenblatt, L. M. (1978). *The reader, the text, the poem: The transactional theory of the literary work*. Carbondale, IL: Southern Illinois University Press.

Rosenblatt, L. M. (1988). The transactional theory of reading and writing. In R. B. Ruddell & N. J. Unrau (Eds.), *Theoretical models and processes of reading* (pp. 1363–1398). Newark, DE: International Reading Association.

Rosenblatt, L. M. (1994). *The reader, the text, the poem: The transactional theory of the literary work*. Carbondale, IL: Southern Illinois University Press.

Roudometof, V. (2016). Theorizing glocalization: Three interpretations. *European Journal of Social Theory, 19*(3), 391–408.

Russell, N. J. C. (2011). Milgram's obedience to authority experiments: Origins and early evolution. *British Journal of Social Psychology, 50*(1), 140–162.

Said, E. W. (1979). *Orientalism*. New York: Vintage.

Said, E. W. (2002). *Reflections on exile and other essays*. Cambridge, MA: Harvard University Press.

Said, E. W. (2004). *Humanism and democratic criticism*. New York: Columbia University Press.

Sam, C., Whiteaker, C., Recht, H., Pogkas, D., Murray, P., Halford, D., & Bryant, E. (2020, March 27). Mapping the Coronavirus outbreak across the world. *Bloomberg*. Retrieved March 27, 2020, from www.bloomberg.com/graphics/2020-coronavirus-cases-world-map/

Sandel, M. J. (2009). *Justice: What's the right thing to do?* New York: Farrar, Straus, and Giroux.

Sartre, J.-P. (2001). What is literature? In V. B. Leitch (Ed.), *The Norton anthology of theory and criticism* (B. Frechtman, Trans., pp. 1336–1349). New York: W. W. Norton. (Original work published 1948).

Schleicher, A. (2019). *PISA 2018: Insights and interpretations*. Paris: OECD.
Scholes, R. (1985). *Textual power: Literary theory and the teaching of English*. New Haven, CT: Yale University Press.
Scholes, R. (1998). *The rise and fall of English: Reconstructing English as a discipline*. New Haven, CT: Yale University Press.
Scholte, J. A. (2005). *Globalization: A critical introduction* (2nd ed.). New York: Palgrave Macmillan.
Sen, A. (2004). Elements of a theory of human rights. *Philosophy & Public Affairs, 32*(4), 315–356.
Sen, A. (2008). Capability and well-being. In D. M. Hausman (Ed.), *The philosophy of economics: An anthology* (3rd ed., pp. 270–294). Cambridge, MA: Cambridge University Press.
Shepherd, E. E. (1937). The survey of world-literature. *English Journal, 26*(4), 337–338.
Shulman, L. (1987). Knowledge and teaching: Foundations of the new reform. *Harvard Educational Review, 57*(1), 1–22.
Sim, M. (2015). Why Confucius' ethics is a virtue ethics. In L. L. Besser & M. Slote (Eds.), *The Routledge companion to virtue ethics* (pp. 63–76). New York: Routledge.
Simpson, J., & Kelly, S. (2013). The teaching of the arts and humanities at Harvard college: Mapping the future. *Harvard Magazine*. Retrieved November 3, 2020, from https://harvardmagazine.com/sites/default/files/mapping the_future_of_the_humanities.pdf
Singer, P. (2011). *Practical ethics*. Cambridge, UK: Cambridge University Press.
Soja, E. W. (2009). Thirdspace: Toward a new consciousness of space and spatiality. In K. Ikas & G. Wagner (Eds.), *Communicating in the third space* (pp. 49–61). New York: Routledge.
Spivak, G. C. (1988). Can the subaltern speak? In C. Nelson & L. Grossberg (Eds.), *Marxism and the interpretation of culture* (pp. 271–316). London: Palgrave Macmillan.
Spivak, G. C. (2003). *Death of a discipline*. New York: Columbia University Press.
Spivak, G. C. (2012). *An aesthetic education in the era of globalization*. Cambridge, MA: Harvard University Press.
Stolper, B. J. R. (1928). Literary perspective to high school pupils. *Teachers College Record, 29*(5), 391–396.
Stolper, B. J. R. (1935). World-literature in the high school. *English Journal, 24*(6), 480–484.
Swenson, J., Young, C. A., McGrail, E., Rozema, R., & Whitin, P. (2006). Extending the conversation: New technologies, new literacies, and English Education. *English Education, 38*(4), 351–369.
Tabb, W. K. (2009). Globalization today: At the borders of class and state theory. *Science & Society, 73*(1), 34–53.
Tagore, S. (2008). Tagore's conception of cosmopolitanism: A reconstruction. *University of Toronto Quarterly*, 77(4), 1070–1084.
Tan, C. (2015). Beyond rote-memorisation: Confucius' concept of thinking. *Educational Philosophy and Theory, 47*(5), 428–439.
Tan, C. (2017). A Confucian conception of critical thinking. *Journal of Philosophy of Education, 51*(1), 331–343.
Tan, T. S. (1898). Chinese problems. *Straits Chinese Magazine, 2*(6), 111–116.
Thiroux, J. P. (2001). *Ethics: Theory and practice*. Upper Saddle River, NJ: Pearson.
Tibbitts, F. (2002). Understanding what we do: Emerging models for human rights education. *International Review of Education, 48*(3/4), 159–171.
Tibbitts, F. (2017). Evolution of human rights education models. In M. Bajaj (Ed.), *Human rights education: Theory, research, praxis* (pp. 69–95). Philadelphia, PA: University of Pennsylvania Press.
Tochon, F., & Munby, H. (1993). Novice and expert teachers' time epistemology: A wave function from didactics to pedagogy. *Teaching and Teacher Education, 9*(2), 205–218.

Tomlinson, J. (1999). *Globalization and culture.* Chicago, IL: University of Chicago Press.

Tu, W. (1994). Embodying the universe: A note on Confucian self-realization. In R. T. Ames, W. Dissanayake, & T. P. Kasulis (Eds.), *Self as person in Asian theory and practice* (pp. 177–186). New York: SUNY Press.

Tucker, M. E. (1998). Religious dimensions of Confucianism: Cosmology and cultivation. *Philosophy East and West, 48*(1), 5–45.

Turco, L. (2000). *The book of forms: A handbook of poetics* (3rd ed.). Handover, NH: University Press of New England.

Turnley, M. (2014, June 3). English Lit students lost for words as exam paper poem contains just punctuation. *Huffington Post.* Retrieved November 3, 2020, from www.huffingtonpost.co.uk/2014/06/03/english-students-shocked-by-poem_n_5436872.html

United Nations. (1948). *Universal declaration of human rights.* Retrieved November 3, 2020, from www.un.org/en/universal-declaration-human-rights/

United Nations. (1993). *The Vienna declaration and programme of action.* Vienna: Declaration Adopted at the World Conference on Human Rights. Retrieved November 3, 2020, from www.un.org/en/development/devagenda/humanrights.shtml

United Nations. (2011). *United nations declaration on human rights education and training.* Retrieved November 3, 2020, from https://digitallibrary.un.org/record/715039?ln=en

United Nations. (2015). *Transforming our world: The 2030 Agenda for sustainable development.* Retrieved November 3, 2020, from https://sustainabledevelopment.un.org/post2015/transformingourworld

United Nations Human Rights Office of the High Commissioner. (2006). *World programme for human rights education: First phase.* Geneva, Switzerland: United Nations.

Van Hooft, S. (2014). *Understanding virtue ethics.* New York: Routledge.

Van Norden, B. W. (2007). *Virtue ethics and consequentialism in early Chinese philosophy.* Cambridge, UK: Cambridge University Press.

Vasudevan, L. M. (2014). Multimodal cosmopolitanism: Cultivating belonging in everyday moments with youth. *Curriculum Inquiry, 44*(1), 45–67.

Vinz, R. (2000). Cautions against canonizing an(other) literature. In R. Mahalingam & C. McCarthy (Eds.), *Multicultural curriculum: New directions for social theory, practice, and policy* (pp. 127–154). New York: Routledge.

Viswanathan, G. (2014). *Masks of conquest: Literary study and British rule in India.* New York: Columbia University Press.

Ward, K. (1971). Kant's teleological ethics. *The Philosophical Quarterly, 21*(85), 337–351.

Watson, J. L. (Ed.). (1997). *Golden arches East: McDonald's in East Asia.* Redwood City, CA: Stanford University Press.

Whitley, D. S. (2009). *Cave paintings and the human spirit: The origin of creativity and belief.* New York: Prometheus Books.

Willmott, H. (1998). Towards a new ethics? The contributions of post structuralism and posthumanism. In M. Parker (Ed.), *Ethics & organizations.* Thousand Oaks, CA: Sage.

Wimsatt, W. K., & Beardsley, M. C. (2001). The intentional fallacy and the affective fallacy. In V. B. Leitch (Ed.), *The Norton anthology of theory and criticism* (pp. 1374–1403). New York: W. W. Norton. (Original work published 1947).

World Health Organization. (2020). *WHO Coronavirus disease dashboard.* Retrieved November 19, 2020, from https://covid19.who.int/

Wu, M. (2013). Ren-li, reciprocity, judgment, and the question of openness to the Other in the Confucian Lunyu. *Journal of Moral Education, 42*(4), 430–442.

Wu, Y. (2018). Facilitating critical thinking skills of Chinese students: A Confucian perspective. In X. Liu & W. Ma (Eds.), *Confucianism reconsidered: Insights for American and Chinese education in the twenty-first century* (pp. 151–166). Albany, NY: SUNY Press.

Yeo, R. (1999). National education in Singapore: Promoting NE in the literature curriculum in secondary schools and junior colleges. In S. H. Chua & W. P. Chin (Eds.), *Localising pedagogy: Teaching literature in Singapore* (pp. 68–78). Singapore: National Institute of Education.

Zembylas, M. (2017). Emotions, critical pedagogy and human rights education. In M. Bajaj (Ed.), *Human rights education: Theory, research, praxis* (pp. 47–68). Philadelphia, PA: University of Pennsylvania Press.

Zhao, T. (2009). A political world philosophy in terms of All-under-heaven (Tian-xia). *Diogenes*, *56*(1), 5–18.

INDEX